YOUR CHINESE HOROSCOPE 2010

NEIL SOMERVILLE

What the Year of the Tiger Holds in Store for You

HARPER
element

TO ROS, RICHARD AND EMILY

HarperElement
An Imprint of HarperCollins*Publishers*
77–85 Fulham Palace Road
Hammersmith, London W6 8JB

www.harpercollins.co.uk

and *HarperElement* are trademarks of
HarperCollins*Publishers* Limited

Published by HarperElement 2009

3

© Neil Somerville 2009

Neil Somerville asserts the moral right to
be identified as the author of this work

A catalogue record for this book is
available from the British Library

ISBN 978-0-00-728146-6

Printed and bound in Great Britain by
Clays Ltd, St Ives plc

Mixed Sources
Product group from well-managed
forests and other controlled sources
www.fsc.org Cert no. SW-COC-1806
© 1996 Forest Stewardship Council
FSC

FSC is a non-profit international organisation established to promote the
responsible management of the world's forests. Products carrying the FSC
label are independently certified to assure consumers that they come
from forests that are managed to meet the social, economic and
ecological needs of present and future generations.

Find out more about HarperCollins and the environment at
www.harpercollins.co.uk/green

CONTENTS

Acknowledgements   v
Introduction   vii
The Chinese Years   ix
Welcome to the Year of the Tiger   xiii

The Rat   2
The Ox   30
The Tiger   58
The Rabbit   86
The Dragon   114
The Snake   142
The Horse   170
The Goat   198
The Monkey   226
The Rooster   254
The Dog   282
The Pig   310

Appendix:
  Relationships between the Signs   340
  Your Ascendant   342
  How to Get the Best from your Chinese Sign
  and the Year   345

ABOUT THE AUTHOR

Neil Somerville is one of the leading writers in the West on Chinese horoscopes. He has been interested in Eastern forms of divination for many years and believes that much can be learned from the ancient wisdom of the East. His annual book on Chinese horoscopes has built up an international following and he is also the author of *What's your Chinese Love Sign?* (Thorsons, 2000), *Chinese Success Signs* (Thorsons, 2001) and *The Answers* (Element, 2004).

Neil Somerville was born in the year of the Water Snake. His wife was born under the sign of the Monkey, his son is an Ox and daughter a Horse.

ACKNOWLEDGEMENTS

In writing *Your Chinese Horoscope 2010* I am grateful for the assistance and invaluable support that those around me have given.

I would also like to acknowledge Theodora Lau's *The Handbook of Chinese Horoscopes* (Harper & Row, 1979; Arrow, 1981), which was particularly useful to me in my research.

In addition to Ms Lau's work, I commend the following books to those who wish to find out more about Chinese horoscopes: Kristyna Arcarti, *Chinese Horoscopes for Beginners* (Headway, 1995); Catherine Aubier, *Chinese Zodiac Signs* (Arrow, 1984), series of 12 books; E. A. Crawford and Teresa Kennedy, *Chinese Elemental Astrology* (Piatkus Books, 1992); Paula Delsol, *Chinese Horoscopes* (Pan, 1973); Barry Fantoni, *Barry Fantoni's Chinese Horoscopes* (Warner, 1994); Bridget Giles and the Diagram Group, *Chinese Astrology* (HarperCollins*Publishers*, 1996); Kwok Man-Ho, *Complete Chinese Horoscopes* (Sunburst Books, 1995); Lori Reid, *The Complete Book of Chinese Horoscopes* (Element Books, 1997); Paul Rigby and Harvey Bean, *Chinese Astrologics* (Publications Division, South China Morning Post Ltd, 1981); Ruth Q. Sun, *The Asian Animal Zodiac* (Charles E. Tuttle Company, Inc., 1996); Derek Walters, *Ming Shu* (Pagoda Books, 1987) and

The Chinese Astrology Workbook (The Aquarian Press, 1988); Suzanne White, *The New Astrology* (Pan, 1987), *The New Chinese Astrology* (Pan, 1994) and *Chinese Astrology Plain and Simple* (Eden Grove Editions, 1998).

───◆◆◆───

As we march into a new year
we each have our hopes, our ambitions and our dreams.

Sometimes fate and circumstance will assist us,
sometimes we will struggle and despair,
but march we must.

For it is those who keep going,
and who keep their aspirations alive,
who stand the greatest chance of securing what they want.

March determinedly,
and your determination will, in some way, be rewarded.

Neil Somerville

───◆◆◆───

INTRODUCTION

The origins of Chinese horoscopes have been lost in the mists of time. It is known, however, that oriental astrologers practised their art many thousands of years ago and even today Chinese astrology continues to fascinate and intrigue.

In Chinese astrology there are 12 signs named after 12 different animals. No one quite knows how the signs acquired their names, but there is one legend that offers an explanation. According to this legend, one Chinese New Year the Buddha invited all the animals in his kingdom to come before him. Unfortunately, for reasons best known to the animals, only 12 turned up. The first to arrive was the Rat, followed by the Ox, Tiger, Rabbit, Dragon, Snake, Horse, Goat, Monkey, Rooster, Dog and finally Pig. In gratitude, the Buddha decided to name a year after each of the animals and that those born during that year would inherit some of the personality of that animal. Therefore those born in the year of the Ox would be hard working, resolute and stubborn, just like the Ox, while those born in the year of the Dog would be loyal and faithful, just like the Dog. While it is not possible that everyone born in a particular year can have all the characteristics of the sign, it is incredible what similarities do occur, and this is partly where the fascination of Chinese horoscopes lies.

In addition to the 12 signs of the Chinese zodiac there are five elements and these have a strengthening or moderating influence upon the signs. Details about the effects of the elements are given in each of the chapters on the 12 signs.

To find out which sign you were born under, refer to the tables on the following pages. As the Chinese year is based on the lunar year and does not start until late January or early February, it is particularly important for anyone born in those two months to check carefully the dates of the Chinese year in which they were born.

Also included, in the appendix, are two charts showing the compatibility between the signs for personal and business relationships and details about the signs ruling the different hours of the day. From this it is possible to locate your ascendant and, as in Western astrology, this has a significant influence on your personality.

In writing this book, I have taken the unusual step of combining the intriguing nature of Chinese horoscopes with the Western desire to know what the future holds, and have based my interpretations upon various factors relating to each of the signs. Over the years in which *Your Chinese Horoscope* has been published I have been pleased that so many have found the sections on the forthcoming year of interest and hope that the horoscope has been constructive and useful. Remember, though, that at all times you are master of your own destiny.

I sincerely hope that *Your Chinese Horoscope 2010* will prove interesting and helpful for the year ahead.

THE CHINESE YEARS

Dog	10 February	1910	to	29 January	1911
Pig	30 January	1911	to	17 February	1912
Rat	18 February	1912	to	5 February	1913
Ox	6 February	1913	to	25 January	1914
Tiger	26 January	1914	to	13 February	1915
Rabbit	14 February	1915	to	2 February	1916
Dragon	3 February	1916	to	22 January	1917
Snake	23 January	1917	to	10 February	1918
Horse	11 February	1918	to	31 January	1919
Goat	1 February	1919	to	19 February	1920
Monkey	20 February	1920	to	7 February	1921
Rooster	8 February	1921	to	27 January	1922
Dog	28 January	1922	to	15 February	1923
Pig	16 February	1923	to	4 February	1924
Rat	5 February	1924	to	23 January	1925
Ox	24 January	1925	to	12 February	1926
Tiger	13 February	1926	to	1 February	1927
Rabbit	2 February	1927	to	22 January	1928
Dragon	23 January	1928	to	9 February	1929
Snake	10 February	1929	to	29 January	1930
Horse	30 January	1930	to	16 February	1931
Goat	17 February	1931	to	5 February	1932
Monkey	6 February	1932	to	25 January	1933
Rooster	26 January	1933	to	13 February	1934

Dog	14 February	1934	to	3 February	1935
Pig	4 February	1935	to	23 January	1936
Rat	24 January	1936	to	10 February	1937
Ox	11 February	1937	to	30 January	1938
Tiger	31 January	1938	to	18 February	1939
Rabbit	19 February	1939	to	7 February	1940
Dragon	8 February	1940	to	26 January	1941
Snake	27 January	1941	to	14 February	1942
Horse	15 February	1942	to	4 February	1943
Goat	5 February	1943	to	24 January	1944
Monkey	25 January	1944	to	12 February	1945
Rooster	13 February	1945	to	1 February	1946
Dog	2 February	1946	to	21 January	1947
Pig	22 January	1947	to	9 February	1948
Rat	10 February	1948	to	28 January	1949
Ox	29 January	1949	to	16 February	1950
Tiger	17 February	1950	to	5 February	1951
Rabbit	6 February	1951	to	26 January	1952
Dragon	27 January	1952	to	13 February	1953
Snake	14 February	1953	to	2 February	1954
Horse	3 February	1954	to	23 January	1955
Goat	24 January	1955	to	11 February	1956
Monkey	12 February	1956	to	30 January	1957
Rooster	31 January	1957	to	17 February	1958
Dog	18 February	1958	to	7 February	1959
Pig	8 February	1959	to	27 January	1960
Rat	28 January	1960	to	14 February	1961
Ox	15 February	1961	to	4 February	1962
Tiger	5 February	1962	to	24 January	1963
Rabbit	25 January	1963	to	12 February	1964
Dragon	13 February	1964	to	1 February	1965

Snake	2 February	1965	to	20 January	1966
Horse	21 January	1966	to	8 February	1967
Goat	9 February	1967	to	29 January	1968
Monkey	30 January	1968	to	16 February	1969
Rooster	17 February	1969	to	5 February	1970
Dog	6 February	1970	to	26 January	1971
Pig	27 January	1971	to	14 February	1972
Rat	15 February	1972	to	2 February	1973
Ox	3 February	1973	to	22 January	1974
Tiger	23 January	1974	to	10 February	1975
Rabbit	11 February	1975	to	30 January	1976
Dragon	31 January	1976	to	17 February	1977
Snake	18 February	1977	to	6 February	1978
Horse	7 February	1978	to	27 January	1979
Goat	28 January	1979	to	15 February	1980
Monkey	16 February	1980	to	4 February	1981
Rooster	5 February	1981	to	24 January	1982
Dog	25 January	1982	to	12 February	1983
Pig	13 February	1983	to	1 February	1984
Rat	2 February	1984	to	19 February	1985
Ox	20 February	1985	to	8 February	1986
Tiger	9 February	1986	to	28 January	1987
Rabbit	29 January	1987	to	16 February	1988
Dragon	17 February	1988	to	5 February	1989
Snake	6 February	1989	to	26 January	1990
Horse	27 January	1990	to	14 February	1991
Goat	15 February	1991	to	3 February	1992
Monkey	4 February	1992	to	22 January	1993
Rooster	23 January	1993	to	9 February	1994
Dog	10 February	1994	to	30 January	1995
Pig	31 January	1995	to	18 February	1996

Rat	19 February	1996	to	6 February	1997
Ox	7 February	1997	to	27 January	1998
Tiger	28 January	1998	to	15 February	1999
Rabbit	16 February	1999	to	4 February	2000
Dragon	5 February	2000	to	23 January	2001
Snake	24 January	2001	to	11 February	2002
Horse	12 February	2002	to	31 January	2003
Goat	1 February	2003	to	21 January	2004
Monkey	22 January	2004	to	8 February	2005
Rooster	9 February	2005	to	28 January	2006
Dog	29 January	2006	to	17 February	2007
Pig	18 February	2007	to	6 February	2008
Rat	7 February	2008	to	25 January	2009
Ox	26 January	2009	to	13 February	2010
Tiger	14 February	2010	to	2 February	2011

NOTE

The names of the signs in the Chinese zodiac occasionally differ, although the characteristics of the signs remain the same. In some books the Ox is referred to as the Buffalo or Bull, the Rabbit as the Hare or Cat, the Goat as the Sheep and the Pig as the Boar.

For the sake of convenience, the male gender is used throughout this book. Unless otherwise stated, the characteristics of the signs apply to both sexes.

WELCOME TO THE
YEAR OF THE TIGER

Powerful, distinctive and fast, the Tiger commands respect
... and fear. No one can ignore – dare ignore – its presence.
The Year of the Tiger can be dramatic. It can be a time of
intense activity, change and, regrettably, possible conflict
and disaster. Events happen quickly in Tiger years and their
effects can be far-reaching.

It was in a Tiger year that the First World War began,
the Cuban missile crisis occurred, Chinese troops invaded
Tibet and, in the last Tiger year, there was fierce fighting in
Kosovo and American air strikes on Sudan and Iraq. This
year is likely to witness further conflict, although with
international action some of the troubles will be brought to
speedy resolution. Also, while some situations will be
grave, politicians will secure some historic settlements. The
last Tiger year saw the Good Friday Agreement which
finally brought peace to Northern Ireland.

In addition to the considerable international activity of
the year, some countries will be undergoing internal
change. Elections held over the year will often bring
changes in government and with these will come sweeping
new initiatives. Also, some leaders could find themselves
under scrutiny for past actions or misdemeanours. It was in
a Tiger year that President Nixon resigned following the
Watergate investigation and that President Clinton faced

impeachment charges. This Tiger year will again see some politicians called to account for their actions or leading members of administrations resigning over policy or for personal reasons. Politically, this promises to be an eventful year.

Industrial matters will also figure prominently, as certain areas struggle with economic pressures or the threat posed by harsh market conditions. The Tiger year will see some difficult times, including the restructuring of some industries and problems manifesting in industrial action. In Britain the General Strike of 1926 and miners' strike of 1974 both occurred during Tiger years and were to have profound consequences. However, while this will be a challenging time for some industries, Tiger years do favour innovation and in some cases are a time for painful but necessary change.

Throughout the year, technology and IT will continue to make major strides and have a significant impact on the lives of individuals and businesses. It was only 12 years ago, in the last Tiger year, that Google founded its search engine, e-commerce began to make an impression and the world's first digital terrestrial television service was launched.

The world of medicine is also likely to be a major beneficiary of some of the year's advances, with pioneering developments and the introduction of new drugs.

In everyday life the Tiger year can also make an impact. Over the year several innovative products are likely to be introduced and go on to have widespread use. The ballpoint and felt-tip pens were both invented in Tiger years, as were the audio cassette, the disposable camera and the much-loved teddy bear. In addition, new and striking fashions will find their way into the shops, with distinctive colours and designs being popular. The Tiger year favours the bold and the bright.

Other features of Tiger years are both the launch and completion of major projects. These can include the regeneration of inner-city areas and industrial wasteland. Previous Tiger years have seen the opening of many famous structures including the Panama Canal, Aswan Dam, Trans-Canada Highway and, in the last Tiger year, the world's longest suspension bridge in Akashi, Japan. This pattern of development will continue in 2010.

In recent years much attention has been focused on global warming and its effect on climate, and again the Tiger year could witness some extremes. Previous Tiger years have been marked by earthquakes, hurricanes, volcanic eruptions and the radiation leak at Chernobyl, and this year will not escape natural or man-made disaster either.

As far as economic activity is concerned, the Tiger year will be volatile. Some gains and rallies will be seen, but following developments in recent years, traders and investors will be cautious, with the markets sensitive to news and reacting accordingly. In 2010 investors will need to remain vigilant.

The vitality of the Tiger year will also be seen in the areas of sport and human achievement. Both the Winter Olympics in Vancouver and FIFA World Cup in South Africa promise much excitement and competitiveness. Some performances are likely to be particularly spectacular and inspiring.

Overall, the Tiger year will certainly be an active one. It will be a time of change but also of considerable opportunity. As far as individuals are concerned, some signs will relish the new possibilities it will open up while others will be uneasy about the developments and the hectic pace of the year. But the Tiger year will create chances for us all, and for those who are prepared to make the most of them this can be significant time. It is a year to be active and alert, to seize opportunities and to use individual talents. For all its problems and difficult moments, it has a lot of potential.

I very much hope you fare well over the next 12 months and are able to make the most of the opportunities this dramatic and frequently exciting year will bring. I wish you well.

YOUR CHINESE
HOROSCOPE 2010

18 FEBRUARY 1912 ~ 5 FEBRUARY 1913		*Water Rat*
5 FEBRUARY 1924 ~ 23 JANUARY 1925		*Wood Rat*
24 JANUARY 1936 ~ 10 FEBRUARY 1937		*Fire Rat*
10 FEBRUARY 1948 ~ 28 JANUARY 1949		*Earth Rat*
28 JANUARY 1960 ~ 14 FEBRUARY 1961		*Metal Rat*
15 FEBRUARY 1972 ~ 2 FEBRUARY 1973		*Water Rat*
2 FEBRUARY 1984 ~ 19 FEBRUARY 1985		*Wood Rat*
19 FEBRUARY 1996 ~ 6 FEBRUARY 1997		*Fire Rat*
7 FEBRUARY 2008 ~ 25 JANUARY 2009		*Earth Rat*

THE
RAT

THE PERSONALITY OF THE RAT

To see,
and to see what others do not see.
That is true vision.

The Rat is born under the sign of charm. He is intelligent, popular and loves attending parties and large social gatherings. He is able to establish friendships with remarkable ease and people generally feel relaxed in his company. He is a very social creature and is genuinely interested in the welfare and activities of others. He has a good understanding of human nature and his advice and opinions are often sought.

The Rat is a hard and diligent worker. He is also very imaginative and is never short of ideas. However, he does sometimes lack the confidence to promote his ideas and this can often prevent him from securing the recognition he deserves.

The Rat is very observant and many Rats have made excellent writers and journalists. The Rat also excels at personnel and PR work and any job that brings him into contact with people and the media. His skills are particularly appreciated in times of crisis, for the Rat has an incredibly strong sense of self-preservation. When it comes to finding a way out of an awkward situation, he is certain to be the one who comes up with a solution.

The Rat loves to be where there is a lot of action, but should he ever find himself in a very bureaucratic or restrictive environment he can become a stickler for discipline and routine. He is also something of an opportunist and is constantly on the lookout for ways in which he can improve his wealth and lifestyle. He rarely lets an opportunity go by and can become involved in so many plans and schemes that he sometimes squanders his energies and achieves very little as a result. He is also rather gullible and can be taken in by those less scrupulous than himself.

Another characteristic of the Rat is his attitude towards money. He is very thrifty and to some he may appear a little mean. The reason for this is purely that he likes to keep his money within his family. He can be most generous to his partner, his children and close friends and relatives. He can also be generous to himself, for he often finds it impossible to deprive himself of any luxury or object he fancies. He is very acquisitive and can be a notorious hoarder. He also hates waste and is rarely prepared to throw anything away. He can be rather greedy and will rarely refuse an invitation to a free meal or a complimentary ticket to a lavish function.

The Rat is a good conversationalist, although he can occasionally be a little indiscreet. He can be highly critical of others – for an honest and unbiased opinion, the Rat is a superb critic – and will sometimes use confidential information to his own advantage. However, as he has such a bright and irresistible nature, most people are prepared to forgive him his slight indiscretions.

Throughout his long and eventful life the Rat will make many friends and will find that he is especially well suited to those born under his own sign and those of the Ox, Dragon and Monkey. He can also get on well with those born under the signs of the Tiger, Snake, Rooster, Dog and Pig, but the rather sensitive Rabbit and Goat will find him a little too critical and blunt for their liking. The Horse and Rat will also find it difficult to get on with each other – the Rat craves security and will find the Horse's changeable moods and rather independent nature a little unsettling.

The Rat is very family orientated and will do anything to please his nearest and dearest. He is exceptionally loyal to his parents and can himself be a very caring and loving parent. He will take an interest in all his children's activities and see that they want for nothing. He usually has a large family.

The female Rat has a kindly, outgoing nature and involves herself in a multitude of different activities. She has a wide circle of friends, enjoys entertaining and is an attentive hostess. She is also conscientious about the upkeep of her home and has good taste in home furnishings. She is most supportive to the other members of her family and, due to her resourceful, friendly and persevering nature, can do well in practically any career she chooses.

Although the Rat is essentially outgoing, he is also a very private individual. He tends to keep his feelings to himself and while he is not averse to learning what other people are doing, he resents anyone prying too closely into his own affairs. He also does not like solitude and if he is alone for any length of time he can easily get depressed.

The Rat is undoubtedly very talented, but he does sometimes fail to capitalize on his many abilities. He has a tendency to become involved in too many schemes and chase after too many opportunities at once. If he can slow down and concentrate on one thing at a time, he can become very successful. If not, success and wealth can elude him. But, with his tremendous ability to charm, he will rarely, if ever, be without friends.

THE FIVE DIFFERENT TYPES OF RAT

In addition to the 12 signs of the Chinese zodiac there are five elements and these have a strengthening or moderating influence on the signs. The effects of the five elements on the Rat are described below, together with the years in which the elements were exercising their influence. Therefore those Rats born in 1960 are Metal Rats, those born in 1972 are Water Rats, and so on.

Metal Rat: 1960
This Rat has excellent taste and certainly knows how to appreciate the finer things in life. His home is comfortable and nicely decorated and he likes to entertain and mix in fashionable circles. He has considerable financial acumen and invests his money well. On the surface he appears cheerful and confident, but deep down he can be troubled by worries that are quite often of his own making. He is exceptionally loyal to his family and friends.

Water Rat: 1912, 1972
The Water Rat is intelligent and very astute. He is a deep thinker and can express his thoughts clearly and persuasively. He is always eager to learn and is talented in many different areas. He is usually very popular, but his fear of

loneliness can sometimes lead him into mixing with the wrong sort of company. He is a particularly skilful writer, but he can get sidetracked very easily and should try to concentrate on just one thing at a time.

Wood Rat: 1924, 1984

The Wood Rat has a friendly, outgoing personality and is popular with his colleagues and friends. He has a quick, agile brain and likes to turn his hand to anything he thinks may be useful. His one fear is insecurity, but given his intelligence and capabilities, this fear is usually unfounded. He has a good sense of humour, enjoys travel and, due to his highly imaginative nature, can be a gifted writer or artist.

Fire Rat: 1936, 1996

The Fire Rat is rarely still and seems to have a never-ending supply of energy and enthusiasm. He loves being involved in some form of action, be it travel, following up new ideas or campaigning for a cause in which he fervently believes. He is an original thinker and hates being bound by petty restrictions or the dictates of others. He can be forthright in his views but can some-times get carried away in the excitement of the moment and commit himself to various undertakings without thinking through all the implications. Yet he has a resilient nature and with the right support can go far in life.

Earth Rat: 1948, 2008

This Rat is astute and very level-headed. He rarely takes unnecessary chances and while he is constantly trying to improve his financial status, he is prepared to proceed slowly and leave nothing to chance. He is probably not as adventurous as the other types of Rat and prefers to remain in familiar territory rather than rush headlong into something he knows little about. He is talented, conscientious and caring towards his loved ones, but at the same time can be self-conscious and worry a little too much about the image he is trying to project.

PROSPECTS FOR THE RAT IN 2010

The Year of the Ox (26 January 2009 to 13 February 2010) will have been a reasonable one for the Rat and in the remaining months he can do himself a lot of good. As so many Rats will have found, the Ox year requires effort, and for those prepared to give that little bit extra, there can be encouraging developments in store.

The Rat's relations with others are particularly well aspected and not only can he look forward to an increasing number of social opportunities at this time but he will also be in demand with family and friends. For those enjoying or perhaps hoping for romance, these can be a promising few months. All Rats should also use any chances they have to talk to others. Whether running over ideas or making arrangements, the Rat can gain a lot from the support and goodwill of those around him.

At work this is a time of application and of focusing on duties and objectives. For those Rats hoping to make progress in their career or looking for a position, October and November could see some interesting possibilities.

The Rat would, though, do well to watch his spending during this period. With his many ideas, he could find his outgoings turning out to be more than anticipated. It would be helpful for him to spread out his purchases and wait for favourable buying opportunities, including post-Christmas sales.

The Year of the Ox will have asked a lot of the Rat but during it he will certainly have had many experiences as well as enjoyed times which will have meant a great deal to him.

The Year of the Tiger begins on 14 February and will be an important one for the Rat. Again, results will need to be worked for and the Rat may not always be at ease with some of the developments of the year, or its pace. However, by remaining alert and being prepared to adapt, he can benefit in many ways.

In his work this is a year of change. Often this will be in the Rat's present place of work, with him benefiting from internal opportunities or the chance to further his duties in some way. Changes in personnel and management can, for some Rats, lead to restructuring and new working practices, but whatever their situation, by making the most of it, they may well be rewarded with the chance to progress. Rats like security and a certain stability, but the Tiger year favours movement and the one thing the Rat will need to be careful of during it is intransigence. To be unwilling to change could undermine his position and prospects. Rats, please take note.

For Rats seeking work or a change in their career, the Tiger year can also present some excellent opportunities. These Rats should not be too restrictive in what they are prepared to consider and if they take advice many could be alerted to possibilities they have not considered before. While these Rats may sometimes despair of ever finding a suitable position or feel daunted by the expectations of a new role, by allowing themselves time and being persistent, they can and will prevail. As the Rat has so often shown, he has the abilities and resourcefulness to triumph over challenges, and he can do so again this year. April, June, September and October could see important developments, but such is the nature of the year that when the Rat sees a position that interests him, he should act quickly. Tiger years can be fast-moving and opportunities need to be grasped as they arise.

Another feature of Tiger years is the travel opportunities they bring. Sometimes these could be connected with work, but many Rats will travel for pleasure during the year. By giving careful thought to their destination and planning ahead, they will often benefit from their time away. Given the nature of the year, if there is a destination the Rat is particularly keen to visit, he should make enquiries and stay alert for offers. Travel will figure strongly for many in 2010.

As far as money matters are concerned, this is a time when good control and advance planning will help the Rat. To do all he wants, he will need to keep control over his everyday spending and avoid succumbing to too many impulse purchases. Budgeting and making allowances for any large purchases – and travel plans – will help. In addition he should avoid unnecessary risks. His luck and judgement may not be as good as in some years. Rats, take note and do be careful.

Being born under the sign of charm, the Rat enjoys company and sets much store by both his family and social life. However, here again the Tiger year calls for care. The Rat needs to be attentive towards others and remain aware of their views and feelings, otherwise misunderstandings could arise. Also, despite his many commitments, he should make sure he spends quality time with others rather than remain too preoccupied with his own concerns. Fortunately, he is usually careful in this respect, but with the aspects as they are and the pressures he may face, this is something he needs to be aware of.

In the Rat's home life this can be a busy year. Not only will many Rats themselves be involved in possible change, particularly in their work, but others in their household could also find themselves under pressure or have problems to contend with. As a result, this is a time when good communication and co-operation will be paramount. Willingness to help and give time to others will make an important difference to the quality of home life. If possible, the Rat should also spread out any accommodation plans or practical activities he may have in mind, rather than cause additional pressure by hurrying them through.

On a social level the Rat will have good opportunities to meet others over the year, particularly as a result of his interests or through his work, with some valuable new friendships being made. For the unattached, romance could add considerable excitement to the year. May, July, August and December will see the most social activity. However, the Rat does need to remain alert, as this is a year when an inadvertent comment could give rise to a misunderstanding or lead to disagreement. Rats, please take note and be careful.

Overall, the Year of the Tiger will be a busy one for the Rat and although there will be times when he will be concerned about developments, by being adaptable and doing his best he can ultimately learn a great deal. This may not be an easy year, but it can be instructive. The Rat will also benefit from the support he receives and the new friendships and contacts he makes, although in his relations with others good communication and awareness will be so very important. A welcome feature of the year will be the travel opportunities that arise and many Rats will have the chance to visit new and often interesting destinations. Despite its pressures, the Tiger year will bring times the Rat will value.

The Metal Rat

This will be an important year for the Metal Rat, not only marking the start of a new decade in his life but also bringing some key decisions and changes. This may not be the easiest or smoothest of years, but its effects can be far-reaching.

One notable aspect of the Metal Rat's nature is his ambition. He is keen and resourceful and able to use his talents in many different ways. Over the year these will continue to serve him well, and by being willing to explore possibilities, whether in his work or personal interests, he will be able to learn a great deal. Although moving away from the familiar may be uncomfortable, what opens up to him this year can prove to be the chance and challenge he now needs.

At work this can be a decisive year. For some Metal Rats there could be significant promotion opportunities, and while these may be something they have been working towards for some time, they could have an impact in several ways. Not only will they entail learning new skills but they could also involve changes to routine and sometimes location. Nevertheless, while personally daunting, these opportunities can give these Metal Rats' career the boost they have been wanting for some time.

For Metal Rats who are content in their present position, again change could beckon. Whether this is brought about through new management, the introduction of new working practices or more senior staff moving on, many Metal Rats will find themselves being given further responsibilities. They may be concerned about their increased role and workload, but by being prepared to adapt and make the most of their situation, they will not only add to their skills but also open up other possibilities for the future. A key feature of the Tiger year is that its effects can be far-reaching.

For those Metal Rats seeking work, either at the start of the Tiger year or during it, again some important possibilities can open up. Securing a position will require effort, and the Tiger year does not always make things easy or straightforward for Rats, but with faith, self-belief and a certain amount of initiative, many will find their tenacity rewarded. Mid-March to the end of April, June and September to mid-November could see considerable activity, but with the fast-moving nature of the Tiger year, ideas and possibilities need to be followed up as they arise.

One of the Metal Rat's strengths is his ability to get on well with people and over the year he should continue to use these skills well. Whether working with others or meeting new people in his line of work, he will impress many with his eager manner and willingness to assist.

As with all Rats in 2010, travel is likely to figure prominently for the Metal Rat, and whether he is travelling for work or pleasure, he should allow time to plan his itinerary and read up about his destination. By going well-prepared, he will make his time away all the more successful. If there is a particular destination that appeals to him, he should talk this over with his loved ones and see what is possible. Some Metal Rats could be tempted to mark their fiftieth year with a special trip or holiday and for many their travels could be one of the highlights of the year.

The Metal Rat is generally careful in money matters, but he should try to make advance provision for his projects and purchases over the year. With good budgeting, he will be able to proceed with many of his plans, but this is a year for careful control, especially with everyday spending.

With the progressive nature of the Tiger year, he should also give some consideration to his interests and recreational pursuits. These bring an important balance to his lifestyle and if there is a particular interest or idea he has been keen to explore, this would be a good year to follow it up. Trying something new or extending his existing knowledge could open up exciting new possibilities both now and in the future. Any Metal Rats who are sedentary for much of the day and do not tend to take much regular exercise would also do well to consider activities that could remedy this. With their fiftieth year marking change and new possibilities, they can benefit from positive action.

In their relations with others, they will find that family, friends and colleagues can all offer useful encouragement and support, but the year still calls for a certain care. In particular the Metal Rat will need to be prepared to consult and listen. To appear too single-minded could not only undermine rapport but also prevent him from benefiting from the opinions of others. In addition, it is important that he spends quality time with his loved ones. In this frequently busy year there is the risk that he might not give the time or attention to others that he has in the past, and this could lead to possible disagreements. With thoughtfulness, this can be a rich and special year, but without, tensions could loom. Metal Rats, do take careful note. Nevertheless, the Tiger year could well be marked by occasions that will mean a great deal to the Metal Rat, including possible celebrations and surprises for his birthday.

He should also make sure his social life does not suffer due to all his activity and should aim to preserve some time for going out and meeting friends as well as treating himself and his loved ones to any social events that appeal. Metal Rats who are alone and would welcome a more active social life will find that positive action can reward them well. By going out, joining interest groups and making a special effort to meet those who are like-minded, they can form some new and often significant friendships. For the unattached, romantic prospects are also promising.

Here again, Tiger years reward those who are prepared to put themselves forward. May, July, August to mid-September and December could see the most social activity.

In general, the Year of the Tiger will be a demanding one for the Metal Rat, particularly in view of some of the changes that will occur. But while the pressures may sometimes be great and there will be times of uncertainty and concern, the year can mark the dawn of a new and important phase. This is a year to be open to possibility, to rise to situations and to keep alert for opportunity. With a willingness to move forward, the Metal Rat can make this an important and personally significant time and one which can also have a positive bearing on the next few years.

TIP FOR THE YEAR
Despite the activity of the year, do make time for those who are important to you. Extra attention and thoughtfulness can make a real difference to the year *and your prospects*.

The Water Rat
The Water Rat is blessed with a great many qualities. He has a willing nature, is prepared to put himself forward and, with the element of Water strengthening his skills as a communicator, he will have a lot in his favour during the Tiger year. To benefit, however, he will need to show flexibility and be prepared to adapt to the situations that arise.

At work, change is indicated, and although many Water Rats will have seen a lot happen in recent years, this period of transition is far from over. Whether settled in a particular position or keen to move on, the Water Rat will need to remain alert and seize opportunities as they occur. In some cases sudden changes in personnel could create openings or new initiatives could give the Water Rat the chance to build on his experience and take on a new role. This is a year for moving forward, even if it may not always be in the exact way the Water Rat had envisaged.

This also applies to those Water Rats seeking work or a change from their present role. The Tiger year can be a time of new starts and by being flexible, considering a wide range of options and talking to those who can advise them, many Water Rats can be alerted to new ways of using their skills and given fresh possibilities to consider. Mid-March to the end of April, June, September and October could see some interesting work developments and the Tiger year favours those who seize the initiative.

Another factor in the Water Rat's favour is his keen and inquisitive mind, and by being prepared to further himself in some way, whether through enrolling on courses, undertaking personal study or trying new subjects or activities, he can help his prospects both now and in the near future.

He would also do well to allow time for recreational pursuits, especially those that allow him to get additional exercise or are in contrast to his usual daily activities. Also, if there are activities that appeal to him, this would be an ideal year to try them out. In 2010 it is important the Water Rat keeps his lifestyle in balance.

Travel will also feature strongly for many Water Rats. Some could benefit from attractive offers they see or could decide to go away at the last moment. However their trips come about, the rest and change of scene can do the Water

Rat a lot of good. For those not able to take a long break, just a few days away or visiting others could be particularly beneficial.

With the possibility of travel and all his current commitments, the Water Rat will need to keep a close watch on his financial situation. This includes making early provision for some of his plans as well as watching his level of spending. This is no year for risks or too many spontaneous purchases.

The activity of the Tiger year will also filter through to the Water Rat's home life and here good communication and co-operation will be more important than ever. Whenever the Water Rat has pressures or is concerned about decisions and possible work changes, it is important that he talks them through with those around him. Not only can loved ones provide understanding and advice but sometimes just the process of talking can help him sort out his own thoughts. This is no year to keep worries to himself. Similarly, if any pressures or domestic problems arise, a willingness to talk can be to the benefit of all. In addition the Water Rat will do much to assist more senior relations, with his thoughtfulness being particularly appreciated. Domestically, this will be a busy year, but despite its pressures it can bring some notable family successes, and the progress of younger relations could be especially delightful.

With all the activity of the year, many Water Rats will be more selective with their socializing than of late, but it is important that they keep in contact with their friends. This is no time for the Water Rat to withdraw into himself and let his social life lapse. May, July, August, December and January are likely to see the most social activity.

The Tiger year will ask a lot of the Water Rat but will also give him the opportunity to develop his strengths and open himself up to new possibilities. By being forward thinking and adapting to the situations that arise, he can make this a constructive and personally satisfying year.

TIP FOR THE YEAR
Pay particular attention to your relations with others. Be open with them. Discuss, talk, consult and help. This is an important time for you and those around you will play a significant and valuable part.

The Wood Rat

The Wood Rat will have accomplished a lot in the last few years and the Tiger year will offer him some interesting opportunities. It may not be a smooth or easy year, but its significance can be far-reaching.

As the Tiger year starts the Wood Rat would do well to take some time to consider his present position and possible next moves. He would find it helpful to talk to others and mention the ideas he is considering. By doing so, he will not only clarify in his own mind what he wants to do but will benefit from the advice and assistance that others can give. As all Rats will find, this is no year for standing still, and by deciding early on what he wants to work towards, the Wood Rat can get the year off to an encouraging start.

At work this could be a particularly important year, with almost all Wood Rats involved in change. Whether this arises through restructuring, opportunities in their present place of work or the decision to move on, many Wood Rats will alter their role in some way. With possible changes to their routine and/or commute, as well as new responsibilities, this can be daunting, but by rising to the challenge the Wood Rat will not only make positive headway but greatly add to his experience.

For Wood Rats who are keen to take their career in a new direction or are seeking work, the Tiger year can bring some interesting possibilities. By seeking advice, exploring options and considering other ways in which they can use their strengths, many Wood Rats will succeed in obtaining a new and often very different position. Persistence will be required, but for the determined this can be a time of positive change. Mid-March to the end of April, June and September to mid-November could see some good opportunities, but with the prevailing aspects the Wood Rat will need to keep alert throughout the year and act quickly when he sees any openings that interest him.

With the Wood Rat's ability to relate so well to others, he should also make the most of the chances he has to network and meet others and, if appropriate, join a professional organization. By getting himself better known he can help his situation and the level of support and advice he receives.

This also applies to his personal interests. If he is able to meet other enthusiasts, whether at special events or by joining a local group, he will find this not only adds to the fun and pleasure his interests can bring but can also lead to him learning and achieving a lot more. By putting himself forward and making the most of his opportunities, he can gain a great deal. In addition, for those who are unattached and would perhaps welcome a more active and fulfilling social life, their interests can be an excellent way to meet those who are similarly minded, and for some, important new friendships or a special romance can follow on. For socializing and meeting others, May, July, August and December could be active and interesting months.

With the busy lifestyle the Wood Rat leads it is also important that he takes good care of himself. This includes having a nutritious and balanced diet as well as taking regular and appropriate exercise. This could be of considerable benefit to him.

The Wood Rat will also need to be careful in money matters. With his current commitments and often expensive plans, he will need to be disciplined in his spending and make early provision for some of the projects he has in mind. Also, where important transactions are concerned, he would do well to check the terms and obligations and, where appropriate, seek advice. This is a year for care and good money management.

Both personally and domestically this will be a busy year, with a lot for the Wood Rat to do and think about. Where necessary, he should be forthcoming and prepared to talk about his concerns. Also, when in company he needs to be attentive and listen closely to others to avoid any possible misunderstanding. However, while the Tiger year does call for a certain awareness, the Wood Rat can look forward to many memorable times with close friends and loved ones. These could include realizing certain hopes and plans as well as enjoying travel and joint activities. Personally, there can be a lot to enjoy this year, but the Wood Rat does need to remain alert and liaise closely with others.

The Wood Rat has many fine talents and knows he has it within him to achieve a great deal. The Tiger year will give him the chance to broaden his experience, learn through change and discover new strengths. It can be an instructive year with far-reaching value – a demanding time, but in many respects a positive one.

TIP FOR THE YEAR

Do not be too restrictive in your outlook and remain open to possibility. Also, consult others and make sure you give time to loved ones. They can play a very special part in your year.

The Fire Rat

The element of Fire gives a sign added determination. Fire signs are the doers of the Chinese zodiac and often have compelling personalities. The Fire Rat certainly has much in his favour, with his earnestness and good people skills being assets that will serve him well throughout his life. During the Tiger year he will have the chance to use his strengths, but he needs to be disciplined. Scattering his energies too widely could affect what he is able to achieve. The Tiger year requires focus.

In the Fire Rat's education, he needs to stay well organized and concentrate on what has to be done. Working steadily throughout the year will not only allow him to fare better but also to learn more. In addition many Fire Rats will be introduced to new subjects or skills, and by applying themselves and working at these, they could discover certain strengths they will be keen to develop in

the future. Educationally, this can be a positive and interesting time, but to benefit the Fire Rat needs to be
committed and make the most of his chances.

This also applies to his interests and recreational
pursuits. If there is a skill that he wants to learn or
improve on, he should find the time to do so. In order to
get results he will need to be disciplined and concentrate on
what he wants to do, even if this may mean cutting back
on other activities. But the effort he makes can reward him
well.

There will also be a good chance for the Fire Rat to get
to know others over the year, especially through his interests, and he may appreciate a special friendship and some
lively and fun times. However, while socially the year will
see some good times, a certain care is needed. If the Fire
Rat should find himself involved in activities or high jinks
he has misgivings about, he should follow his better judgement. Similarly, if he has concerns over any matter,
whether educationally or personally, rather than dwell on
it by himself he should talk to those in a position to help
and advise. Fire Rats, do take note and remember that
support and advice are available to you.

Many Fire Rats will also have the opportunity to travel
during the year and whether their trips are connected with
their studies or a holiday, they can add some excitement
and interest to the year.

As far as the Fire Rat's domestic life is concerned, he
needs to be open and communicative. Those around him
will often be keen to encourage and help him, but to
benefit he does need to be forthcoming. If he is also
prepared to contribute to home life, he can generate a

better understanding with his loved ones and enjoy more as a result. Again, it is worth the Fire Rat making the effort. Whether in his home life, his interests or his schoolwork, the more involved he is, the more he can benefit.

For Fire Rats born in 1936, this is a year for deciding on plans and carrying them out. If the Fire Rat lets himself get distracted, there is a risk that chances could slip by and he could find himself not able to make as much of the year as he would like. His ideas could concern almost any area of his life – perhaps modifications to his home, hobbies and projects he wants to pursue, travel or some other area of interest – but by giving some thought to what he wants to do and putting in the effort, he can enjoy some satisfying times. Also, sharing thoughts with those close to him can lead to more happening as well as to offers of additional support.

Another factor in the Fire Rat's favour will be the way he keeps himself informed. This can lead to hearing of opportunities or offers that are ideal for him or benefits that could help his present situation. This is a year to be aware and open to possibility.

Whether born in 1936 or 1996, this can be a rewarding year for the Fire Rat, but it is one requiring effort and discipline. However, if he focuses on what he wants to do, makes the most of the support of those close to him and seizes his opportunities, he will often be pleased with the results his efforts and diligence can bring.

TIP FOR THE YEAR
Use your time and opportunities wisely and concentrate on what you have to do. The greater the focus, the better and more satisfying the results.

The Earth Rat

The Tiger year is a busy and eventful one and the Earth Rat, with his measured approach, will be well placed to benefit from it.

For Earth Rats in work this is a year to keep their wits about them, including keeping informed of developments and remaining aware of proposals under consideration. This way, when changes do take place or openings arise, the Earth Rat will be able to consider his position, assess the implications and act. Although some may prefer to continue with their present duties, this is no year to bury their heads in the sand and they should aim to remain aware and, importantly, be flexible.

For some Earth Rats, the changes that occur could involve taking on new responsibilities, often in a more supervisory role. Here their extensive experience will be a great asset. Other Earth Rats may find themselves affected by new working practices or having to vary their role in some way. If they are willing to adapt, these changes will often give them the chance to extend their skills and will bring some interesting new challenges. This is no year for standing still, and for any Earth Rats who have become staid in their present role, the Tiger can often bring the change they need.

There will, though, be some Earth Rats who will decide to take advantage of retirement options, consider reducing their work schedule or look for a more convenient position. By considering various possibilities, making enquiries and talking to contacts, many could be successful in securing a new position with duties very different from those they have done before. A key feature of the Tiger year is that it can open up new possibilities. April, June, September and October could see some important decisions, but throughout the year opportunities need to be seized when they arise.

This can also be a rewarding year as far as the Earth Rat's personal interests are concerned and if there is an idea he has been nurturing, a subject that appeals to him or a skill he would like to improve, this is a year to follow this up. In particular, those Earth Rats who reduce their work commitments will find that by giving themselves new objectives and using their additional free time in a purposeful way, they will get much value out of what they do. Being observant and good communicators, Rats are particularly known for their writing abilities, and any Earth Rats who are interested in exploring their skills will find they can be the source of much pleasure. Again, a key element of the year is to seize the initiative *and take action*.

The Earth Rat will also find his interests bringing him into contact with others and can look forward to a variety of social occasions over the year. Any Earth Rats who are lonely or have neglected their social life in recent years will find that becoming more active and perhaps joining a local interest group will bring an improvement to their situation. May, July, August and December could be the busiest months socially as well as good ones for meeting others.

The Earth Rat's domestic life is also likely to see much activity during the year and any accommodation ideas he may have need to be discussed and planned well in advance. If he decides to move, ample time needs to be allowed for the moving process to take place, and the earlier preparations can be made, the better. Throughout the year it is also important that the Earth Rat consults others about his plans, otherwise misunderstandings could arise. This also applies to any pressures or concerns he may have. This is very much a time for openness. However, busy though domestic life may be, there will be many occasions the Earth Rat will thoroughly enjoy, including marking the achievements of someone dear. For some this could include celebrating the birth of a grandchild.

Travel is also well aspected and the Earth Rat should make the most of any opportunities or invitations that come his way. By remaining alert, he could particularly benefit from special offers and last-minute breaks.

In matters of finance, however, he will need to remain vigilant and should keep particular control over his spending. For those Earth Rats who retire or lessen their working commitments, there could be financial adjustments to consider and where important paperwork is concerned, the Earth Rat will need to check the details thoroughly and take advice should anything concern him. Financially, this is a time to be careful and disciplined.

Overall, the Year of the Tiger will be an active one for the Earth Rat, bringing change but with it the opportunity to explore new possibilities. With a willing attitude and the support of others, he can make this a special and often personally rewarding time.

TIP FOR THE YEAR
This can be a time of opportunity but to benefit you need to be flexible and mindful of others. Explore new possibilities and look at ways of furthering your interests. This can be a promising and important year. Use it well.

FAMOUS RATS

Ben Affleck, Ursula Andress, Louis Armstrong, Lauren Bacall, Shirley Bassey, Kathy Bates, Irving Berlin, Silvio Berlusconi, Kenneth Branagh, Marlon Brando, Charlotte Brontë, Jackson Browne, George H. W. Bush, Glen Campbell, David Carradine, Jimmy Carter, Aaron Copland, Cameron Diaz, David Duchovny, Duffy, Noël Edmonds, T. S. Eliot, Eminem, Colin Firth, Clark Gable, Liam Gallagher, Al Gore, Hugh Grant, Geri Halliwell, Lewis Hamilton, Thomas Hardy, Prince Harry, Haydn, Charlton Heston, Buddy Holly, Mick Hucknall, Henrik Ibsen, Jeremy Irons, Samuel L. Jackson, Jean-Michel Jarre, Scarlett Johansson, Gene Kelly, Avril Lavigne, Jude Law, Gary Lineker, Lord Andrew Lloyd Webber, Ian McEwan, Katie Melua, Claude Monet, Richard Nixon, Ozzy Osbourne, Sean Penn, Sir Terry Pratchett, Ian Rankin, Lou Rawls, Burt Reynolds, Jonathan Ross, Rossini, William Shakespeare, Donna Summer, James Taylor, Leo Tolstoy, Henri Toulouse-Lautrec, Spencer Tracy, Carol Vorderman, the Prince of Wales, George Washington, the Duke of York, Emile Zola.

6 FEBRUARY 1913 ⁓ 25 JANUARY 1914	*Water Ox*
24 JANUARY 1925 ⁓ 12 FEBRUARY 1926	*Wood Ox*
11 FEBRUARY 1937 ⁓ 30 JANUARY 1938	*Fire Ox*
29 JANUARY 1949 ⁓ 16 FEBRUARY 1950	*Earth Ox*
15 FEBRUARY 1961 ⁓ 4 FEBRUARY 1962	*Metal Ox*
3 FEBRUARY 1973 ⁓ 22 JANUARY 1974	*Water Ox*
20 FEBRUARY 1985 ⁓ 8 FEBRUARY 1986	*Wood Ox*
7 FEBRUARY 1997 ⁓ 27 JANUARY 1998	*Fire Ox*
26 JANUARY 2009 ⁓ 13 FEBRUARY 2010	*Earth Ox*

THE
OX

THE PERSONALITY OF THE OX

The more considered the way,
the more considerable the journey.

The Ox is born under the signs of equilibrium and tenacity. He is a hard and conscientious worker and sets about everything he does in a resolute, methodical and determined manner. He has considerable leadership qualities and is often admired for his tough and uncompromising nature. He knows what he wants to achieve in life and, as far as possible, will not be deflected from his ultimate objective.

The Ox takes his responsibilities and duties very seriously. He is decisive and quick to take advantage of any opportunity that comes his way. He is also sincere and places a great deal of trust in his friends and colleagues. He is, nevertheless, something of a loner. He is a quiet and private individual and often keeps his thoughts to himself. He also cherishes his independence and prefers to set about things in his own way rather than be bound by the dictates of others or influenced by outside pressures.

The Ox tends to have a calm and tranquil nature, but if something angers him or he feels that someone has let him down, he can have a fearsome temper. He can also be stubborn and obstinate and this can lead him into conflict with others. Usually he will succeed in getting his own way, but should things go against him he is a poor loser and will take any defeat or setback badly.

The Ox is often a deep thinker and rather studious. He is not particularly renowned for his sense of humour and does not take kindly to new gimmicks or anything too innovative. He is too solid and traditional for that and prefers to stick to the more conventional norm.

His home is very important to him and in some respects he treats it as a private sanctuary. His family tends to be closely knit and the Ox will make sure that each member does their fair share around the house. He tends to be a hoarder, but he is always well organized and neat. He also places great importance on punctuality and there is nothing that infuriates him more than to be kept waiting, particularly if it is due to someone's inefficiency. The Ox can be a hard taskmaster!

Once settled in a job or house the Ox will quite happily remain there for many years. He does not like change and he is also not particularly keen on travel. He does, however, enjoy gardening and other outdoor pursuits and he will often spend much of his spare time out of doors. He is usually an excellent gardener and whenever possible will make sure he has a large area of ground to maintain. He usually prefers to live in the country than the town.

Due to his dedicated and dependable nature the Ox will usually do well in his chosen career, providing he is given enough freedom to act on his own initiative. He invariably does well in politics, agriculture and in careers that need specialized training. He is also very gifted artistically and many Oxen have enjoyed considerable success as musicians or composers.

The Ox is not as outgoing as some and it often takes him a long time to establish friendships and feel relaxed in another person's company. His courtships are likely to be long, but once he is settled he will remain devoted and loyal to his partner. He is particularly well suited to those born under the signs of the Rat, Rabbit, Snake and Rooster. He can also establish a good relationship with the Monkey, Dog, Pig and another Ox, but he will find that he has little in common with the whimsical and sensitive Goat. He will also find it difficult to get on with the Horse, Dragon and Tiger – the Ox prefers a quiet and peaceful existence and those born under these three signs tend to be a little too lively and impulsive for his liking.

The female Ox has a kind and caring nature, and her home and family are very much her pride and joy. She always tries to do her best for her partner and can be a most conscientious and loving parent. She is an excellent organizer and a very determined person who will often succeed in getting what she wants in life. She usually has a deep interest in the arts and is often a talented artist or musician.

The Ox is a very down-to-earth character. He is sincere, loyal and unpretentious. He can, however, be rather reserved and to some he may appear distant and aloof. He has a quiet nature, but underneath he is very strong-willed and ambitious. He has the courage of his convictions and is often prepared to stand up for what he believes to be right, regardless of the consequences. He inspires confidence and trust and throughout his life he will rarely be short of people who are ready to support him.

THE FIVE DIFFERENT TYPES OF OX

In addition to the 12 signs of the Chinese zodiac there are five elements and these have a strengthening or moderating influence on the signs. The effects of the five elements on the Ox are described below, together with the years in which the elements were exercising their influence. Therefore those Oxen born in 1961 are Metal Oxen, those born in 1913 and 1973 are Water Oxen, and so on.

Metal Ox: 1961

This Ox is confident and very strong-willed. He can be blunt and forthright in his views and is not afraid of speaking his mind. He sets about his objectives with a dogged determination, but he can become so involved in his various activities that he can be oblivious to the thoughts and feelings of those around him, and this can sometimes be to his detriment. He is honest and dependable and will never promise more than he can deliver. He has a good appreciation of the arts and usually has a small circle of very good and loyal friends.

Water Ox: 1913, 1973

This Ox has a sharp and penetrating mind. He is a good organizer and sets about his work in a methodical manner. He is not as narrow-minded as some of the other types of Ox and is more willing to involve others in his plans and aspirations. He usually has very high moral standards and is often attracted to careers in public service. He is a good judge of character and has such a friendly and persuasive manner that he usually experiences little difficulty in securing his objectives. He is popular and has an excellent way with children.

Wood Ox: 1925, 1985

The Wood Ox conducts himself with an air of dignity and authority and will often take a leading role in any enterprise in which he becomes involved. He is very self-confident and is direct in his dealings with others. He does, however, have a quick temper and has no hesitation in speaking his mind. He has tremendous drive and willpower and an extremely good memory. He is particularly loyal and devoted to the members of his family and has a most caring nature.

Fire Ox: 1937, 1997

The Fire Ox has a powerful and assertive personality and is a hard and conscientious worker. He holds strong views and has very little patience when things do not go his own way. He can also get carried away in the excitement of the moment and does not always take into account the views of those around him. He nevertheless has many leadership qualities and will often reach positions of power, eminence and wealth. He usually has a small group of loyal and close friends and is very devoted to his family.

Earth Ox: 1949, 2009

This Ox sets about everything he does in a sensible and level-headed manner. He is ambitious but also realistic in his aims and is often prepared to work long hours in order to secure his objectives. He is shrewd in financial and business matters and is a very good judge of character. He has a quiet nature and is greatly admired for his sincerity and integrity. He is also very loyal to his family and friends and his views are often sought.

PROSPECTS FOR THE OX IN 2010

The Year of the Ox (26 January 2009 to 13 February 2010) holds encouraging prospects for the Ox and in the remaining months he can accomplish a great deal. However, to make the most of this time he will need to be open and pay special attention to his relations with others. The Ox often has a tendency to set about his activities in his own way – some Oxen are particularly independent – but to get the most from the remaining months of the Ox year he should make the most of his chances to meet others. Many Oxen can look forward to some rewarding occasions in their home life at this time and these can often be all the more special due to a family celebration earlier in the year. For many Oxen, 2009 can be a personally memorable year. For those enjoying romance this can be an exciting time, while those who are unattached could find their social life becoming much busier.

This likelihood of social activity also applies to the Ox's work, and in the closing months of the year he would do well to liaise with colleagues and make the most of his chances to network. By raising his profile, he can benefit from some fine opportunities. For those seeking work this is also a time to be active and explore openings. The Ox year is very rewarding of effort and the Ox himself, determined and resolute, will be well placed to benefit from it. The key, however, will be his relations with others.

The Year of the Tiger starts on 14 February and will be a mixed one for the Ox. He likes to plan and be methodical and organized, but in the Tiger year events can happen quickly. The Ox may be concerned about some of the developments and this will not be an easy time for him, but as he has so often shown, he is made of stern stuff and, with care, he can gain a lot from what happens over the year.

In his work he will need to keep alert. Although he may prefer to concentrate on what needs to be done, he could find he has to contend with delays, increased bureaucracy and sometimes the unhelpful attitude of others. In addition he may have to adapt to new working procedures and personnel. For one so conscientious and so keen to stick to the tried and tested, this can be difficult. However, by putting in the effort, the Ox will find his fortitude will prevail and he may well emerge with much to his credit. This can include headway made under difficult conditions, personal success, skills mastered or new responsibilities secured. The going will sometimes be tough, but the Ox is a doer and survivor and over the year he will have a good chance to demonstrate his strengths.

Although many Oxen will remain with their present employer, they will often have the chance to vary their role and in the process learn about other aspects of their work. However, for those eager to make a change, the Tiger year can be an important one. Securing a new position will not be easy, but by widening their options, seeking advice and being prepared to adapt and learn, they will find their persistence paying off, with many being offered an interesting position with the potential for future development. March, April, September and November could see some good opportunities. Work-wise, this is, though, a year when all Oxen will need to keep their wits about them and adapt to situations as they arise.

The Ox will also need to be his usual cautious self when dealing with money matters. Events can happen quickly this year and bring unexpected costs. These could include repairing or replacing items, increased accommodation costs or debts that need paying. In 2010 the Ox will need to keep vigilant, check the terms and implications of any major purchase or transaction and use his money prudently. Making early provision for his outgoings will help. Money-wise, this is a year for good planning and the avoidance of risk.

A more satisfying part of the year will concern the Ox's personal interests and although he will have many demands on his time, it is important he gives himself the chance to enjoy recreational pursuits. These can be particularly good ways for him to relax and take his mind off other pressures. Some interests can also have pleasing social benefits and throughout this busy year the Ox owes it to himself to preserve time for activities that bring him pleasure.

He will also very much enjoy aspects of his home life, especially shared activities and interests. When major purchases or accommodation decisions need to be made, considering options jointly will lead to better choices that can be appreciated by all. In addition, family treats and trips out as well as a possible holiday can do the Ox and his loved ones good as well as provide the opportunity to unwind.

However, while the Tiger year can bring some pleasing times, it is still one for care. Over the year the Ox does need to listen closely to his loved ones, watch his some-times independent tendencies and, if tired or under pres-sure, try not to take his irritation out on others. Without care, disagreements could flare up and this is something all Oxen need to be wary of. When experiencing any prob-lems or pressures, they will find that being open and forth-coming will give others more chance to help and understand.

The Ox will also need to tread carefully in social situa-tions, as an inadvertent comment or lapse could cause problems. Those Oxen enjoying romance need to be partic-ularly aware and attentive. However, despite the cautionary aspects, the Ox will thoroughly enjoy many social occa-sions and his socializing can do him a lot of good. March, April, June and August could see the most social activity.

The main advice for the Ox this year is to proceed care-fully. This is a time of volatility and although the Ox prefers to follow carefully laid plans, he will need to adapt and make the best of situations as they arise. During the year he will face new challenges, but in the process he will learn a lot, discover new strengths and possibly take up new interests as well as take satisfaction in the progress he makes.

The Metal Ox

The element of Metal gives the Ox added determination. Always keen to make the most of himself, the Metal Ox sets about his activities with diligence and commitment. While he will continue to do so in 2010, the Tiger year may be a challenging one for him. Problems, delays and obstacles may all affect his plans, and parts of the year are likely to be frustrating. However, opportunities and interesting choices can follow on from the events that take place.

Throughout the year the Metal Ox will need to keep alert to all that is going on around him. This is no time for him to be so immersed in his own activities that he is oblivious to the views of others. To prevent problems, he needs to be aware and show flexibility.

This particularly applies to his work situation. Although many Metal Oxen will be satisfied with their present position and happy to continue with their duties, over the year they will feel the effects of change, whether through the introduction of new procedures or alterations to their existing role. The Metal Ox will often be concerned about the implications and pace of what happens, but will be faced with moving with the times and making the best of his situation. Nevertheless, some could find the changes give them the chance to further their experience and widen their role. In addition, others will often look to the Metal Ox for advice, and by assisting and doing what he can, he can improve his reputation. While this can sometimes be a difficult and frustrating year for him, there will still be scope to make progress and to use his considerable experience to good effect.

For Metal Oxen who are keen to change their employer, as well as those seeking work, the Tiger year can work in curious ways. Openings will be limited and these Metal Oxen must not be too restrictive in the type of position they pursue. However, an opportunity could arise in an unexpected manner, possibly through the Metal Ox seeing an advert by chance, making a tentative enquiry or being alerted to a possible opening by a colleague or friend. With the aspects as they are, opportunities can come along at almost any time, but late February to April, September and November could be important months.

Another important factor in how the Metal Ox fares will be his attitude towards others. He does possess an independent streak, but in work situations he does need to liaise with others and communicate readily. This is not a year when he can afford to be isolated or too removed from what is happening.

This advice also applies to his personal interests. By meeting other enthusiasts, whether by attending events and gatherings or joining a local group, he could find himself being helped and encouraged. Also, by preserving time for his interests, he will be helping to keep his lifestyle in balance.

The Metal Ox would also do well to give some consideration to his well-being and, especially if sedentary for much of the day, seek advice on appropriate exercise. If he is reliant on convenience food, he could find that a more balanced diet would boost his energy levels. To keep himself on good form, he would find it well worth giving some attention to his current way of life.

He should also try to go away for a break during the year. The rest and change of scene can do him a lot of good and even if he is not able to travel too far, he will appreciate the chance to see places that are new to him. If he is able to combine a holiday with an interest or event, this can bring extra meaning to his time away.

This will be a busy year as far as his domestic life is concerned and good co-operation and communication will be needed between family members. Throughout the year it is also important that the Metal Ox is open and prepared to share any pressures or concerns he may have. Not only can this lead to more offers of support, but it can also help rapport and understanding. Should any tensions or differences of opinion arise, taking the time to talk these through can be of great help. Tiger years are active ones and it is important that quality time is preserved for home life. If the Metal Ox has any ideas for shared activities, including home or garden improvements, he should put them forward, as they will often be appreciated. By being aware and open he will play a central and valued role in his domestic life.

As far as financial matters are concerned, this is a year for vigilance. Not only should the Metal Ox keep a close watch on his budget and make allowance for forthcoming expenses, but he should also be thorough with paperwork. This includes checking any forms he may be required to complete and the terms of any agreements he may enter into, as well as making sure essential policies are kept up to date. The Tiger year is not one for carelessness or risk.

Overall, this will be a demanding and sometimes disruptive year for the Metal Ox. Changes may suddenly arise and he could feel buffeted by events or situations outside his control. However, by being willing to adapt, he can often learn from them. And while the Tiger year may not be an easy one, the Metal Ox's hard-fought achievements will be something that he can build on and enjoy more fully in following years.

TIP FOR THE YEAR
Pay attention to your relations with others. Listen to their views and be open and communicative. Also, spend time on your interests. They can do you a lot of good as well as keep your lifestyle in balance.

The Water Ox

This will be a mixed year for the Water Ox. He may well find himself under increased pressure and certain plans may be more difficult to realize than he had hoped. However, while there will be times of disappointment and sometimes despair, there will also be some very special moments and personal successes. This may not be an easy year, but it can be an important and illuminating one.

At work this will be a demanding year and while the conscientious Water Ox will often want to be left to carry out his own duties, distractions and delays are likely to arise. In addition he could find his work is not made any easier by the attitude of some colleagues or a lack of resources or other support. Some of the year will test his forbearance. However, one of his qualities is that he is no quitter. He is prepared to work hard, and by doing what he can, he will not only overcome some of the year's obstacles but also have the opportunity to learn new skills. In addition his fortitude will often impress others and when opportunities arise many Water Oxen will find themselves well positioned to benefit. 'Problems are opportunities in disguise,' as the saying goes, and this will hold very true for the Water Ox this year.

Water Oxen who are anxious to change their job or who are seeking work could find it particularly helpful to consult those in a position to help. These could be career advisers, employment agencies or professional organizations, but by drawing on the advice available and widening their options, these Water Oxen may be offered an interesting new challenge. The Tiger year may be demanding, but the chances will be there. March, April, September and November could see some interesting possibilities.

Throughout the year, though, the Water Ox will need to be careful in financial matters. He could face some additional expenses, including costs for repairing and replacing equipment as well as helping with the activities of others. As a result he will need to keep a close watch on his spending and whenever possible save in advance. He should also check forms and financial agreements thoroughly and follow up anything that is unclear. This is no year for risk.

One of the most satisfying areas of the year will be the personal projects the Water Ox decides to set himself. For more creative Water Oxen, these could involve making items or using their skills in new ways, but whatever the Water Ox chooses to do, in this often busy year it is important he preserves time for activities he enjoys. Any Water Oxen who have let their interests lapse in recent times would do well to consider rectifying this. Also, Tiger years do favour the new and it could be that a pursuit that has recently become popular could be very suitable.

The Water Ox's domestic life will also see a lot of activity over the year and he will do much to assist others. Younger relations in particular could be facing academic pressures and here the Water Ox's encouragement and understanding will be particularly valued. Sometimes more senior relations will also look to the Water Ox for assistance and while he will again do much to help, there will be times when he will be torn in several directions and have to rush from one matter to another. There could also be some situations that concern him and add to the pressure. When this happens, or he has decisions preying on his mind, or is worried about the attitudes of others, it is important that he is forthcoming. With discussion, problems can often be resolved, tensions eased and decisions made. In this demanding year, openness and co-operation are essential.

While there will be some particularly busy times during the year, there will, however, also be some occasions which will mean a great deal to the Water Ox. An academic success, some progress made or a holiday or break can all bring a great deal of pleasure as well as be good for domestic rapport and understanding.

It is also important that the Water Ox does not feel so busy that he has to cut back on his socializing over the year. This not only helps keep his lifestyle in balance but can also give him the opportunity to get to know others. The unattached and those hoping for a more fulfilling social life will find that by going out and giving themselves the chance to meet others, their positive actions can lead to an improvement in their situation. March, April, June and August to early September could see the most social activity.

Overall, the Tiger year will be fast-moving and there will be times when the Water Ox will feel concerned about developments or under pressure. However, by doing what he can and rising to the challenges of the year he will gain important experience which he will be able to build on in the future. This is a time to remain alert, be prepared to adapt and remain mindful of others.

TIP FOR THE YEAR

Although you will have many demands on your time, do not let these prevent you from developing your interests. These can bring balance to your lifestyle as well as offer much personal satisfaction. Also, at busy or worrying times, do draw on the assistance of others. This can help you in many ways.

The Wood Ox

There are two words that it would be helpful for the Wood Ox to keep in mind this year: 'awareness' and 'flexibility'. This will be a busy year and throughout the Wood Ox will need to remain alert and be prepared to adapt. He may have firm ideas and objectives, but to stay too wedded to these could hinder his progress.

One area which will see change will be work. Those Wood Oxen who have been in the same position for some time may well feel ready for a change at some point during the year. For many, this will be with their present employer and their in-house knowledge will make them strong candidates for promotion. Others will choose to look for greater responsibilities elsewhere, but whatever the

Wood Ox does, this is a year favouring progress and personal development. Many Wood Oxen will be successful in securing a new position and taking on a more fulfilling role, and a lot will be expected of them, including learning new duties and, for some, altering their routine. The early days could be daunting and tiring. However, by having faith in their abilities and rising to the challenge, these Wood Oxen will often find their new role allows them to discover strengths which will become part of their onward development. Progress made this year can have important long-term benefits. Even those Wood Oxen who decide to remain in their existing role will find that developments will often require them to adapt and this will help prepare them for future possibilities.

For Wood Oxen seeking work, the Tiger year will not be easy. Patience and persistence will be required and there will be times when these Wood Oxen will feel despondent, especially when certain applications do not go their way. However, by drawing on the advice available, widening their options and showing initiative at interview, many will find their tenacity rewarded by the offer of a job that may be different from what they have done before, and this can be of great future value. Late February to the end of April, September and November could see some interesting openings, but opportunities do need to be seized when they arise.

The progress the Wood Ox makes in his work can lead to an increase in income over the year. However, while this will be welcome, the Wood Ox will need to remain disciplined in his spending. With his existing outgoings and plans for the future, this is no time to succumb to too many temptations. Also, if he should enter into any agreement or contract during the year, he does need to check the terms and obligations carefully. This is a year to be thorough and vigilant.

With his often demanding schedule, it is also important that the Wood Ox gives some consideration to taking sufficient exercise and having a well-balanced diet. To neglect his well-being or drive himself too hard could leave him prone to minor ailments or lacking his usual energy. He should also allow himself time for recreational pursuits rather than feel he needs to be continually active. His interests can bring him great pleasure and enjoyment.

In his relations with others, this can be an eventful year. For some Wood Oxen this could include parenthood and the considerable adjustments this can involve, while others could be involved in a move with their partner to more suitable accommodation and some will decide to marry. For many this will be a busy and special year, with a lot to do, plan and look forward to. Throughout, it is important that the Wood Ox is open, communicative and considerate. Decisions will need to be shared, plans sometimes adjusted and compromises reached. But with care and mindfulness, this can be a positive and exciting year.

Nevertheless, there will be some Wood Oxen who will be unhappy with their personal situation. Perhaps a relationship is unfulfilling or a friendship not as strong or as special as it once was. For some, the Tiger year can bring difficult decisions and uncertain times. However, as the proverb reminds us, 'Fortune turns like a wheel,' and for the few Wood Oxen who experience difficulties this year, disappointments will pass and fresh opportunities often open up, including, for those who are alone, meeting someone very special. Demanding though the Tiger year may sometimes be, it can have far-reaching significance. March, April, June and August could see the most social activity.

Overall, the Wood Ox will need to remain alert, vigilant and flexible over the Tiger year. But he will often be able to build on his accomplishments in the future, especially in the following and more favourable Rabbit year.

TIP FOR THE YEAR
Consult, communicate and be aware. Also be prepared to adapt to situations as they arise. This way you can learn a great deal and often find opportunities beginning to open up for you. Also, do be attentive to those who are special to you. This will add a lot to your year.

The Fire Ox

The Fire Ox has a determined nature and during his life his great sense of purpose and many skills will lead to him achieving a great deal. However, as we all know, some years are better than others, and for the Fire Ox this will be one of the more challenging ones.

For the Fire Ox born in 1997 this is a year for commitment and hard work. In his education a lot will be expected of him, with much to learn and many new skills to master. It will sometimes be difficult for the young Fire Ox to cope with such a wide variety of subjects as well as fit in all the other things he wants to do. Also, while he has his strengths, some subjects could be a struggle and cause him some anguish. The Tiger year will be demanding, but it is by being stretched and challenged that the Fire Ox can learn a lot, and over the year he will not only make important progress but also improve his awareness and general confidence.

Another benefit of the year will be the way in which the Fire Ox will be able to build on certain skills. Whether these involve physical and sporting activities, music, drama or some other area, by making the most of the facilities available to him, he can make considerable progress. Through commitment, he will learn and benefit. Some Fire Oxen could also find they are encouraged to make more of a certain talent and if they take the chances they are offered, what they do now can be of both present and future value.

In view of all the Fire Ox's activities and pressures it is also important that he is forthcoming and talks over any problems or concerns he has with those who are able to help, either at home or at school. This way he can be better supported. In addition there could be occasions when he finds himself at odds with others. Sometimes what he wants to do may clash with something that others have arranged, or attitudes may differ over certain matters. At such times some give and take will be needed. However, if the young Fire Ox is willing to be open and join in with various activities, there will be much for him to appreciate, particularly in his home life.

He can also look forward to many enjoyable times with his friends and will welcome their support and camaraderie. He will also be reassured in the knowledge that he is not alone in some of the difficulties he may be facing.

Overall, the Tiger year will be a demanding one for Fire Oxen born in 1997, but by rising to the challenges and making the most of their opportunities, ideas and strengths, this can be a year when they will grow, develop and get to learn a great deal. And the commitment and effort they put in will provide them with a solid foundation on which to build in following years.

For Fire Oxen born in 1937, this will be a variable year. The Fire Ox does like to forge ahead and set about his activities in specific ways, but during the year he may have to reconsider some of his plans. In some cases others may suggest different approaches to certain tasks or it may be that changes to situations mean he has to look again at what he wants to do. As he will discover, the Tiger year is not one for intransigence, and showing greater flexibility will not only lead to more being achieved but ultimately to more being to his advantage.

However, while the Tiger year calls for increased awareness, it can also bring some personally rewarding times. Many Fire Oxen will particularly delight in some family news and events during the year, with shared interests and activities bringing much pleasure. The Fire Ox is also likely to have the chance to go away, and whether staying with relations or going away for a holiday, his travels can often add extra interest to the year.

When dealing with important finance and paperwork, though, the Fire Ox will need to be his usual thorough self as well as check anything which is unclear. This is a time when he should draw on the assistance and advice available to him.

Generally, the more senior Fire Ox will need to be flexible in his planning this year and mindful of the views of those around him. With care and awareness, however, the Tiger year can still contain a great many pleasures, especially in terms of shared interests, family news and activities.

Whether born in 1937 or 1997, the Fire Ox will find the year will require effort, flexibility and a willingness to make the most of his situation and opportunities. It is by being willing rather than steadfast that both the younger and more senior Fire Ox can get the best from the year and take pleasure in their achievements.

TIP FOR THE YEAR
Be accommodating in your approach. Adapt to situations and listen closely to others. Despite the mixed aspects a lot can go in your favour, but this is a year for flexibility and awareness.

The Earth Ox

One of the main traits of the Earth Ox is that he is perceptive. He is good at appraising situations and realistic in his aims, and in the Tiger year his talents will serve him well. By being adaptable and keeping his wits about him, he can emerge from the year with a lot to his credit.

For those Earth Oxen in work this can be a challenging time. Many will face change, possibly due to internal reorganization and the introduction of new initiatives and systems. Also, due to their experience, some could find themselves being given additional responsibilities. Workwise, a lot will be asked of the Earth Ox and this will be very much a year for making the most of his situation and rising to the tasks given. These may not always be easy and some Earth Oxen will not be helped by delays, increased bureaucracy or the pettiness and unhelpful attitude of those around them. For these Earth Oxen parts of the year will be frustrating, but again it is a case of focusing on what needs to be done and resisting any irritations and distractions that arise.

Many Earth Oxen will remain with their current employer over the year, but for those keen to move, alter their working commitments or find work, the Tiger year can be daunting. In some cases there could be few suitable vacancies and when they do arise the Earth Ox could find himself facing stiff competition. However, one of the main features of the Tiger year is that it favours personal development and by being willing to widen the scope of what they are prepared to consider, many Earth Oxen will be given the chance to use their skills in different ways. The Earth Ox's alert and perceptive nature will be of great help in keeping him informed of developments and possibilities. With the aspects as they are, chances need to be taken when they arise, but March, April, September and November could see some interesting possibilities.

In all the Earth Ox tackles this year, it is important that he is thorough. This is no time for risks or shortcuts, particularly when dealing with paperwork or forms which have financial implications. Earth Oxen, do take note. In addition, with any expensive purchase or plan he is considering, the Earth Ox should avoid rush. In some cases by waiting for more favourable buying opportunities he could save himself considerable outlay or find something that better meets his requirements. Many Earth Oxen are careful in financial matters, but sometimes the general pace of the Tiger year could make the Earth Ox act before he has considered all the implications. This is not a time for him to lower his usually cautious guard.

A more positive aspect of the year concerns the Earth Ox's personal interests and he should allow himself the time to both enjoy and develop these. Not only can they bring him satisfaction and be a source of relaxation, but they can also have additional benefits. For those Earth Oxen who enjoy creative activities, new ideas and projects could be especially absorbing.

The Earth Ox's interests can also bring him into contact with others, and by going to gatherings and events he will often enjoy himself and welcome the opportunity to meet other enthusiasts. In addition, when he has invitations to social occasions or sees events that appeal to him, he should follow these up. Although some Earth Oxen may be tempted to stay at home, their social life can bring an important balance to their lifestyle. Late February to the end of April, June and August could be particularly interesting months for socializing.

In the Earth Ox's domestic life, this is a year to be attentive to the views of others. The Earth Ox does like to hold sway and make the decisions, but while those around him are grateful for all he does, it is important that he regularly consults them over plans and ideas as well as listens closely to their suggestions. Without care and mindfulness, misunderstandings or differences of opinion could arise which, with more discussion, could have been avoided. In addition, some plans could need altering as situations change, and again the Earth Ox will need to be accommodating. This is very much a year to be alert, flexible and liaise with others. However, despite the cautionary aspects, the Earth Ox's domestic life will certainly have some meaningful times, including any holidays or breaks he is able to take with his loved ones.

Given the hectic pace of the year, the Earth Ox could also find it helpful to give some consideration to his well-being, including making sure he takes regular exercise and has a balanced diet, though he should seek medical guidance before making any modifications.

Generally, the Tiger year will be a demanding one for the Earth Ox and throughout he will need to remain alert and adapt to changing situations. However, with his perceptive and adroit nature, he can get a lot from the year, particularly in terms of exploring and developing some of his skills and interests.

TIP FOR THE YEAR

This can be a fast-moving year with changes taking place, situations altering and plans sometimes having to be modified. To benefit, keep alert and be flexible.

FAMOUS OXEN

Lily Allen, Hans Christian Andersen, Gemma Arterton, Johann Sebastian Bach, Warren Beatty, Kate Beckinsale, David Blaine, Napoleon Bonaparte, Albert Camus, Jim Carrey, Charlie Chaplin, George Clooney, Natalie Cole, Bill Cosby, Tom Courtenay, Tony Curtis, Diana, Princess of Wales, Marlene Dietrich, Walt Disney, Patrick Duffy, Jane

Fonda, Edward Fox, Michael J. Fox, Peter Gabriel, Elizabeth George, Richard Gere, Ricky Gervais, Handel, King Harald V of Norway, Adolf Hitler, Dustin Hoffman, Hal Holbrook, Anthony Hopkins, Billy Joel, King Juan Carlos of Spain, John Key, B. B. King, Keira Knightley, Mark Knopfler, Burt Lancaster, Jessica Lange, Heather Locklear, Kate Moss, Alison Moyet, Eddie Murphy, Paul Newman, Jack Nicholson, Leslie Nielsen, Barack Obama, Gwyneth Paltrow, Oscar Peterson, Paula Radcliffe, Robert Redford, Lionel Richie, Wayne Rooney, Tim Roth, Rubens, Meg Ryan, Amanda Seyfried, Jean Sibelius, Sissy Spacek, Bruce Springsteen, Meryl Streep, Lady Thatcher, Alan Titchmarsh, Scott F. Turow, Vincent van Gogh, Minette Walters, Zoë Wanamaker, Sigourney Weaver, the Duke of Wellington, Arsène Wenger, W. B. Yeats.

26 JANUARY 1914 ∿ 13 FEBRUARY 1915   *Wood Tiger*

13 FEBRUARY 1926 ∿ 1 FEBRUARY 1927   *Fire Tiger*

31 JANUARY 1938 ∿ 18 FEBRUARY 1939   *Earth Tiger*

17 FEBRUARY 1950 ∿ 5 FEBRUARY 1951   *Metal Tiger*

5 FEBRUARY 1962 ∿ 24 JANUARY 1963   *Water Tiger*

23 JANUARY 1974 ∿ 10 FEBRUARY 1975   *Wood Tiger*

9 FEBRUARY 1986 ∿ 28 JANUARY 1987   *Fire Tiger*

28 JANUARY 1998 ∿ 15 FEBRUARY 1999   *Earth Tiger*

14 FEBRUARY 2010 ∿ 2 FEBRUARY 2011   *Metal Tiger*

THE
TIGER

THE PERSONALITY OF THE TIGER

It's
the zest,
the enthusiasm,
the giving the little bit more,
that makes the difference.
And opens up so much.

The Tiger is born under the sign of courage. He is a charismatic figure and usually holds very firm views. He is strong-willed and determined and sets about most of his activities with tremendous energy and enthusiasm. He is very alert and quick-witted and his mind is forever active. He is a highly original thinker and is nearly always brimming with new ideas or full of enthusiasm for some new project or scheme.

The Tiger adores challenges and loves to get involved in anything that he thinks has an exciting future or that catches his imagination. He is prepared to take risks and does not like to be bound either by convention or the dictates of others. He likes to be free to act as he chooses and at least once during his life he will throw caution to the wind and go off and do the things he wants to do.

The Tiger does, however, have a somewhat restless nature. Even though he is often prepared to throw himself wholeheartedly into a project, his initial enthusiasm can soon wane if he sees something more appealing. He can also be rather impulsive and there will be occasions in his life when he acts in a manner he later regrets. If he were to think things through or be prepared to persevere in his various activities, he would almost certainly enjoy a greater degree of success.

Fortunately the Tiger is lucky in most of his enterprises, but should things not work out as he hoped, he is liable to suffer from severe bouts of depression and it will often take him a long time to recover. His life often consists of a series of ups and downs.

He is, however, very adaptable. He has an adventurous spirit and rarely stays in the same place for long. In the early stages of his life he is likely to try his hand at several different jobs and he will also change his residence fairly frequently.

The Tiger is very honest and open in his dealings with others. He hates any sort of hypocrisy or falsehood. He is also well known for being blunt and forthright and has no hesitation in speaking his mind. He can be rebellious at times, particularly against any form of petty authority, and while this can lead him into conflict with others, he is never one to shrink from an argument or avoid standing up for what he believes is right.

The Tiger is a natural leader and can rise to the top of his chosen profession. He does not, however, care for anything too bureaucratic or detailed, and he does not like to obey orders. He can be stubborn and obstinate and throughout his life he likes to retain a certain amount of independence in his actions and be responsible to no one but himself. He likes to consider that all his achievements are due to his own efforts and he will not ask for support from others if he can avoid it.

Ironically, despite his self-confidence and leadership qualities, he can be indecisive and will often delay making a major decision until the very last moment. He can also be sensitive to criticism.

Although the Tiger is capable of earning large sums of money, he is rather a spendthrift and does not always put his money to its best use. He can also be most generous and will often shower lavish gifts on friends and relations.

The Tiger cares very much for his reputation and the image that he tries to project. He carries himself with an air of dignity and authority and enjoys being the centre of attention. He is very adept at attracting publicity, both for himself and for the causes he supports.

The Tiger often marries young and he will find himself best suited to those born under the signs of the Pig, Dog, Horse and Goat. He can also get on well with the Rat, Rabbit and Rooster, but will find the Ox and Snake a bit too quiet and serious for his liking, and he will be highly irritated by the Monkey's rather mischievous and inquisitive ways. He will also find it difficult to get on with another Tiger or a Dragon – both partners will want to dominate the relationship and could find it difficult to compromise on even the smallest of matters.

The Tigress is lively, witty and a marvellous hostess at parties. She takes great care over her appearance and is usually most attractive. She can be a very doting mother and while she believes in letting her children have their freedom, she makes an excellent teacher and will ensure that her children are well brought up and want for nothing. Like her male counterpart, she has numerous interests and likes to have sufficient independence and freedom to go off and do the things she wants to do. She has a most caring and generous nature.

The Tiger has many commendable qualities. He is honest, courageous and often a source of inspiration to others. Providing he can curb the wilder excesses of his restless nature, he is almost certain to lead a fulfilling and satisfying life.

THE FIVE DIFFERENT TYPES OF TIGER

In addition to the 12 signs of the Chinese zodiac there are five elements and these have a strengthening or moderating influence on the signs. The effects of the five elements on the Tiger are described below, together with the years in which the elements were exercising their influence. Therefore those Tigers born in 1950 and this year are Metal Tigers, those born in 1962 are Water Tigers, and so on.

Metal Tiger: 1950, 2010
The Metal Tiger has an assertive and outgoing personality. He is very ambitious and while his aims may change from time to time, he will work relentlessly until he has obtained what he wants. He can, however, be impatient for results and become highly strung if things do not work out as he would like. He is distinctive in his appearance and is admired and respected by many.

Water Tiger: 1962

This Tiger has a wide variety of interests and is always eager to experiment with new ideas or satisfy his adventurous nature by going off to explore distant lands. He is versatile, shrewd and has a kindly nature. He tends to remain calm in a crisis, although he can be annoyingly indecisive at times. He communicates well with others and through his many capabilities and persuasive nature usually achieves what he wants in life. He is also highly imaginative and is often a gifted orator or writer.

Wood Tiger: 1914, 1974

The Wood Tiger has a friendly and pleasant personality. He is less independent than some of the other types of Tiger and more prepared to work with others to secure a desired objective. However, he does have a tendency to jump from one thing to another and can easily become distracted. He is usually very popular, has a large circle of friends and invariably leads a busy and enjoyable social life. He also has a good sense of humour.

Fire Tiger: 1926, 1986

The Fire Tiger sets about everything he does with great verve and enthusiasm. He loves action and is always ready to throw himself wholeheartedly into anything that catches his imagination. He has many leadership qualities and is capable of communicating his ideas and enthusiasm to others. He is very much an optimist and can be most generous. He has a likeable nature and can be a witty and persuasive speaker.

Earth Tiger: 1938, 1998

This Tiger is responsible and level-headed. He studies everything objectively and tries to be scrupulously fair in all his dealings. Unlike other Tigers, he is prepared to specialize in certain areas rather than get distracted by other matters, but he can become so involved in what he is doing that he does not always take into account the opinions of those around him. He has good business sense and is usually very successful in later life. He has a large circle of friends and pays great attention to both his appearance and his reputation.

PROSPECTS FOR THE TIGER IN 2010

The Year of the Ox (26 January 2009 to 13 February 2010) may have been an often frustrating one for the Tiger. During it, activities and plans may not have proceeded as quickly or as well as he would have liked and he could also have faced some disappointments. In the closing months he will need to remain careful. With his prospects about to show a distinct improvement in his own year, this is no time to jeopardize his situation through unnecessary risks or impulsive action.

At work the Tiger will often face a growing workload and should remain focused on his duties. Although this will not always be an easy time, by showing commitment and giving his best he can help his prospects in the future. All Tigers should also make the most of any opportunity they have to add to their experience. Skills and knowledge acquired now can be instrumental in their later progress.

November 2009 could see some interesting developments, but the real rewards of the Tiger's efforts will come through next year.

Socially, the Tiger will find himself in demand as the Ox year draws to a close, with chances to meet up with others and social events to look forward to. December and January will be busy months. In addition his home life will see much activity. Here the Tiger will need to liaise well with others and, when possible, spread out his various activities. Should he find himself in any fraught situation (not helped by pressure or tiredness), he will need to tread carefully. With the aspects as they are, this is a time for caution and tact. Tigers, be warned – enjoy the many good times the year end can bring, but do be mindful of the views of others.

Overall, the Ox year will have been a demanding one for many Tigers, but with the approach of their own year the tide will begin to turn very much in their favour.

The Year of the Tiger starts on 14 February and will be an encouraging one for the Tiger. It will give him the chance to take his ideas and skills further as well as enjoy some pleasing personal developments. This is *his* year and it is one of considerable promise.

For Tigers who are starting the year feeling dissatisfied, this is very much a time to draw a firm line under past disappointments and focus on the present. For many the year can mark the start of a new chapter in their lives and with a positive and willing attitude, they will find that a lot can open up for them.

At work the Tiger's prospects are far more promising than of late, and those Tigers who are feeling frustrated or staid in their present role will find that new chances can quickly arise. These may include promotion opportunities as more senior colleagues move on or new challenges elsewhere, but if the Tiger actively seizes his opportunities, important progress can be made.

This also applies to those Tigers seeking work. Although some may feel hurt by what they have recently experienced, again it is a case of drawing a firm line under the past and concentrating on the present. Also, when looking for a position, these Tigers would do well to show initiative and resolve. This includes finding out more about the actual work involved, so they can emphasize any relevant experience and be well informed at interview. In addition, training or refresher courses and expert advice could be helpful. With determination and commitment, they will find some excellent opportunities coming their way. March, May, July and September could see some interesting developments, but with the encouraging aspects throughout the year, opportunities can arise quickly and at almost any time.

The Tiger's progress at work can also lead to a rise in income and financially this is a much-improved year. Many Tigers could enjoy some additional good fortune, with an activity, interest, idea or hunch rewarding them well. In addition, if there is something particular the Tiger wants to buy, it would be to his advantage to keep alert. Over the year many Tigers could be fortunate in spotting bargains. However, while the Tiger can fare well financially, he should use any upturn to help his overall position rather than fritter it away. This includes looking to reduce any borrowings he may have as well as taking advantage of tax incentives to set something aside for the longer term.

With this being a favourable year, the Tiger should also consider treating himself to a holiday or some time away. Not only can a break do him considerable good, but by choosing his destination carefully, he will often have a lot of fun. Again, this is a year to make good use of his opportunities.

The Tiger's personal life will also see a lot of activity and there will be good opportunities to make some significant new friends. For unattached Tigers, their own year can mark the start of a wonderful romance which could come about almost as if ordained by fate. Friendships and, for some, romance can mean a lot to the Tiger this year, with April to June, August and December being especially active and often special months. Any Tiger who is alone or has had some personal difficulty or sadness to bear will find his own year can see a brightening in his situation, with new friendships or interests being of real value.

An important aspect of the Tiger's personality is that he does like to keep active and in his domestic life he will often have ideas he wants to carry out. However, despite his eagerness, these should not be rushed, and major home purchases or plans need to be thought through and costed carefully. With good planning, far better choices will often be made.

With this being a year for change, some Tigers may be tempted to move, and those who do will again need to allow time and avoid haste. However, whether the Tiger moves or remains in his present accommodation, 2010 will see a lot of practical activity, with many a Tiger being the instigator of some ambitious plans.

The Tiger can also look forward to some particularly special moments during the year, with personal news and family occasions to celebrate. And despite all the activity, by preserving time to spend with his loved ones, he can make this a gratifying and often eventful year.

The aspects are very much on the Tiger's side this year, with opportunities to make more of his talents as well as enjoy the realization of his plans and the times he spends with others. This will be a busy year but a special one.

The Metal Tiger

This is the Metal Tiger's own year and one which holds considerable promise for him. It is a year for forging ahead with plans as well as enjoying some personal achievements. The Metal Tiger will fare well and will also benefit from some strokes of good fortune.

Almost as soon as the Tiger year begins, if not a few weeks before, many Metal Tigers will detect a change in their fortunes. After being frustrated by some of the problems and pressures of the Ox year, they will begin to feel more determined and hopeful. And as one who likes to get on and do things, the Metal Tiger will realize that to make the changes he wants, he should act. Certainly, this is very much a year favouring initiative.

At work this is a time of change and opportunity. For those Metal Tigers who have felt frustrated in recent times, their own year can bring them the openings they have long been wanting. Some could find themselves ideally placed for promotion. For those who do take on new responsibilities, their new role will often allow them to concentrate on the areas in which their strengths lie.

Most Metal Tigers will remain with their present employer over the year and benefit from opportunities that arise there, but those who would prefer to change or reduce their working commitments could also enjoy some fortuitous chances. Sometimes good friends or close contacts could alert them to an ideal opportunity, or by making enquiries they could discover a position that is perfect for them. As many will find, once they start to take action, possibilities will emerge. March, May, July and September could see some interesting developments. These Metal Tigers should also not allow any applications that do not go their way to weaken their resolve. Opportunities can arise in curious ways in their own year and it is a time to remain persistent and alert.

Conversely, however, some Metal Tigers will retire this year. Those who do would do well to give serious consideration to the activities they would now like to pursue. With some clear objectives, these Metal Tigers will often revel in the opportunity to do what they want.

As far as personal interests are concerned, all Metal Tigers should look to develop what they do in some way. New challenges could be especially satisfying and should there be a particular interest that appeals to him, the Metal Tiger should follow it up. With good use of time and opportunity, he will find his actions and interests can add a great deal of pleasure and purpose to the year.

The Metal Tiger can also look forward to some interesting travel opportunities. In addition to a special holiday, possibly to mark his sixtieth birthday, he could have chances to go away for a short break or receive invitations to visit others. Although some of his travelling could be arranged at short notice, he can look forward to visiting some interesting destinations as well as enjoying himself while away.

With his own year having an element of luck, if he sees a competition that interests him, he would also do well to enter it. His own year can have some pleasant surprises in store.

Throughout the year the Metal Tiger will be grateful for the support of those around him, with his domestic life being both active and meaningful. However, with some of the ideas he has and decisions he will need to make, he does need to be open and communicative. This way, more can be decided, arranged and looked forward to. In addition, with some Metal Tigers deciding to move or make improvements to their home, if decisions are shared and all play their part, plans will often be all the easier to carry out. The Metal Tiger will also be grateful for the encouragement he is given for some of his own activities, and others may well have surprises in store to mark his sixtieth birthday. Over the year the love, support and goodwill shown him will be special and mean a great deal to him.

He will also enjoy an increase in social activity, particularly arising from an interest he pursues. By making the most of opportunities to meet other enthusiasts, as well as taking up invitations, he can look forward to some interesting and pleasurable occasions. Any Metal Tiger who is keen to lead a fuller social life or make new friends will find that positive action will reward him well. For some who are unattached, a new friendship could turn to romance and add a definite sparkle to the year. Social opportunities could occur at almost any time, some with little warning, but April to June, August, December and early January could be particularly active and special months.

The Metal Tiger's own year contains many positive aspects but, as with any year, problems can still arise and disappointments sometimes occur. In 2010 these will often come as a result of rush or unnecessary risk, and despite the Metal Tiger's natural enthusiasm, he does need to be wary of acting without sufficient thought or consultation. Particularly in financial matters, when dealing with paperwork or making important decisions, he will need to be thorough, attentive and prepared to check anything which may be unclear.

In most respects, though, this will be a highly favourable year for the Metal Tiger, and by using his time and opportunities well, he can accomplish a great deal as well as look forward to some personally rewarding times.

TIP FOR THE YEAR
Give some thought to what you want to do. With clear aims and ideas, a lot can open up for you. This is your year and it can bring you much good fortune.

The Water Tiger

The Water Tiger will have much in his favour this year. With his Tiger enthusiasm combined with the Water element making him an effective communicator, important doors will open up for him, allowing him to accomplish a great deal. After the muted progress some will have experienced of late, this is a time when they will be able to reap some well-deserved and sometimes overdue rewards.

One important feature of the year is that it will give the Water Tiger a greater chance to act on his ideas and to use his strengths. If there is a specific objective that he has been keen to realize or changes he has been considering, now is the time to keep alert and explore possibilities. As many Water Tigers will find, once they start to take action, developments can quickly follow on.

At work the Tiger year can be particularly significant. For some Water Tigers, important opportunities can beckon, even though these may be different from what they may have envisaged. For some these could entail considerable change and upheaval, but to compensate, these Waters Tigers will often feel invigorated by the challenge they are now presented with.

For Water Tigers who are feeling staid and unfulfilled at work, this can also be the year when their career enjoys a new lease of life. Opportunities in their present place of work could allow some to switch to something different and broaden their skills, while others, by making enquiries, could find a more fulfilling position with another employer. Again, once the Water Tiger has made the conscious decision to make a change, he will be setting important – and unstoppable – wheels in motion.

For Water Tigers seeking work, the Tiger year can also bring some interesting opportunities. A major feature of the year is that it will give many the chance to develop their skills in new ways. March, May, July and September to mid-October could see the best opportunities, but such is the nature of the Tiger year that possibilities can open up quickly and at almost any time. As far as work matters are concerned, this is a year to keep alert and be ready to act.

With the encouraging aspects, the Water Tiger will also find this a favourable year to develop certain personal interests or skills. Those who are creative could find this a particularly inspiring time, with some exciting ideas to explore. If they are able to promote or display any of their work, they could be encouraged by the response.

The Tiger year can also bring some unexpected travel opportunities and, in addition to a main break or holiday, the Water Tiger could receive invitations to visit others or find his work giving him the chance to travel. Over the year many Water Tigers can look forward to visiting some interesting destinations and areas new to them.

The Water Tiger's progress over the year can lead to an improvement in his financial situation and this may well lead to him deciding to go ahead with certain plans or purchases he has been considering. However, he should still keep a close watch on his spending and where possible consider setting something aside for the longer term. Money saved now, sometimes enhanced through tax relief, could become a welcome asset in years to come. Also, the Water Tiger should be wary of risk or complacency. Despite the encouraging aspects, misjudgements could still occur, and time does need to be allowed for planning major purchases. Water Tigers, take note and do manage your money wisely.

This will be a special year in the Water Tiger's domestic life, often being marked by some important family news or celebration. The Water Tiger will enjoy playing a key part, particularly in making arrangements. Also, throughout the year he will do much to help and advise close relations, with his time and insights being valued. However, with many Water Tigers experiencing change in their work and others in their household leading equally busy schedules, it is important that there is good co-operation and a sharing of household tasks. As with any year, pressures, problems and differences of opinion will sometimes raise their head, but if there is a willingness to talk these through, they will not detract from this often rewarding time.

The Water Tiger's work, interests and circle of friends will also give rise to some social occasions over the year and he will often enjoy the company of those who are like-minded. For Water Tigers who would welcome a more fulfilling social life, the Tiger year can see a transformation in their situation and, for some, the chance of an important new friendship or romance. Again, if the Water Tiger is active, a lot can open up for him. April to June, August and December to early January will see the most social activity.

Overall, this is a year of considerable potential for the Water Tiger and by seizing his opportunities, he can make important progress. With determination, goodwill and good luck, this can be a successful and progressive year.

TIP FOR THE YEAR
Take the initiative. Believe in yourself and what you want. By making decisions and taking action, you can take advantage of some important developments and will find that opportunities will often quickly follow on.

The Wood Tiger

This is a year of considerable opportunity for the Wood Tiger, although just how much he achieves is partly dependent on him. As a Wood Tiger, he has a keen nature and is interested in many things, but without care, he can spread his energies too widely. To reap the rewards of this favourable time, he does need to remain focused and disciplined.

As the Tiger year starts, it would help him to have some idea of what he wants to accomplish during it. This could be related to almost any area of his life, but with some thoughts in mind he will not only make better use of his time and energy but also be alert to the right actions to take. By planning ahead, he will be able to get far more out of the year.

The Wood Tiger's work prospects are especially promising, with important opportunities opening up. Sometimes, as a result of work he has recently been engaged on, his employer could look to him to take on a greater role. Many Wood Tigers will find themselves being trained for and offered promotion this year. Such are the aspects that one step up could be the prelude to others and, particularly for the ambitious, this can be a year of substantial headway and some great personal and well-deserved success.

For Wood Tigers who feel there are limited openings in their current place of work and want to further their experience elsewhere, again some very good opportunities will be available. By making enquiries and, if appropriate, talking to contacts, they could be alerted to some ideal positions. By having a clear idea of what they want to do and taking that all-important first step, they will find possibilities soon opening up for them.

This also applies to those Wood Tigers seeking work. Although some may have become dispirited about their prospects in recent times, by maintaining belief in themselves, they will find their drive, initiative and commitment will often prevail and give them the chance they have been wanting. For some this will be in a totally different area than before but will nevertheless set their career off on a potentially rewarding track. This is a year of scope and possibility. Opportunities can arise quickly, with March, May, July and September seeing some interesting developments.

The progress the Wood Tiger makes at work will lead to a rise in income and some Wood Tigers could receive funds from another source or find a personal interest supplementing their means. However, to reap the benefits of any upturn, the Wood Tiger will need to manage his money carefully. It would be helpful for him to look ahead and make provision for more expensive plans and outlays. Also, if entering into an agreement, he does need to check the terms and implications. The aspects may be on his side, but this is still not a year for risks or proceeding on a hurried or ad hoc basis. With clear ideas and good management, the Wood Tiger will fare much better financially.

For many Wood Tigers, accommodation matters will figure prominently over the year, including a possible move. Here again, costs need to be considered and early provision made for new obligations. However, while moving or carrying through plans will bring pressure, what is achieved can underline the progressive nature of the year.

Such are the aspects that many Wood Tigers can also look forward to a personal celebration during the year. For some this could be a personal or family success, a decision to marry or, if currently alone, the start of a serious relationship. This can indeed be a special and personally exciting time. Also, throughout the year the Wood Tiger will be well supported by those close to him. At times of pressure he will find it helpful to share his concerns and will benefit from the advice and assistance given.

In return the Wood Tiger will do a lot for others during the year and for those Wood Tigers with more senior relations, the time and help they are able to give will be more appreciated than they may realize. For those who are parents, the encouragement and care given to their children will not only be important in terms of their physical development but will also strengthen rapport and understanding.

With the Wood Tiger's relations with others being favourably aspected this year, he can also look forward to some pleasurable social occasions and opportunities to meet others. For the unattached, romance or an important new friendship could transform their year. April, June, August and December could see the most social activity, but whenever the Wood Tiger has invitations or sees events that appeal to him, he should try to go. Not only can these often be highly enjoyable, but they can also bring balance to his lifestyle. There will also be opportunities to travel during the year, although, as with so much in 2010, planning ahead will enable the Wood Tiger to do more.

On a cautionary note, when taking part in physical activities, whether sport, recreation, lifting or undertaking strenuous tasks, the Wood Tiger will need to take care and follow the correct procedures. Similarly, if he experiences a spate of hectic days and late nights, he should make sure he allows himself the chance to rest and catch up, as well as pay attention to his well-being and diet. Taking good care of himself will enable him to enjoy this positive year.

Generally, this is a year of considerable promise for the Wood Tiger, with successes and sometimes celebrations in his personal life to enjoy, while in his work there will be good opportunities to progress. To benefit fully he will need to keep focused and act on his ideas and the very good opportunities that will come his way. But with his own keen nature, backed by the support of those around him, this can be a positive and rewarding year.

TIP FOR THE YEAR
Be disciplined. With resolve and purpose, a lot can open up for you. Use your time and opportunities wisely and you will be rewarded well.

The Fire Tiger

Whether it is because this is the Year of the Tiger or due to his own ambitious nature, the Fire Tiger will be keen to make much of the next 12 months. He realizes that achieving his aims not only rests on his willingness to act but also to put himself forward. And his determination, energy and considerable qualities will lead to some significant developments during the year and times of personal happiness.

The Fire Tiger's relations with others will be particularly special and for those with a partner there will often be some exciting plans to look forward to. These could involve a change of accommodation or celebrating some personal or family news. In addition, giving time to each other and sharing interests and love and understanding can bring extra meaning and importance to the year.

For Fire Tigers who are unattached, the year is also encouragingly aspected, with many feeling the effects of Cupid's arrow. A chance encounter could quickly develop into a serious romance, with some meeting their soul mate and future partner. For any Fire Tigers who are nursing disappointment over a relationship that has foundered, there will be a good chance of meeting someone who will become significant. The Tiger year contains many favourable developments and the Fire Tiger's personal life is particularly highlighted.

The Fire Tiger will also find his interests and recreational pursuits giving rise to some good social opportunities. Here again, any Fire Tigers who are alone or would like new friendships will find that by going out and becoming more involved in interests they enjoy, they can be well rewarded with an upturn in their social life. April to June, August, December and early January could see the most social activity, but in most months there will be things for the Fire Tiger to do, with spontaneity and unexpected occasions adding to the excitement of the year.

Throughout the year it is also important that the Fire Tiger draws on the assistance of family members. In addition to providing support and encouragement, more senior relations will often be pleased to advise on certain decisions or give additional help. Over this full and busy year Fire Tigers would do well to remember this and be prepared to ask.

This is also a favourable year as far as the Fire Tiger's work prospects are concerned and he should not only keep alert for ways to advance but also be prepared to put himself forward. Often important progress can be made with his present employer and some Fire Tigers will be offered the chance to train for greater responsibilities.

Work prospects are also promising for Fire Tigers who decide to move elsewhere or are seeking a position. By obtaining advice from employment agencies and professional organizations and stressing their experience at interview, they will find some interesting opportunities can arise. This is a good time for the Fire Tiger to look at different ways of using his strengths. March, May, July and September could see some positive developments, but when the Fire Tiger sees an opening that interests him, he should be quick to act.

Over the year he should also make the most of chances to network and meet others in similar lines of work to his own. Whether through courses, joining an organization or being introduced to others, by getting himself known and impressing those he meets, he can do much to help his present position and future prospects. In addition, colleagues who have similar interests could become long-standing friends.

The Fire Tiger's progress at work can also help him financially. However, as with many of his sign, he does spend his money easily and has a most generous streak. Over the year it would be helpful for him to keep a close watch on his outgoings and save towards specific requirements. He should also be wary of risk or entering into agreements before he has had time to check the implications. If he has any doubts he should seek advice. Financially, this is a year when good management will reward him well.

Overall, the Tiger year is a highly favourable one for the Fire Tiger, giving him the opportunity to make more of himself, advance his career and enjoy positive relations with many. This is his year and it is one in which he can show his many fine qualities.

TIP FOR THE YEAR

This is no time for standing still. Seek out ways to make more of your skills and strengths. With willingness, a lot can open up for you. Also, enjoy your positive relations with others. Their support and encouragement can have a positive bearing on how you fare.

The Earth Tiger

This will be a pleasing year for the Earth Tiger with good opportunities for him to enjoy and develop certain interests and skills. In addition, his family and social life will be important, with a variety of occasions to look forward to.

For Earth Tigers born in 1998 this can be an especially important year. In their education there will be many opportunities to try out new skills, have extra lessons and courses in areas of particular interest (including sport and music) and enjoy the other activities their school can offer. By making the most of these facilities, the young Earth Tiger will not only have fun but also be furthering his education. With a positive and keen attitude, he can make considerable progress this year.

The Earth Tiger should also aim to make the most of his hobbies and interests. By spending time on what he enjoys, he will take much satisfaction from what he can achieve. Also, if a new subject or activity appeals to him, he should find out more. This is very much a year for discovering and developing talents.

With his active and outgoing nature, the Earth Tiger will also enjoy the companionship of many people, and his interests will allow him to meet others. Particularly for those Earth

Tigers who are feeling alone or are in a new environment, a friendship made this year can prove special and enduring.

While the aspects are encouraging, should the Earth Tiger have any concerns or be keen to try out or develop certain activities, it is important that he lets others know. Those close to him are keen to see him make the most of his potential, but for them to do so, the Earth Tiger will need to be forthcoming and receptive to assistance and advice given.

Another highlight of the year will be the travel opportunities it will bring, and many young Earth Tigers will enjoy the chance to visit somewhere new. For some, the excitement they get from travelling will whet their appetite for more and be something that stays with them for a great many years.

This can also be a rewarding year for the Earth Tiger born in 1938, with travel opportunities again adding interest to the year. If the more senior Earth Tiger sees a holiday, special offer or short break that appeals to him, or receives an invitation to visit others, he should follow it up. Not only will he enjoy the social opportunities and companionship his travels bring but also the often interesting attractions he gets to see.

The Earth Tiger will also value his relations with those around him, and by talking over his ideas, he will not only gain more support but also stand a good chance of his suggestions being taken further. Not only will he benefit from the assistance of others over the year but he will also be glad to reciprocate by giving time and encouragement to those close to him. As far as his domestic life is concerned, this will be a positive and personally rewarding year.

In addition, the Earth Tiger will derive much pleasure from his interests over the year and by setting himself some aims and projects he will often delight in the ways in which he can use his knowledge. If there is a local group or society that interests him, it could be worth him getting in contact. That way he can also benefit from the social opportunities his interests can bring.

This also applies to Earth Tigers who are alone and would welcome new friends or a more rewarding activity to fill their time. By making enquiries, seeing what is available in their area and taking positive action, they can benefit from the opportunity to get to know others. The Tiger year holds much promise, but it does call on the Earth Tiger to act.

As far as finance is concerned, the Earth Tiger could have some sizeable outgoings over the year, perhaps due to travel, replacing equipment and/or changes to his accommodation. At such times he will need to keep a close watch on costs and, when applicable, obtain estimates and quotations. Despite the favourable aspects of the year, this is no time for risk or carelessness. Earth Tigers, please take note.

Overall, the Tiger year offers considerable opportunity to the Earth Tiger, whether born in 1938 or 1998, particularly in allowing him to carry through ideas and further certain interests. He will be helped by the supportive attitude of those close to him and this will not only encourage him but also bring some often meaningful occasions. This is very much a year for making the most of opportunities.

As an Earth Tiger you possess a keen and adventurous nature. Use your inquisitive streak to discover and learn. By following up your ideas and opportunities, you can make this a very satisfying and personally rewarding year.

FAMOUS TIGERS

Paula Abdul, Debbie Allen, Kofi Annan, Sir David Attenborough, Queen Beatrix of the Netherlands, Victoria Beckham, Beethoven, Tony Bennett, Tom Berenger, Chuck Berry, Jon Bon Jovi, Sir Richard Branson, Matthew Broderick, Emily Brontë, Garth Brooks, Mel Brooks, Isambard Kingdom Brunel, Agatha Christie, Charlotte Church, Phil Collins, Robbie Coltrane, Sheryl Crow, Tom Cruise, Penelope Cruz, Charles de Gaulle, Leonardo DiCaprio, Emily Dickinson, David Dimbleby, Dwight Eisenhower, Queen Elizabeth II, Enya, Roberta Flack, Frederick Forsyth, Jodie Foster, Megan Fox, Crystal Gayle, Buddy Greco, Germaine Greer, Ed Harris, Hugh Hefner, William Hurt, Ray Kroc, Stan Laurel, Jay Leno, Matt Lucas, Groucho Marx, Karl Marx, Marilyn Monroe, Demi Moore, Alanis Morissette, Rafael Nadal, Jeremy Paxman, Marco Polo, Beatrix Potter, Renoir, Kenny Rogers, the Princess Royal, Dame Joan Sutherland, Dylan Thomas, Liv Ullman, Jon Voight, Julie Walters, H. G. Wells, Oscar Wilde, Robbie Williams, Dr Rowan Williams, Tennessee Williams, Sir Terry Wogan, Stevie Wonder, William Wordsworth.

14 FEBRUARY 1915 ～ 2 FEBRUARY 1916   *Wood Rabbit*

2 FEBRUARY 1927 ～ 22 JANUARY 1928   *Fire Rabbit*

19 FEBRUARY 1939 ～ 7 FEBRUARY 1940   *Earth Rabbit*

6 FEBRUARY 1951 ～ 26 JANUARY 1952   *Metal Rabbit*

25 JANUARY 1963 ～ 12 FEBRUARY 1964   *Water Rabbit*

11 FEBRUARY 1975 ～ 30 JANUARY 1976   *Wood Rabbit*

29 JANUARY 1987 ～ 16 FEBRUARY 1988   *Fire Rabbit*

16 FEBRUARY 1999 ～ 4 FEBRUARY 2000   *Earth Rabbit*

THE
RABBIT

THE PERSONALITY OF THE RABBIT

Whenever
Wherever
With whoever.
Always I try to understand.
Without this one flounders.
But with understanding,
at least you have a chance.
A good chance.

The Rabbit is born under the signs of virtue and prudence. He is intelligent, well mannered and prefers a quiet and peaceful existence. He dislikes any sort of unpleasantness and will try to steer clear of arguments and disputes. He is very much a pacifist and tends to have a calming influence on those around him. He has wide interests and usually a good appreciation of the arts and the finer things in life. He also knows how to enjoy himself and will often gravitate to the best restaurants and nightspots in town.

The Rabbit is a witty and intelligent speaker and loves being involved in a good discussion. His views and advice are often sought by others and he can be relied upon to be discreet and diplomatic. He will rarely raise his voice in anger and will even turn a blind eye to matters that displease him just to preserve the peace. He likes to remain on good terms with everyone, but he can be rather sensitive and takes any form of criticism very badly. He will also be the first to get out of the way if he sees any form of trouble brewing.

The Rabbit is a quiet and efficient worker and has an extremely good memory. He is very astute in business and financial matters, but his degree of success often depends on the conditions that prevail. He hates being in a situation which is fraught with tension or where he has to make sudden decisions. Wherever possible he will plan his various activities with the utmost care and a good deal of caution. He does not like to take risks and does not take kindly to change. Basically, he seeks a secure, calm and stable environment, and when conditions are right he is more than happy to leave things as they are.

The Rabbit is conscientious and because of his methodical and ever-watchful nature he can often do well in his chosen profession. He makes a good diplomat, lawyer, shopkeeper, administrator or priest, and he excels in any job where he can use his superb skills as a communicator. He tends to be loyal to his employers and is respected for his integrity and honesty, but if he ever finds himself in a position of great power he can become rather intransigent and authoritarian.

The Rabbit attaches great importance to his home and will often spend a lot of time and money maintaining and furnishing it and fitting it with all the latest comforts – the Rabbit is very much a creature of comfort! He is also something of a collector and there are many Rabbits who derive much pleasure from collecting antiques, *objets d'art* or anything else which catches their eye or particularly interests them.

The female Rabbit has a friendly, caring and considerate nature, and will do all in her power to give her home a happy and loving atmosphere. She is also very sociable and enjoys holding parties and entertaining. She has a great ability to make the maximum use of her time and although she involves herself in numerous activities, she always manages to find time to sit back and enjoy a good read or a chat. She has a great sense of humour, is very artistic and is often a talented gardener.

The Rabbit takes considerable care over his appearance and is usually smart and well turned out. He also attaches great importance to his relations with others and matters of the heart are particularly important to him. He will rarely be short of admirers and will often have several serious romances before he settles down. He is not the most faithful of signs, but he will find that he is especially well suited to those born under the signs of the Goat, Snake, Pig and Ox. Due to his sociable and easy-going manner he can also get on well with the Tiger, Dragon, Horse, Monkey, Dog and another Rabbit, but he will feel ill at ease with the Rat and Rooster, as both these signs tend to speak their mind and be critical in their comments and the Rabbit just loathes any form of criticism or unpleasantness.

The Rabbit is usually lucky in life and often has the happy knack of being in the right place at the right time. He is talented and quick-witted, but he does sometimes put pleasure before work and wherever possible will opt for the easy life. He can at times be a little reserved and suspicious of the motives of others, but generally will lead a long and contented life and one which – as far as possible – will be free of strife and discord.

THE FIVE DIFFERENT TYPES
OF RABBIT

In addition to the 12 signs of the Chinese zodiac there are five elements and these have a strengthening or moderating influence on the signs. The effects of the five elements on the Rabbit are described below, together with the years in which the elements were exercising their influence. Therefore those Rabbits born in 1951 are Metal Rabbits, those born in 1963 are Water Rabbits, and so on.

Metal Rabbit: 1951
This Rabbit is capable, ambitious and has very definite views on what he wants to achieve in life. He can occasionally appear reserved and aloof, but this is mainly because he likes to keep his thoughts to himself. He has a quick and alert mind and is particularly shrewd in business matters. He can also be very cunning in his actions. He has a good appreciation of the arts and likes to mix in the best circles. He usually has a small but very loyal group of friends.

Water Rabbit: 1963
The Water Rabbit is popular, intuitive and keenly aware of the feelings of those around him. He can, however, be rather sensitive and tends to take things too much to heart. He is very precise and thorough in everything he does and has an exceedingly good memory. He tends to be quiet and

at times rather withdrawn, but he expresses his ideas well and is highly regarded by his family, friends and colleagues.

Wood Rabbit: 1915, 1975

The Wood Rabbit is likeable, easy-going and very adaptable. He prefers to work in a group rather than on his own and likes to have the support and encouragement of others. He can, however, be rather reticent in expressing his views and it would be in his own interests to become a little more open and let others know how he feels on certain matters. He usually has many friends, enjoys an active social life and is noted for his generosity.

Fire Rabbit: 1927, 1987

The Fire Rabbit has a friendly, outgoing personality. He likes socializing and being on good terms with everyone. He is discreet and diplomatic and has a very good understanding of human nature. He is also strong-willed and provided he has the necessary backing he can go far in life. He does, not, however, suffer adversity well and can become moody and depressed when things are not working out as he would like. He has a particularly good manner with children, is very intuitive and there are some Fire Rabbits who are even noted for their psychic ability.

Earth Rabbit: 1939, 1999

The Earth Rabbit is a quiet individual, but he is nevertheless very astute. He is realistic in his aims and is prepared to work long and hard in order to achieve his objectives. He has good business sense and is invariably lucky in financial matters. He also has a most persuasive manner and usually experiences little difficulty in getting others to fall in with his plans. He is held in high esteem by his friends and colleagues and his views are often sought and highly valued.

PROSPECTS FOR THE RABBIT IN 2010

The Year of the Ox (26 January 2009 to 13 February 2010) will have been a demanding one, with the Rabbit often facing increased pressures and some frustrating times. However, as it draws to a close, many Rabbits will start to see some encouraging developments.

Domestically and socially, there will be an increase in activity, with chances for the Rabbit to meet friends and relations he does not often see as well as go to events he will particularly appreciate. September and November could see some interesting social opportunities. Also, those close to the Rabbit could offer useful advice over a matter that has been concerning him and he will be grateful for the assistance given and the way certain problems can now be eased or resolved.

Another feature of the closing months of the Ox year will be the travel opportunities that arise. Many Rabbits will be able to take a holiday or short break or stay with relatives or friends. This, too, can lead to some pleasant occasions, with the Rabbit benefiting from the rest and change of scene.

In work matters the Ox year will often have been demanding and the Rabbit could have found progress difficult. October and November could see some interesting openings, but the main value of the Ox year will be the additional experience the Rabbit can gain.

The Year of the Tiger starts on 14 February and will be an interesting one for the Rabbit. Although he may sometimes be concerned about the heady pace of events, he will be able to do well and often turn situations to his advantage. Also, the following year is his own year and during the last quarter of the Tiger year many Rabbits will experience a shift in their favour as projects they have been working on reach a successful conclusion or new possibilities start to open up. The Tiger year is one of preparation and a prelude to better times ahead.

Tiger years are characterized by activity and, like most signs, the Rabbit will need to keep his wits about him. This is no time to absorb himself so much in his own activities that he is not aware of what is going on around him. Fortunately the Rabbit is usually perceptive, but to get the most from this year he does need to keep alert and be prepared to act quickly.

This will be especially true in his work situation. Opportunities can suddenly open up for him, either through staff leaving and promotion opportunities becoming available or chances arising to cover for colleagues who are unexpectedly away. By being swift in putting himself forward, the Rabbit can impress others and make headway. As the proverb reminds us, 'It is the early bird that catches the worm,' and the more quickly the Rabbit acts, the better his prospects.

Many Rabbits will be able to make progress in their present place of work, with March, May and the closing months of the year presenting some good opportunities. However, the aspects are also encouraging for those who are keen to move elsewhere or are seeking a position. By making enquiries and considering other possibilities, they could uncover the ideal opportunity. Again, these Rabbits should remember that time is of the essence and they will need to act swiftly. Such is the nature of the year that even if one application does not go their way, another could soon appear in its place.

Another important benefit of the year is that it will allow the Rabbit to further his experience and if he is offered training or sees courses that could help him progress, he should take these up. With his own auspicious year following, any skills or qualifications he can gain now can prove a very useful asset in the near future.

The Rabbit is generally careful when dealing with money matters and correspondence, and over the year he should not relax his usually disciplined approach. Sometimes, with all the activity, there could be the temptation to rush or not be as attentive as usual, but this could lead to problems. When dealing with finance or important paperwork, the Rabbit will need to be thorough, check what is involved and, if necessary, take advice.

With the pace and pressures of the year he should also try to keep his lifestyle in balance. This includes allowing time for interests, and if sedentary for much of the day, making up for this by taking regular exercise. Many Rabbits could also derive pleasure from a personal goal they set themselves, perhaps developing an existing interest or learning a new skill.

The Rabbit can also look forward to some pleasing social occasions, and changes in his work or introductions made through existing friends could help widen his social circle. April, May and November to January could see some good social opportunities. However, while his social life will be generally positive, at some time during the year the Rabbit could become concerned about a close friend. Here his ability to empathize will be an important asset and over the year many Rabbits will demonstrate the true value of friendship and win the lasting gratitude of another.

The Rabbit's domestic life will be fairly active over the year and his organizational abilities will be of great help. However, while he may be willing, it is important that he does not shoulder too much by himself. He may be willing and conscientious, but there is a limit to all he can fit in. Rabbits, do remember this and ask for help at busy times. Similarly, if anything is concerning the Rabbit, he should seek advice. However, although home life will be busy, it will also bring the Rabbit much pleasure and by spending time with his loved ones on interests, projects or perhaps a holiday, he will find the Tiger year bringing some special and meaningful family times.

In general, the Year of the Tiger is an active and fast-moving one and will see the Rabbit involved in many activities. However, while sometimes demanding, it is a time when the Rabbit can make good progress, gain new experience and take a lot of personal satisfaction in his achievements. And as the Tiger year draws to a close, he will not only start to reap the rewards of some of his efforts but also sense an important shift in his favour which will gather momentum as his own auspicious year approaches.

The Metal Rabbit

This will be a pleasing year for the Metal Rabbit, and while he will not be immune from the fast pace or sudden developments that characterize the Tiger year, a lot can go in his favour. He will have the chance to develop particular strengths and his achievements can bring him a great deal of satisfaction.

At work the Tiger year can bring change and quite a few Metal Rabbits will find their skills and in-depth knowledge in demand as new tasks and opportunities arise. As they will discover, Tiger years are not ones for standing still!

Although many Metal Rabbits will remain with their present employer, for those who are keen to move, perhaps so they have less commuting, or are seeking work, again the Tiger year can open up some interesting possibilities. By registering with various employment agencies and not being too restrictive in what they are prepared to consider, many will be given what can be an interesting opportunity that is very different from what they have previously been doing. Although this could involve a steep learning curve and the early days and weeks may be daunting, by making the most of the challenge, these Metal Rabbits will often enjoy the chance to prove themselves in a new way. Late February and March, May and the closing months of the year could see some important developments, but such is the nature of the Tiger year that opportunities could occur at any time and need to be grasped as they arise. Also, the Metal Rabbit should not lose heart if some applications do not go his way. Persistence will prevail and, as many will find, sometimes a successful opportunity could appear in a most fortuitous way.

The Metal Rabbit is usually careful when dealing with finance and important paperwork and in the Tiger year he must not let his vigilance slip. Over the year documents and policies need to be attended to carefully and kept safely. An oversight or delay could be to the Metal Rabbit's detriment. Metal Rabbits, take note and if you have any concerns, seek appropriate advice. Throughout the year you need to be your thorough self, particularly with decisions affecting the longer term.

An expense many Metal Rabbits will have during the year will be their accommodation. Sometimes there could be repair costs or the Metal Rabbit could decide to replace some equipment or furnishings. When there is time enough, he should obtain several quotations as well as consider his options. The more thorough he is, the better. With accommodation matters featuring strongly this year, some Metal Rabbits may decide to move, and here they could get caught up in the fast pace of the Tiger year. For months nothing may happen then all of a sudden terms are agreed and there is a bout of frenzied activity. A lot can happen in Tiger years, and often very quickly.

With all the activity, the Metal Rabbit will be particularly grateful for the support of those around him. In his home life everyone will need to work together, and with major undertakings, the more these can be talked through in advance, the better for all. Throughout the year the Metal Rabbit needs to remain open and communicative. This way more support and understanding can be given, and discussion can also help ease certain worries or pressures.

However, while the Tiger year will be busy it can also be rewarding, with some fine family moments to enjoy. The progress of a younger relation could especially delight the Metal Rabbit and he should try to take a holiday or break with his loved ones during the year. The change and rest this brings will do everyone good.

In view of the busy nature of the year the Metal Rabbit may be selective in his socializing, but it is important that he does not deny himself the opportunity to go to events that appeal to him or to keep in contact with friends. His social life can bring an important balance to his lifestyle. Also, the Tiger year will give many Metal Rabbits the chance to develop certain hobbies or skills and they will often be able to widen their social circle as a result. April, May and November to mid-January could see the most social activity, with the closing months of the year being an often personally rewarding time.

The Year of the Tiger will ask a lot of the Metal Rabbit, but it will also be one of opportunity. By making the most of the situations that arise, he will often have the opportunity to develop his talents in new ways. This is a year to move with the times, but for many Metal Rabbits it will be a positive, interesting and personally rewarding one.

TIP FOR THE YEAR

With the busy nature of the year, do keep your lifestyle in balance. Spend quality time with loved ones and allow time for recreational pursuits. Also, be communicative and liaise well with those around you. With greater openness, you will be helped and encouraged in a variety of ways.

The Water Rabbit

There is a Chinese proverb which is very apt for the Water Rabbit this year: 'Diligence is a priceless treasure and caution is a talisman for survival.' The Water Rabbit is both diligent and cautious. He likes to be sure of his ground and does not take change or risk lightly. However, in the Tiger year he could find himself in some fast-developing situations with important decisions to take. Here his judgement – and diligence – will serve him well.

In his work this will be a time of change and, for some, upheaval. Over the year many Water Rabbits will find the nature of their responsibilities changing, possibly due to new procedures being introduced or the Water Rabbit being given fresh objectives or promotion opportunities. Whatever happens, almost all Water Rabbits will find themselves involved in change this year, and while they may have certain misgivings, by making the best of their situation and seizing any chances to further their experience, their achievements can be the prelude to further advances, particularly in the auspicious Rabbit year that follows.

Most Water Rabbits will remain with their current employer, but for those who consider the time is right for change or who are seeking work, the Tiger year will be an important one. Obtaining a new position will not be easy or straightforward. Opportunities could be limited and competition fierce. However, the Water Rabbit does have particular advantages. He not only has good self-belief but, with Water as his element, is an effective communicator. And it is by remaining persistent and stressing his skills and experience at interview that he may well secure the opportunity he has been wanting. It may take time, but

March, May to early June and the closing months of the year could see some important developments.

The Water Rabbit can also strengthen his prospects by taking advantage of any training he may be offered or refresher courses he may be eligible for. By keeping his skills up to date and adding to his knowledge, he will be helping both his present and future situation. If there is a particular skill or qualification he feels may be useful and he could perhaps acquire in his spare time, he should work towards this, as it will not only represent an investment in himself but also help to open up other possibilities.

In addition, this can be a rewarding year for personal interests. Many Water Rabbits will have the opportunity to use their communication skills again and for those who enjoy writing or other expressive pursuits, any work they put forward could meet with an encouraging response. With the year favouring personal development, going on courses and expanding his interests could reward the Water Rabbit well. In this busy year time allowed for recreational pursuits will be important, pleasurable and often beneficial in other ways.

The Tiger year can also give rise to travel opportunities. Sometimes these will be connected with work and could involve the Water Rabbit travelling at short notice, but where possible, he should also aim to go away for a break. The rest and respite from all the activity will do him good.

The Water Rabbit is generally careful in money matters and in 2010 he should not let his vigilance slip. Financial forms and important paperwork need to be dealt with thoroughly and promptly and if the Water Rabbit has any uncertainties it is important that he seeks clarification.

Also, when considering any expensive purchase or transaction, he should check the terms carefully. There may be pressures on his time, but financial matters do need to be handled with caution.

With his friendly and approachable manner the Water Rabbit is usually able to get on well with people and his personable skills will serve him well again this year. In his work he will often have the chance to meet new colleagues and he will impress others as well as find many setting much store by his advice. His personal interests, too, can bring him some good social opportunities. Water Rabbits who would welcome a more fulfilling social life will find that by going out more and maybe joining interest groups, activities and courses in their area, they can make an important difference to their situation. Late March to May and November to mid-January are likely to see the most social activity.

The Tiger year proceeds at a fast pace and this will also apply to the Water Rabbit's domestic life. In view of all the activity, there will need to be good liaison and co-operation between family members. The Water Rabbit should also make sure everyone does their fair share around the home, and if he has any concerns or is under pressure, he should let others know. With openness and willingness to help, home life, while busy, will be meaningful and contain some particularly special times, including some surprises. The advice and support the Water Rabbit is able to give both younger and more senior relations will be of particular value, with his ability to empathize again being appreciated.

Overall, this will be a busy year for the Water Rabbit, but what he achieves can be significant in the longer term. This can be an instructive and personally rewarding year and will prepare the way for the success that awaits in 2011.

TIP FOR THE YEAR
Be open to possibility. In this fast-moving year opportunities can arise suddenly and by being prepared to consider and act on these, you can make useful progress. Also, use your abilities to communicate and connect with people. Your relations with others can be another satisfying element to your year.

The Wood Rabbit

The Wood Rabbit is ambitious, with many aims and hopes he is keen to realize. He is also realistic and as situations change he is prepared to adapt. As he recognizes, there are many ways to the top and if he has to alter his route he will do so. During the Tiger year his adaptable and willing nature will serve him well.

At work there is likely to be considerable change, with new possibilities opening up. Some Wood Rabbits could, because of their experience and in-house knowledge, be well placed for promotion or trained for a new role. Sometimes what is offered could be different from what the Wood Rabbit had intended, but by making the most of his opportunities he will not only be advancing his career but also gaining valuable new experience. In addition, with his prospects being encouraging next year, what he can achieve now can stand him in excellent stead for the future.

One of the Wood Rabbit's strengths is his ability to relate well to people, and by showing himself a committed team member and using his chances to network, he will impress many over the year and improve his reputation and prospects.

For Wood Rabbits who are seeking work or hoping to move on from their present employment, the Tiger year can take a curious course. By registering with agencies, keeping alert for vacancies and widening their options, many will obtain a position that is different from what they have done before. Although this may initially be daunting, the Wood Rabbit's ability to adapt and learn can again serve him well, not only in allowing him to add to his experience but also to discover new strengths. The Tiger year may have some unexpected twists, but these can be instrumental in the Wood Rabbit's future success. March, May and the closing months of the year could see some chances opening up, but with the fast-moving nature of the year the Wood Rabbit will need to keep alert and act quickly whenever opportunities arise.

With so much that the Wood Rabbit does this year being of future value, if there are any skills or courses he feels could be useful and can pursue in his own time, he should follow them up. The Tiger year very much favours personal growth.

The Wood Rabbit should also give some consideration to his well-being over the year. If sedentary for long periods during the day, he should seek advice on the most appropriate ways to exercise, and if reliant on fast food, consider switching to a more balanced diet. With the pressures and pace of the year, he does need to look after himself. Wood Rabbits, do take note.

The Wood Rabbit should also be his thorough self when dealing with money matters. Although progress made at work will often bring an increase in income, with accommodation expenses, personal and family commitments and his own plans, he will have many demands on his resources. As a result he should remain disciplined in his spending and keep watch on his outgoings. He also needs to attend to financial paperwork carefully, checking on details and keeping important documents filed away safely. This is no time to be lax and if he experiences problems or uncertainties, he should seek advice. In money matters, this is a year for care.

With his friendly nature the Wood Rabbit enjoys positive relations with many people and over the year he will enjoy and value his social life. In view of some of the pressures and decisions of the year, he will often welcome the chance to talk to long-standing friends, some of whom will be able to help and advise. Certain of his interests can also lead to him meeting others and enjoying the chance to exchange ideas as well as attend what can be some pleasurable occasions. The Tiger year is also well aspected for those Wood Rabbits who would welcome a more fulfilling social life. By involving themselves in more local activities, they can make some potentially important friendships. April, May and November to mid-January could see the most social activity.

The Wood Rabbit's domestic life will also be active and sometimes demanding. With the various commitments of those in his household, there will often be a lot to arrange and keep track of. To help, there needs to be good communication, and if the Wood Rabbit is under pressure or senses another family member is concerned about some matter, it is important any tensions are raised and discussed. This way more help and understanding can be given, with a worry shared being very much a worry halved.

However, while the Wood Rabbit's domestic life may be busy, it will also contain many pleasurable times, including shared interests, personal successes, completed household projects and a possible holiday or break. Domestic life may be full this year, but it can be very satisfying.

Overall, the Year of the Tiger will be an important one for the Wood Rabbit and by adapting to situations as they arise and using his strengths to advantage, he can make good headway and help his prospects, especially for the favourable Rabbit year which follows.

TIP FOR THE YEAR

Be flexible in your outlook, as some interesting and some-times unexpected opportunities can arise this year. Also, develop your skills and interests and make the most of your social and networking opportunities. Positive action can be to your present *and* future benefit.

The Fire Rabbit

This will be an exciting and fast-moving year for the Fire Rabbit, with some often special developments in his personal life. The Tiger year has considerable potential and throughout the Fire Rabbit will need to keep his wits about him and make the most of these interesting times.

The Fire Rabbit loves company; he listens and is inter-ested in people, and others respond well to him. And in the Tiger year he will find himself in demand. Whether going to parties or other social events or just meeting up to chat with friends, he will find his social life bringing him bring a great deal of pleasure. Fire Rabbits who, perhaps because of work, have to move to a new area will find this will give them the chance to meet others and make some significant friendships. For socializing, April, May and the final months of the year could see the most activity as well as bring good opportunities to meet others.

Affairs of the heart are also well aspected and whether the Fire Rabbit already has a partner or meets someone special over the year, the Tiger year can be an exciting and often romantic one. For any Fire Rabbits who have had some recent personal sadness to bear, the Tiger year can see an improvement in their situation, particularly in the second half of the year.

The Fire Rabbit will also be encouraged by the support he is given during the year and will find it helpful to talk his plans over with family members. Those senior to him often have much experience behind them and could suggest possibilities or approaches the Fire Rabbit may not have considered.

Although the Fire Rabbit's relations with others will generally be positive during the year, there could still be certain matters that concern him. A friend or loved one could have a problem and the Fire Rabbit could find himself in a delicate situation. At such times he should be guided by his instincts but also remember that he is not alone and professional advice is available. Simply talking to another person via a helpline could be especially helpful. Fire Rabbits, if necessary, do remember this.

The Fire Rabbit will also derive much pleasure from his interests, especially those that take him out of doors, have a social element to them or allow him to explore his creativity. Although there will be many demands on his time over the year, he should make sure he gives himself the chance to enjoy and develop these.

Another pleasurable aspect of 2010 will be some of the travel opportunities that arise. The Fire Rabbit may be tempted by an offer he sees, receive invitations to visit others or decide to go away almost on a whim. However it comes about, his travelling will often be good fun as well as offer the chance to relax and unwind.

For Fire Rabbits studying for qualifications, the Tiger year will require focus and discipline. Tiger years can bring distractions and to do well the Fire Rabbit will need to concentrate on what he has to do and plan his work and revision carefully. Fortunately the Fire Rabbit has a very diligent nature, but it is worth him putting in the effort this year as well as keeping in mind what he is working towards and the opportunities that certain qualifications can bring.

The Tiger year can also be significant for the Fire Rabbit's work prospects. For those already set on a particular career, this is an excellent year in which to further their skills and broaden their experience. And when opportunities arise to take on further training or responsibilities, by showing initiative and the desire to move ahead, the Fire Rabbit will be doing his prospects a lot of good.

The year can also be important for those Fire Rabbits who are not fulfilled in their present position or are looking for work. By keeping alert and remaining open to possibility, many could secure a job which not only offers the opportunity of learning new skills but could also be a platform for later development. Openings can arise suddenly and by being prepared to act quickly, many Fire Rabbits can make progress that can be of great value, especially in the following Year of the Rabbit. Late February to March, May and the last quarter of the year could see some interesting developments.

The Fire Rabbit will often have the means to do a lot of what he wants over the year although he will need to keep track of his spending and be careful with larger purchases or transactions. This is no year for risk or paying scant attention to small print and the terms and repayments he may be taking on. When in doubt over any financial matter it would be worth him seeking guidance.

Overall, this is a year of considerable opportunity for the Fire Rabbit and by showing commitment and willingness, he can make good headway as well as gain much useful experience. He knows he has it in him to accomplish a great deal and the effort he makes now can set him firmly on the way towards some of his longer-term ambitions. And throughout the year he will particularly value his relations with those close to him and enjoy some special times.

TIP FOR THE YEAR
What you can learn now can bear sizable fruit. Have fun this year but also do yourself proud and make good use of your current opportunities.

The Earth Rabbit

The Earth Rabbit has a quiet and thoughtful nature and likes to set about his activities carefully and without fuss. However, the Tiger year is fast paced and during it the Earth

Rabbit could find himself caught up in sudden developments and having to rethink plans and approaches. This is very much a year when he will need to be alert and aware.

One area which is likely to feature prominently is accommodation. Some Earth Rabbits will decide to move to a place that better suits their requirements and the Tiger year will ask a lot of them. Not only will there be considerable sorting to be done (and the sooner this is started the better), but a lot of time will be spent looking for a suitable place to move to as well as in finding a buyer for their own home. There will be times of pressure, despair and important decisions, but when all is agreed, events could move surprisingly quickly and the Earth Rabbit be keen to settle into his new home and area.

For Earth Rabbits who are content where they are, again the active nature of the Tiger year will come to the fore and they will be keen to proceed with certain changes to their home. These could include replacing equipment and furnishings. The Earth Rabbit will particularly delight in making selections in home furnishings and décor, and his fine taste and judgement will lead to some pleasing purchases. For almost all Earth Rabbits this will be a year which will see much practical activity and some upheaval at home, but despite the pressure and disruption, the Earth Rabbit will often delight in what is achieved and the benefits that follow on.

With all the activity, there are, though, two important points to be stressed. The Earth Rabbit does need to deal with financial transactions carefully and study the terms and implications of any agreements he may enter into. This is not a time to make assumptions or rush matters that could have important repercussions. Similarly, should he receive any paperwork about pensions, benefits or taxes which could affect his position, he should deal with this promptly and check anything that may be unclear. Earth Rabbits, do take note, remain thorough and, where necessary, draw on the advice of experts.

The other area that requires care is physical safety when undertaking strenuous activities. When lifting, moving heavy or cumbersome objects or gardening, the Earth Rabbit needs to follow correct procedures and, when possible, draw on the assistance of others. Earth Rabbits, again take note and do not take risks where your own well-being is concerned.

More positively, the Tiger year can bring some good travel opportunities for the Earth Rabbit, with some arising at short notice. Although the methodical Earth Rabbit may prefer more time to prepare, taking up an unexpected invitation to stay with someone, a bargain travel opportunity or the suggestion of a short break can all add fun and extra meaning to the year. The Tiger year has a strong element of spontaneity.

Throughout the year the Earth Rabbit will be grateful for the support of those close to him. With some of the decisions that need taking and the plans he wants to carry out, their input, advice and practical help will be important and sometimes reassuring. Although accommodation matters can make this a busy year, it will also contain some family occasions which will be particularly special to him. Domestically, the last quarter of the year will be especially active.

Over the years the Earth Rabbit will also have built up considerable knowledge about certain of his interests and the Tiger year will give him a good chance both to use and enjoy this. This could be through pursuing a particular activity, developing an idea, carrying out a project or sharing his enthusiasm and skills with others, but by giving time to what he enjoys, the Earth Rabbit can take much personal satisfaction from the year. In addition, his interests can sometimes have a strong social element that the Earth Rabbit will find enjoyable and helpful. For those who move, it would be well worth finding out about local societies or interest groups in their area.

For Earth Rabbits born in 1999 the Tiger year can be an active one, with some important changes taking place. For some this could involve a change of school and starting a new range of subjects as well as learning new skills. For the conscientious Earth Rabbit who has a tendency to keep his feelings to himself, parts of the year could be daunting. However, he should remember he is not alone and many around him will have similar concerns. By allowing themselves time to adjust these young Earth Rabbits will quickly realize that with change comes a wealth of opportunity and the Tiger year will introduce them to new possibilities and skills that they will be able to develop and often take much pleasure in.

Whether born in 1939 or 1999, this can be an eventful year for the Earth Rabbit. There will be pressures, changes and also some good opportunities, and by keeping alert and making the most of unfolding situations, he will often find events going in his favour. Throughout the year he should remember that those around him can offer support, which can be helpful in these active but often satisfying times.

TIP FOR THE YEAR

For the senior Earth Rabbit, be careful and thorough when conducting important transactions or dealing with paperwork which could have financial implications. And for all Earth Rabbits, enjoy and develop your interests and if possible, share your enthusiasm with others. With awareness and willingness, a lot can happen for you this year.

FAMOUS RABBITS

Margaret Atwood, Drew Barrymore, David Beckham, Harry Belafonte, Pope Benedict XVI, Ingrid Bergman, St Bernadette, Jeff Bezos, Gordon Brown, Nicolas Cage, Lewis Carroll, Fidel Castro, John Cleese, Confucius, Marie Curie, Johnny Depp, Albert Einstein, George Eliot, W. C. Fields, James Fox, Sir David Frost, Cary Grant, Edvard Grieg, Oliver Hardy, Seamus Heaney, Tommy Hilfiger, Bob Hope, Whitney Houston, Helen Hunt, John Hurt, Anjelica Huston, Chrissie Hynde, Enrique Inglesias, Clive James, Henry James, Sir David Jason, Angelina Jolie, Michael Jordan, Michael Keaton, John Keats, Lisa Kudrow, Gina Lollobrigida, George Michael, Sir Roger Moore, Andrew Murray, Mike Myers, Brigitte Nielsen, Graham Norton, Michelle Obama, Jamie Oliver, George Orwell, Edith Piaf, Brad Pitt, Sidney Poitier, Romano Prodi, Ken Russell, Elisabeth Schwarzkopf, Neil Sedaka, Jane Seymour, Neil Simon, Frank Sinatra, Sting, Quentin Tarantino, J. R. R. Tolkien, KT Tunstall, Tina Turner, Luther Vandross, Queen Victoria, Muddy Waters, Orson Welles, Hayley Westenra, Walt Whitman, Robin Williams, Kate Winslet, Tiger Woods.

3 FEBRUARY 1916 〜 22 JANUARY 1917   *Fire Dragon*

23 JANUARY 1928 〜 9 FEBRUARY 1929   *Earth Dragon*

8 FEBRUARY 1940 〜 26 JANUARY 1941   *Metal Dragon*

27 JANUARY 1952 〜 13 FEBRUARY 1953   *Water Dragon*

13 FEBRUARY 1964 〜 1 FEBRUARY 1965   *Wood Dragon*

31 JANUARY 1976 〜 17 FEBRUARY 1977   *Fire Dragon*

17 FEBRUARY 1988 〜 5 FEBRUARY 1989   *Earth Dragon*

5 FEBRUARY 2000 〜 23 JANUARY 2001   *Metal Dragon*

THE
DRAGON

THE PERSONALITY OF THE DRAGON

I like giving things a go.
Sometimes I succeed,
sometimes I fail.
Sometimes the unexpected happens.
But it is the giving things a go
and the stepping forward
that make life so interesting.

The Dragon is born under the sign of luck. He is a proud and lively character and has a tremendous amount of self-confidence. He is also highly intelligent and very quick to take advantage of any opportunities. He is ambitious and determined and will do well in practically anything he attempts. He is also something of a perfectionist and will always try to maintain the high standards he sets himself.

The Dragon does not suffer fools gladly and will be quick to criticize anyone or anything that displeases him. He can be blunt and forthright in his views and is certainly not renowned for being either tactful or diplomatic. He does, however, often take people at their word and can occasionally be rather gullible. If he ever feels that his trust has been abused or his dignity wounded, he can sometimes become very bitter and it will take him a long time to forgive and forget.

The Dragon is usually very outgoing and is particularly adept at attracting attention and publicity. He enjoys being in the limelight and is often at his best when he is confronted by a difficult problem or tense situation. In some respects he is a showman and he rarely lacks an audience.

His views are highly valued and he invariably has something interesting – and sometimes controversial – to say.

He also has considerable energy and is often prepared to work long and unsocial hours in order to achieve what he wants. He can, however, be rather impulsive and does not always consider the consequences of his actions. He also has a tendency to live for the moment and there is nothing that riles him more than to be kept waiting. The Dragon hates delay and can get extremely impatient and irritable over even the smallest of hold-ups.

The Dragon has an enormous faith in his abilities, but he does run the risk of becoming over-confident and unless he is careful he can sometimes make grave errors of judgement. While this may prove disastrous at the time, he does have the tenacity and ability to bounce back and pick up the pieces again.

The Dragon has such an assertive personality, so much willpower and such a desire to succeed that he will often reach the top of his chosen profession. He has considerable leadership qualities and will do well in positions where he can put his own ideas and policies into practice. He is usually successful in politics, show business, as the manager of his own department or business, and in any job that brings him into contact with the media.

The Dragon relies a tremendous amount on his own judgement and can be scornful of other people's advice. He likes to feel self-sufficient and there are many Dragons who cherish their independence to such a degree that they prefer to remain single throughout their lives. However, the Dragon will often have numerous admirers and many will be attracted by his flamboyant personality and striking looks. If he does marry, he will usually marry young, and will find himself particularly well suited to those born under the signs of the Snake, Rat, Monkey and Rooster. He will also find that the Rabbit, Pig, Horse and Goat make ideal companions and will readily join in with many of his escapades. Two Dragons will also get on well together, as they will understand each other, but the Dragon may not find things so easy with the Ox and Dog, as both will be critical of his impulsive and somewhat extrovert manner. He will also find it difficult to form an alliance with the Tiger, for the Tiger, like the Dragon, tends to speak his mind, is very strong-willed and likes to take the lead.

The female Dragon knows what she wants in life and sets about everything she does in a determined and positive manner. No job is too small for her and she is often prepared to work extremely hard to secure her objectives. She is immensely practical and somewhat liberated. She hates being bound by routine and petty restrictions and likes to have sufficient freedom to go off and do what she wants to do. She will keep her house tidy, but is not one for spending hours on housework – there are far too many other things that she prefers to do. Like her male counterpart, she has a tendency to speak her mind.

The Dragon usually has many interests and enjoys sport and other outdoor activities. He also likes to travel and often prefers to visit places that are off the beaten track rather than head for popular tourist attractions. He has a very adventurous streak in him and providing his financial circumstances permit – and the Dragon is usually sensible with his money – he will travel considerable distances during his lifetime.

The Dragon is a very flamboyant character and while he can be demanding of others and in his early years rather precocious, he will have many friends and will nearly always be the centre of attention. He has charisma and so much confidence that he can often become a source of inspiration to others. In China he is the leader of the carnival and he is also blessed with an inordinate share of luck.

THE FIVE DIFFERENT TYPES OF DRAGON

In addition to the 12 signs of the Chinese zodiac there are five elements and these have a strengthening or moderating influence on the signs. The effects of the five elements on the Dragon are described below, together with the years in which the elements were exercising their influence. Therefore those Dragons born in 1940 and 2000 are Metal Dragons, those born in 1952 are Water Dragons, and so on.

Metal Dragon: 1940, 2000
This Dragon is very strong-willed and has a particularly forceful personality. He is energetic, ambitious and tries to be scrupulous in his dealings with others. He can also be blunt and to the point and usually has no hesitation in speaking his mind. If people disagree with him or are not prepared to co-operate, he is more than happy to go his own way. The Metal Dragon usually has very high moral values and is held in great esteem by his friends and colleagues.

Water Dragon: 1952

This Dragon is friendly, easy-going and intelligent. He is quick-witted and rarely lets an opportunity slip by. However, he is not as impatient as some of the other types of Dragon and is prepared to wait for results rather than expect everything to happen at once. He has an understanding nature and is willing to share his ideas and co-operate with others. His main failing is a tendency to jump from one thing to another rather than concentrate on the job in hand. He has a good sense of humour and is an effective speaker.

Wood Dragon: 1964

The Wood Dragon is practical, imaginative and inquisitive. He loves delving into all manner of subjects and can quite often come up with some highly original ideas. He is a thinker and a doer and has the drive and commitment to put many of his ideas into practice. He is more diplomatic than some of the other types of Dragon and has a good sense of humour. He is very astute in business matters and can also be most generous.

Fire Dragon: 1916, 1976

This Dragon is ambitious, articulate and has a tremendous desire to succeed. He is a hard and conscientious worker and is often admired for his integrity and forthright nature. He is very strong-willed and has considerable leadership qualities. He can, however, rely a bit too much on his own judgement and fail to take into account the views and feelings of others. He can also be rather aloof and it would certainly be in his own interests to let others join in more with his various activities. He usually enjoys music, literature and the arts.

Earth Dragon: 1928, 1988

The Earth Dragon tends to be quieter and more reflective than some of the other types of Dragon. He has a wide variety of interests and is keenly aware of what is going on around him. He also has clear objectives and usually has no problems in obtaining support and backing for any of his ventures. He is very astute in financial matters and is often able to accumulate considerable wealth. He is a good organizer, although he can at times be rather bureaucratic and fussy. He mixes well with others and has a large circle of friends.

PROSPECTS FOR THE DRAGON IN 2010

There is a Chinese proverb which is especially apt for the Dragon in the Ox year (26 January 2009 to 13 February 2010). It is, 'Slow and steady wins the race,' and although the Dragon may despair at some of the delays and situations that arise, by adapting to the Ox year's steady pace he can still make this a constructive time.

In his work the Dragon will have a good chance to demonstrate his skills in what can be a busy few months.

September could see some encouraging developments, while for those seeking change or looking for work, their best chances will be in the areas where they have most experience.

The Dragon can also fare reasonably well in financial matters and could be particularly fortunate in certain purchases made towards the end of the year. It would be worth him keeping alert for favourable buying opportunities.

With his outgoing nature, he can look forward to an increasing number of social occasions, with August, December and January being particularly active times. For those enjoying romance, the last quarter of the year could be especially interesting.

In the Dragon's home life, time spent sharing activities and plans will be much appreciated. With a lot happening as the year draws to an end, the more that can be decided in advance, the better. There could also be a pleasant surprise in store for some Dragons in the final weeks of the year.

The Tiger year starts on 14 February and has a vitality and energy to it which will suit the Dragon well. No longer feeling so restricted and with ideas and possibilities to pursue, he will be keen to make the most of the next 12 months.

Many Dragons will be keen to progress at work. With the experience they have built up, they will feel ready for new challenges. Almost as soon as the Tiger year begins, if not shortly before, many will be starting to consider possibilities, look for vacancies or make applications. This is very much a time for progress and the Dragon will be keen to take the initiative. However, as he will quickly find, the Tiger year proceeds in curious ways. Sometimes there will be lulls and a lack of response to his applications, but then all a sudden there will be a spate of activity and several expressions of interest. Also, the Dragon could find he is passed over for some positions for which he thought he was a strong candidate, yet pursued for those where he thought he had less chance. Although sometimes baffling, this is very much a year for making the most of opportunities *as they arise*. With willingness and persistence, many Dragons will be successful in furthering their career this year.

For Dragons who are seeking a change from their present role as well as those looking for a position, the Tiger year holds considerable scope. These Dragons will often have the chance to prove themselves in a new capacity and, in the process, considerably widen their skills. A lot can open up for them this year, with March, April, August and November seeing some good opportunities.

However, while this is a year of exciting possibility, the Dragon does need to be careful and alert. In setting about his duties he needs to be his thorough self and wary of jumping to conclusions or taking risks. He should also work closely with colleagues rather than too independently. With the pace and activity of the Tiger year, lapses and oversights can easily occur. Dragons, take note. Benefit from the encouraging and progressive aspects of the year, but do remain thorough and alert.

This also applies to financial matters. Thanks to their progress at work, many Dragons will enjoy a rise in income and some could also benefit from an additional sum during the year. However, the Tiger year does call for discipline. This includes budgeting for more major expenses as well as avoiding too many impulse purchases. Without watchfulness, ad hoc spending could quickly mount up and result in the Dragon having to cut back on other activities. Also, if he is tempted to speculate, he needs to check the implications. This is no year to push his luck too far.

The Dragon will also need to be careful in his relations with others. Although these will mostly go well, sometimes problems could arise. In his home life the Dragon could find busy schedules and work pressures leading to tiredness and tension, and with so many competing demands, quality time could begin to suffer. He does need to be aware of this and, although busy, allow time for family life. The Dragon is usually mindful in this respect, but in the Tiger year it is best to be forewarned.

Despite these cautionary words, there will be much for the Dragon to value in his home life, including home or garden projects, individual family successes and maybe a special celebration or family get-together during the year. Also, where possible, all Dragons should aim to go away with their loved ones for a break. The Tiger year very much favours activity and holidaying in a new area can do everyone a lot of good.

As far as affairs of the heart are concerned, again the Dragon needs to tread carefully. With care, romances can flourish over the year and bring considerable happiness, but should the Dragon start to take the love of another for granted or not be as aware or mindful as he usually is, then problems can arise. Dragons, do take note and be attentive.

Relations with others may need care, but the Tiger year will still contain many social occasions which the Dragon will enjoy as well as opportunities to get to know others. March, April, July and August could see the most social activity, including some invitations which take the Dragon by surprise.

In such a busy year, it is important that the Dragon takes good care of himself. This includes taking regular exercise, paying attention to his diet and allowing himself time for recreational pursuits. With the Tiger year encouraging innovation and adventure, if there is a new activity or interest that appeals to him, he should take the time to find out more. In this busy year it is important that he keeps his lifestyle in balance.

Overall, the Tiger year promises to be a full one, and while the Dragon will value the chance to make more of himself, he will still need to be watchful and alert. Without care, difficulties and misunderstandings could arise which, with greater consideration, could often have been avoided. Dragons, do take note. Enjoy some well-deserved success, but do be mindful.

The Metal Dragon

This can be an interesting and positive year for the Metal Dragon, although throughout he will need to watch his independent tendencies. To remain too rigid in his approach could mean that he is not always able to make the most of his opportunities. In this active year, he does need to show flexibility as well as consult others.

One area which is particularly well aspected is travel. There will not only be chances for the Metal Dragon to meet up with others, including some he has not seen for a considerable while, but he could also get the chance to visit places he has long wanted to see. The Tiger year possesses an adventurous and active quality, and by making enquiries and keeping alert for travel offers, the Metal Dragon will enjoy what he is able to do and the spontaneity of some of what happens.

Another benefit of the Metal Dragon's travels will be the chance to socialize, and those who are alone will especially welcome the chance to meet others. Over the year some valuable new friendships can be made.

With the emphasis of the Tiger year on trying things out, the Metal Dragon should also spend some time enjoying and developing his interests. For those Metal Dragons who favour more expressive pursuits, including photography, art, writing or other creative activities, this can be an especially rewarding year. Some could extend their knowledge by enrolling on a course or taking up something new. By using his skills the Metal Dragon can derive much satisfaction from his personal interests. As with travel, they can also give rise to some social opportunities, with late February to April, July and August being active and favourable times.

With 2010 also marking a new decade in their life, many Metal Dragons will find themselves the centre of attention, with loved ones keen to celebrate. However, here again some ideas that others have could mean the Metal Dragon has to rearrange certain plans and show flexibility. Also, if he has any thoughts on either the marking of his seventieth birthday or other activities he would like to carry out over the year, it is important that he lets others know. With openness and discussion, much more can be realized. In addition, with the aspects as they are, the Metal Dragon does need to listen carefully to the views and advice of those close to him. He may have his own ideas, but to prevent possible discord, it would be to his advantage to be open-minded. Also, should he have concerns over any matter, he could find it helpful to talk these over with those able to offer expert advice. While not an adverse year, the Tiger year can still bring its problems, and when facing these, the Metal Dragon should remember he is not alone.

During the year the Metal Dragon will take particular delight in following the activities of close family members and, if a grandparent, could support his grandchild or grandchildren in a special way. There may be a considerable gap in years, but the bond may be meaningful and constructive.

With his practical nature the Metal Dragon could also feel inspired to carry out some projects on his home over the year. Much can be accomplished, but the Metal Dragon does need to consult those around him and listen to their views. With co-operation and the pooling of ideas and energies, shared projects can bring everyone much pleasure.

With travel possibilities, home improvements and recreational pursuits, the Metal Dragon would do well to keep track of his outgoings and, where possible, make early allowance for forthcoming expenses. This is a year for careful financial management. In addition he should be prompt and thorough when dealing with paperwork and seek advice if he has any uncertainties. The Tiger year is one to be alert.

For Metal Dragons born in 2000, the Tiger year has great potential. With his active and eager nature, the young Metal Dragon will often enjoy the opportunities that open up for him and whether learning academic subjects or enjoying more physical activities, he can take a lot from the year. The one thing to watch is the tendency of some Metal Dragons to be single-minded. Although they may be enthusiastic, they must not let this stop them from being open to instruction, from asking in case of difficulty and from listening to those who speak from experience. For the risk-taker or overly complacent, the Tiger year can pose problems. Young Metal Dragons, do take note. This can be an exciting year with great fun to be had, but do be open to advice.

Whether born in 1940 or 2000, this will be an active year for the Metal Dragon. New possibilities will open up and the Metal Dragon will benefit from a lot of his activities. In addition, both younger and more senior Metal Dragons will value the social opportunities the year will bring as well as the support and encouragement they are given. Throughout they do need to listen to loved ones and show flexibility. But for a great many this new decade can get off to a positive and promising start.

TIP FOR THE YEAR

Watch your independent tendencies. With support, so much more can open up for you. Also, look to develop your ideas and creative talents, and enjoy the love and affection of others. The start of this new decade in your life can be personally very special.

The Water Dragon

There is a Chinese proverb which reminds us, 'With aspirations you can go anywhere; without aspirations you can go nowhere,' and the Water Dragon is certainly one with aspirations. Over the years he will have accomplished a great deal and enjoyed some personal successes of which he can be truly proud. And as the Tiger year starts, many Water Dragons will feel ready to move forward once more. The Tiger year is one of hope and action and the Water Dragon will be well placed to make headway.

For those Water Dragons in work this can be an interesting year. Change is on the way and whether this comes through new management, fresh initiatives or sudden vacancies, there will be opportunities for the Water Dragon to take on greater responsibilities. Sometimes his new duties could be very different from those he has done before and there will be much for him to learn, but a key feature of the Tiger year is that it will give the Water Dragon the chance to move ahead and use his strengths in new ways. For some, the events of the year can give their career the fresh impetus they have been wanting for a long time.

The Tiger year also holds interesting prospects for those Water Dragons seeking work as well as those looking for more major change. With a determined approach, they can find the Tiger year delivering in some often surprising ways. These Water Dragons should not be too restrictive in the type of position they are prepared to consider, and by keeping alert and registering with employment agencies as well as making their own enquiries, they will find that doors *will* open for them. The Tiger year is very rewarding of initiative and with the Water Dragon's earnest and persistent nature, he may well be able to make the change he has been wanting. March to early May, August and November could see some good work possibilities, but such is the nature of the Tiger year that opportunities could arise with little warning and need to be acted upon quickly.

Another satisfying area of the year will be the Water Dragon's personal interests and if there are any skills he wants to learn or improve on or activities he has considered starting, this would be a good time to take action. Many Water Dragons have a liking for the outdoors and for those who enjoy gardening or walking or follow sport, the Tiger year is encouragingly aspected.

There will also be good travel opportunities for many Water Dragons, sometimes arising at short notice. Where possible, the Water Dragon should try to take advantage of these, even if it means rearranging other activities. The spontaneous Tiger year is not always a respecter of existing plans!

The Water Dragon will face some additional expenses over the year, perhaps as a result of extra travelling, helping a family member or home improvements, and he should keep a close watch on his outgoings and make allowance for forthcoming expenses. With good management he will be able to proceed as he wishes, although if lax in controlling his spending, he may need to make adjustments later. He also needs to be disciplined when dealing with financial paperwork and important correspondence. The Tiger year is not one for carelessness or risk.

With his active and outgoing nature the Water Dragon enjoys good relations with many people and in both his domestic and social life he can look forward to many pleasing occasions. In his home life he will be keen to support some younger relations and his judgement and ability to empathize will be particularly valued. Some Water Dragons could also have celebrations in store with the birth of a grandchild or the marriage of a close relation. For many the Tiger year will contain some special family moments.

In his social life the Water Dragon will find himself in increasing demand, with his interests, work and friends all bringing opportunities to go out. There can also be a certain unpredictability to what happens, with the Water Dragon sometimes deciding to go out on a whim or receiving an invitation at comparatively short notice. For the unattached, a new friendship or possible romance could result from a chance encounter. Such are the ways of the Tiger year. March, April, July and August could see the most social activity.

However, while there will be much for the Water Dragon to enjoy, no year is without its problems and the Tiger year will be no exception. When in company, whether that of family, friends or colleagues, the Water Dragon does need to remain alert. Being inattentive or preoccupied or making an ill-judged remark could lead to problems. As a Chinese proverb reminds us, 'What is said can't be unsaid,' and throughout the year the Water Dragon does need to be his aware and tactful self.

Overall, the Tiger year will be a full and interesting one for the Water Dragon and by looking to use his skills and strengths to advantage, he will find his efforts bringing positive results. This is very much a year for pursuing aspirations, and with determination, but also mindfulness, it can be a special and often rewarding time.

Look ahead, but be open to new possibilities. With a willingness to learn and adapt, you can make important headway and use your skills and talents in more satisfying ways.

The Wood Dragon

This can be a positive year for the Wood Dragon, although it also comes with a warning. He can fare well and benefit from the very good opportunities the year will bring, but it is essential he keeps his lifestyle in balance. If he devotes too much attention to one area of his life, problems could start to occur in another. In the Tiger year the Wood Dragon does need to be aware of this and manage his time and commitments carefully.

This is particularly the case in his domestic life. Although he and others in his household may sometimes be working long hours and contending with many pressures, it is important that regular time is preserved for talking and being together. With some of the possibilities that are likely to open up for the Wood Dragon over the year, discussing the implications will also be helpful to everyone. Over the year the time and attention the Wood Dragon and his loved ones can give to one another can make a considerable difference and should not be underestimated. This is a year for involvement *and* quality time. It could also be marked by several pleasing developments. These could not only include some of the Wood Dragon's own achievements but also the academic progress or news of a younger relation. With travel favourably indicated, the Wood Dragon should also try to take a holiday with his loved ones over the year.

He should also aim to keep in regular contact with friends, as well as go to social events that appeal to him. This can be another helpful way for him to keep his lifestyle in balance. He may also be assisted by the advice certain friends can give. March, April and July to early September could be the most active months socially and in this busy year it is important he does not allow other demands on his time to stop him from enjoying social occasions. For Wood Dragons who are alone, especially those who have had some recent personal difficulty, the Tiger year could have some surprises in store, with an important friendship or romance suddenly developing. Events can move quickly this year and in often fortuitous and unexpected ways.

The Tiger year can also be significant as far as the Wood Dragon's work prospects are concerned. There may be reorganization and restructuring in his place of work (this happens a lot in Tiger years) or changes may result from colleagues moving on. Many Wood Dragons will find themselves well placed to benefit. While some of the duties they take on will be challenging and personally demanding, they will give them an excellent chance to gain experience as well as increase their options for the future. The Tiger year can be both progressive and instructive.

For Wood Dragons who are keen to move on from where they are or are seeking work, this is a time to cast their net wide. Their quest will not be easy, but with persistence, belief and initiative, many will not only succeed in getting a new position but one with considerable potential. Progress made now can often have great significance in following years. March to early May, August and

November will see the best opportunities and they should be acted upon quickly.

The Wood Dragon will, however, need to be vigilant in money matters this year. If he does not already do so, it would be worth him keeping a set of accounts so he can keep track of his position. Without care, outgoings could be greater than anticipated and over the year he would do well to keep sensible control over the purse-strings as well as budget ahead where possible. This is not a year for risk or proceeding too much on an ad hoc basis.

With the various demands on his time it is also important that the Wood Dragon does not neglect his recreational pursuits, especially those that give him the chance to relax and unwind or to take additional exercise. He should not drive himself so hard or have so many commitments that he misses out on the pleasure and very real benefits his personal interests can bring.

The Tiger year will be a busy and eventful one for the Wood Dragon, with chances to make headway in his work and widen his experience. Some family news and personal success will mean a great deal. However, with the demands of the year it is so very important that the Wood Dragon keeps his lifestyle in balance. Sometimes this may be akin to a juggling act, but by prioritizing and remaining focused, he can make this a rewarding year which can also have considerable future value.

TIP FOR THE YEAR
Be willing to adapt. Also, preserve time for yourself and those important to you and to enjoy the rewards you work so hard for. Prioritize and keep your lifestyle in balance.

The Fire Dragon

The element of Fire can give a sign greater impetus and resolve, and for the Fire Dragon, this adds to his already determined qualities. Fire Dragons are not ones for holding back. They like to seize the initiative, take action and be involved in whatever is going on. And with the opportunities the Tiger year can produce, this promises to be an interesting and eventful year for them.

One area which will see some important developments will be work. Although many Fire Dragons will feel settled in their career and have made good progress in recent years, the Tiger year can open up new possibilities. For some, their employers will encourage them to develop particular strengths and offer training or give them the chance to take on greater responsibilities. This could sometimes involve a considerable change in duties, but take their career to a new level.

Many Fire Dragons will make progress with their present employer, but for those who feel opportunities are limited where they are or are seeking work, again the Tiger year can bring important opportunities. By keeping alert for possibilities and registering with various employment agencies, many Fire Dragons will succeed in getting an interesting new position which will give them a chance to prove themselves in a different capacity and increase the range of possibilities open to them later on. The year's emphasis on change, progress and challenge will suit the Fire Dragon personality and many of them will benefit from it.

Also, if difficulties or disappointments do occur, the Fire Dragon should not lose heart. By maintaining self-belief and remaining persistent, he *will* prevail. No journey is ever smooth and despite the encouraging aspects, the Fire Dragon can expect some bumps along the way. For work matters, March to early May, August and November could see some interesting developments.

One of the key features of the year will be the way in which the Fire Dragon can broaden his skills, and he can reinforce this positive aspect by undertaking research and study on his own initiative. Similarly, if there is a subject or activity that appeals to him, whether of a work or more recreational nature, he should follow this up. If he is willing to move forward, his actions can bring him considerable satisfaction as well as often having both present and future benefit.

Although the Fire Dragon often keeps himself active, it would also be worth him giving some consideration to his well-being, including reviewing his level of exercise and the quality of his diet. If he feels either could be improved, it would be worth him seeking medical guidance. To make the most of the year, he does need to keep himself on good form.

The progress the Fire Dragon makes at work can bring an increase in his income and some Fire Dragons will also receive a further sum or gift. However, the Tiger year is one for financial care. Without discipline, spending can creep up and the Fire Dragon may not always put his money to its best use. In 2010 he should be wary of impulse buys, watch his outgoings and take the time to consider more sizeable purchases. In addition he should attend to matters which have financial implications carefully and get advice when necessary. Financially, this is a year to be thorough and disciplined.

As far as his home life is concerned, this will be a happy, busy and eventful year. Others will often look to him for advice and assistance and be particularly grateful for what he is able to do. With his practical nature, he will often have accommodation projects to tackle as well as ideas he wants to get underway. However, while he will get a lot done over the year, he does need to allow sufficient time for practical undertakings. In this busy year, good planning and spreading activities out will be helpful. Also, with the demands of an often busy work schedule and other commitments, there will be times when he will feel tired and tense or not be able to give as much attention to domestic matters as he would like. He does need to be mindful of this and keep his lifestyle in good balance. Fire Dragons, take note and preserve quality time for home life and loved ones.

It is also important that the Fire Dragon keeps in regular contact with friends and does not deprive himself of the pleasure social occasions can bring. Amid all the activity, he needs to allow time for fun and recreation. For the unattached, the Tiger year can also have an exciting element, with a chance encounter quickly becoming significant. Late February to April, July and August could see the most social activity and some good chances to meet others.

Overall, the Year of the Tiger has much potential for the Fire Dragon and will give him the chance to develop both personally and in his career. Over the year there will be good opportunities for him, and by rising to the challenge, he can benefit both in the present and the longer term. However, over this busy year he does need to make sure he gives time to his loved ones and keeps his lifestyle in balance.

TIP FOR THE YEAR

Look to further your experience and develop your skills. What you achieve now can prepare the way for further opportunities. Also, value your home life, friends and interests. These are treasures in your life and need your time and attention.

The Earth Dragon

This is a year of considerable promise for the Earth Dragon. However, while the aspects are on his side, he will still need to exercise caution and think through his actions. To take risks or become too carefree could cause problems as well as undermine his prospects. This is a progressive year, but one that calls for self-discipline.

The Earth Dragon has a friendly and outgoing manner and many think highly of him. Over the year his ability to relate to others will serve him well. With many Earth Dragons likely to be involved in change this year, these skills will often give them the opportunity to make new friends and work contacts. For the unattached, particularly those who would welcome romance, this can be an exciting year. Late February to April and July to early September could see the most social activity.

However, the Tiger year does have its paradoxes and while the Earth Dragon will often find himself in demand, the year does call for care. Taking friendships for granted, making assumptions or being less than attentive will be noted and could undermine the rapport and goodwill the Earth Dragon enjoys. Similarly, if he is tempted to stray or let another person down, problems can ensue. Earth Dragons, take careful note. Relations with others can be positive and bring considerable happiness, but lapses have the potential for undoing much of the goodwill you have built up.

Earth Dragons currently enjoying romance can often find this becoming more special as the year progresses, but again care and mindfulness are so important. This is a year to cherish those who are special by listening, sharing and spending time together. With care, the Tiger year can bring some memorable and happy times.

The Tiger year is also known for its energy and vitality. This is a year for action and quite a few interesting possibilities can open up for the Earth Dragon. Many Earth Dragons will take advantage of special travel offers and get to visit some often interesting destinations. Sometimes trips could be arranged at short notice and the spontaneity will add to the fun and adventure.

In addition the Earth Dragon's personal interests are also favourably aspected and over the year he will not only enjoy spending time on these but also adding to his knowledge and skills. For the more creative, this is an excellent year to promote their talents. Many will receive an encouraging response.

In work matters the Tiger year is also one of considerable possibility and will enable many Earth Dragons to move ahead in their career. Some will be encouraged by their present employer to take on additional responsibilities and make more of certain skills, while others may prefer to try a different type of work. This is certainly a year for change and for seizing chances to broaden skills.

For Earth Dragons seeking work the Tiger year can also present some good openings, although to benefit they should not be too restrictive in what they are prepared to consider. This is a year to be flexible and willing to make the most of what becomes available. In addition, the Earth Dragon should remain persistent. Sometimes a new role could entail a heavy workload, but this is no time for giving up too easily or opting out. By remaining determined, showing commitment and proving his reliability, the Earth Dragon will be doing his reputation and prospects considerable good. As the Chinese proverb reminds us, 'Diligence leads to riches,' and in the Tiger year effort and commitment will lead to both present and future success. Opportunities could arise at almost any time, but late February to early May, August and November could see some key developments.

In money matters, the Earth Dragon will need to be disciplined. In order to proceed with certain plans he will need to keep a close watch on his everyday spending and commitments. This is not a year for risk or spending too freely.

In general, the Earth Dragon can fare well in the Tiger year and during it there will be some very good opportunities for him to pursue. By making the most of these and being willing to learn, he will not only be helping his present situation but also paving the way to future growth. He will also enjoy other aspects of the year, including the pleasure his interests, skills and, for some, creative talents can bring. His social life and relations with others can also be a source of much happiness, although in company he does need to remain his attentive and thoughtful self. This can be a good year, but it calls for discipline and awareness.

TIP FOR THE YEAR

Use your opportunities to meet others and make new friends and work contacts. Some of these can come to be important in the future. Also, show commitment. This way you will not only impress others but also learn more and be able to take greater satisfaction in your achievements.

FAMOUS DRAGONS

Maya Angelou, Jeffrey Archer, Joan Armatrading, Joan Baez, Count Basie, Maeve Binchy, Sandra Bullock, James Coburn, Courteney Cox, Bing Crosby, Russell Crowe, Roald Dahl, Salvador Dali, Charles Darwin, Neil Diamond, Bo Diddley, Matt Dillon, Christian Dior, Placido Domingo, Fats Domino, Kirk Douglas, Faye Dunaway, Lee Evans, Dan Fogler, Bruce Forsyth, Sigmund Freud, Graham Greene, Che Guevara, James Herriot, Paul Hogan, Joan of Arc, Boris Johnson, Tom Jones, Immanuel Kant, Martin Luther King, John Lennon, Abraham Lincoln, Elle MacPherson, Queen Margrethe II of Denmark, Andrew Motion, Hosni Mubarak, Florence Nightingale, Nick Nolte, Sharon Osbourne, Al Pacino, Gregory Peck, Pelé, Edgar Allan Poe, Vladimir Putin, Keanu Reeves, Sir Cliff Richard, George Bernard Shaw, Martin Sheen, Alicia Silverstone, Ringo Starr, Princess Stephanie of Monaco, Dave Stewart, Karlheinz Stockhausen, Shirley Temple, Maria von Trapp, Andy Warhol, Raquel Welch, the Earl of Wessex, Mae West.

23 JANUARY 1917 ⌒ 10 FEBRUARY 1918	*Fire Snake*
10 FEBRUARY 1929 ⌒ 29 JANUARY 1930	*Earth Snake*
27 JANUARY 1941 ⌒ 14 FEBRUARY 1942	*Metal Snake*
14 FEBRUARY 1953 ⌒ 2 FEBRUARY 1954	*Water Snake*
2 FEBRUARY 1965 ⌒ 20 JANUARY 1966	*Wood Snake*
18 FEBRUARY 1977 ⌒ 6 FEBRUARY 1978	*Fire Snake*
6 FEBRUARY 1989 ⌒ 26 JANUARY 1990	*Earth Snake*
24 JANUARY 2001 ⌒ 11 FEBRUARY 2002	*Metal Snake*

THE
SNAKE

THE PERSONALITY OF THE SNAKE

I think
And think some more.
About what is,
About what can be,
About what may be.
And when I am ready,
Then I act.

The Snake is born under the sign of wisdom. He is highly intelligent and his mind is forever active. He is always planning and always looking for ways in which he can use his considerable skills. He is a deep thinker and likes to meditate and reflect.

Many times during his life he will shed one of his famous Snake skins and take up new interests or start a completely different job. The Snake enjoys a challenge and he rarely makes mistakes. He is a skilful organizer, has considerable business acumen and is usually lucky in money matters. Most Snakes are financially secure in their later years, provided they do not gamble – the Snake has the distinction of being the worst gambler in the whole of the Chinese zodiac!

The Snake generally has a calm and placid nature and prefers the quieter things in life. He does not like to be in a frenzied atmosphere and hates being hurried into making a quick decision. He also does not like interference in his affairs and tends to rely on his own judgement rather than listen to advice.

At times the Snake can appear solitary. He is quiet, reserved and sometimes has difficulty in communicating with others. He has little time for idle gossip and will certainly not suffer fools gladly. He does, however, have a good sense of humour and this is particularly appreciated in times of crisis.

The Snake is certainly not afraid of hard work and is thorough in all that he does. He is very determined and can occasionally be ruthless in order to achieve his aims. His confidence, willpower and quick thinking usually ensure his success, but should he fail it will often take a long time for him to recover. He cannot bear failure and is a very bad loser.

The Snake can also be evasive and does not willingly let people into his confidence. This secrecy and distrust can sometimes work against him and it is a trait that all Snakes should try to overcome.

Another characteristic of the Snake is his tendency to rest after any sudden or prolonged bout of activity. He burns up so much nervous energy that he can, if he is not careful, be susceptible to high blood pressure and nervous disorders.

It has sometimes been said that the Snake is a late starter in life and this is mainly because it often takes him a while to find a job in which he is genuinely happy. However, he will usually do well in any position that involves research and writing and where he is given sufficient freedom to develop his own ideas and plans. He makes a good teacher, politician, personnel manager and social adviser.

The Snake chooses his friends carefully and while he keeps a tight control over his finances, he can be particularly generous to those he likes. He will think nothing of buying expensive gifts or treating his friends or loved ones to the best theatre seats in town. In return he demands loyalty. The Snake is very possessive and can become extremely jealous and hurt if he finds his trust has been abused.

The Snake is also renowned for his good looks and is never short of admirers. The female Snake in particular is most alluring. She has style, grace and excellent (and usually expensive) taste in clothes. A keen socializer, she is likely to have a wide range of friends and the happy knack of impressing those who matter. She has numerous interests and her opinions are often highly valued. She is generally a calm person and while she involves herself in many activities, she likes to retain a certain amount of privacy in her undertakings.

Affairs of the heart are very important to the Snake and he will often have many romances before he finally settles down. He will find that he is particularly well suited to those born under the signs of the Ox, Dragon, Rabbit and Rooster. Provided he is allowed sufficient freedom to pursue his own interests, he can also build up a very satisfactory relationship with the Rat, Horse, Goat, Monkey and Dog, but he should try to steer clear of another Snake as they could very easily become jealous of each other. The Snake will also have difficulty in getting on with the honest and down-to-earth Pig, and will find the Tiger far too much of a disruptive influence on his quiet and peace-loving ways.

The Snake certainly appreciates the finer things in life. He enjoys good food and often takes a keen interest in the arts. He also enjoys reading and is invariably drawn to subjects such as philosophy, political thought, religion or the occult. He is fascinated by the unknown and his enquiring mind is always looking for answers. Some of the world's most original thinkers have been Snakes, and although he may not readily admit it, the Snake is often psychic and relies a lot on intuition.

The Snake is certainly not the most energetic member of the Chinese zodiac. He prefers to proceed at his own pace and to do what he wants. He is very much his own master and throughout his life he will try his hand at many things. He is something of a dabbler, but at some time – usually when he least expects it – his hard work and efforts will be recognized and he will invariably meet with the success and the financial security he so desires.

THE FIVE DIFFERENT TYPES OF SNAKE

In addition to the 12 signs of the Chinese zodiac there are five elements and these have a strengthening or moderating influence on the signs. The effects of the five elements on the Snake are described below, together with the years in which the elements were exercising their influence. Therefore those Snakes born in 1941 and 2001 are Metal Snakes, those born in 1953 are Water Snakes, and so on.

Metal Snake: 1941, 2001
This Snake is quiet, confident and fiercely independent. He often prefers to work on his own and will only let a privileged

few into his confidence. He is quick to spot opportunities and will set about achieving his objectives with an awesome determination. He is astute in financial matters and will often invest his money well. He also has a liking for the finer things in life and a good appreciation of the arts, literature, music and food. He usually has a small group of extremely good friends and can be generous to his loved ones.

Water Snake: 1953

This Snake has a wide variety of interests. He enjoys studying all manner of subjects and is capable of undertaking quite detailed research and becoming a specialist in his chosen area. He is highly intelligent, has a good memory and is particularly astute when dealing with business and financial matters. He tends to be quietly spoken and a little reserved, but he does have sufficient strength of character to make his views known and attain his ambitions. He is very loyal to his family and friends.

Wood Snake: 1965

The Wood Snake has a friendly temperament and a good understanding of human nature. He is able to communicate well and often has many friends and admirers. He is witty, intelligent and ambitious. He has numerous interests and prefers to live in a quiet, stable environment where he can work without too much interference. He enjoys the arts and usually derives much pleasure from collecting paintings and antiques. His advice is often highly valued, particularly on social and domestic matters.

Fire Snake: 1917, 1977

The Fire Snake tends to be more forceful, outgoing and energetic than some of the other types of Snake. He is ambitious, confident and never slow in voicing his opinions – and he can be very abrasive to those he does not like. He does, however, have many leadership qualities and can win the respect and support of many with his firm and resolute manner. He usually has a good sense of humour, a wide circle of friends and a very active social life. He is also a keen traveller.

Earth Snake 1929, 1989

The Earth Snake is charming, amusing and has a very amiable manner. He is conscientious and reliable in his work and approaches everything he does in a level-headed and sensible way. He can, however, tend to err on the cautious side and never likes to be hassled into making a decision. He is adept in dealing with financial matters and is a shrewd investor. He has many friends and is very supportive towards the members of his family.

PROSPECTS FOR THE SNAKE IN 2010

The Year of the Ox (26 January 2009 to 13 February 2010) can be an exacting one for the Snake and during it he will have faced pressures and considerable challenges. However, despite its demanding nature, he can still get much value from the remaining months.

One of the key benefits of the Ox year is the way the Snake will be able to add to his knowledge, and if he has the chance of training or can study by himself, he will not only find this personally satisfying but also helpful both now and in the future. Investing time in himself will reward him well.

In his work October could see some interesting possibilities, and by concentrating on his duties and developing his skills, he can make the last quarter of the year quite constructive.

The Snake is usually careful in financial matters, but with an increasing number of end-of-year expenses likely, he would do well to keep track of his spending and spread out some of his purchases.

He can also look forward to some fine domestic and social occasions as the Ox year draws to a close. By being more open and using his chances to meet others and talk over ideas, he could be helped in often surprising ways. This is very much a time for him to overcome some of his more reserved Snake tendencies and be forthcoming. He can also look forward to some special family occasions towards the end of the year, with the chance to meet or hear from someone he has not had contact with for some time.

The Year of the Tiger starts on 14 February and will be a mixed one for the Snake. Snakes like to proceed at a steady and measured pace. They are not ones for frenzy or rush, but during the Tiger year they will find themselves caught up in swift-moving developments and will need to adapt as best they can.

Almost all areas of the Snake's life will feel the effects of the year's vigour, but one in particular will be his work. The Tiger year favours change and for many Snakes this could involve adapting to new ways of working or having to alter their role or routine in some way. Events can happen quickly in Tiger years and the Snake will need to keep alert and be willing to act as situations unfold.

Almost as soon as the Tiger year begins quite a few Snakes will find themselves with important work choices to make, with February and March seeing considerable activity. Further opportunities could occur in June and November, but such is the nature of the Tiger year that the Snake could be involved in change at almost any time.

For Snakes who are seeking work or keen to move away from their present position, perhaps because of some of the changes taking place or a lack of suitable opportunities, the Tiger year can be a tricky one. Not only will competition be fierce but opportunities could be limited. There will be frustrating times, but these Snake should remember that situations can change quickly in the Tiger year and one moment they could be full of despair and the next cele-brating a job offer. As the saying goes, 'You never know what's around the corner,' and the Tiger year can quite suddenly present an excellent opportunity.

Whatever his work situation, in view of the changes of the year the Snake would do well to watch his independent tendencies and communicate and co-operate readily with colleagues. To appear too isolated could undermine his position as well as deny him some of the support that is available. When seeking work or considering a change, he should talk to those in a position to give good advice. This is not a year to act too much on his own. Snakes, do take note.

This need for care also applies to money matters. Expenses can arise suddenly in the Tiger year – perhaps repair costs, the need to replace equipment or the decision to go ahead with certain purchases. Although in some cases the Snake will need to take quick decisions, he should still check the terms and implications of any agreement he may enter into. Rush is not part of the Snake psyche, and without care, he may make mistakes and misjudgements. He should also aim to set money aside for specific plans, including travel and a possible holiday, and, if he is able, take advantage of tax relief to add to savings or a pension policy. With good management, he will be able to enjoy what he saves towards.

The Tiger year is an innovative one and the Snake will not only feel its effects in his work but also in the other opportunities it opens up. These include the chance to try out new interests and recreational pursuits, and while some may not come to anything, at least the Tiger year will give many Snakes some interesting new experiences. This is very much a year favouring an open mind. In addition the Snake will appreciate any short breaks or holidays he is able to take. There will be the chance for many Snakes to visit areas new to them as well as enjoy a rest from everyday routine.

The Snake's relations with others will be generally positive and constructive this year, but some Snakes could find themselves being drawn into awkward situations or giving advice to someone concerning a complex matter. At such times the Snake should choose his words carefully and think through the implications of his response. Fortunately he is by nature astute and thoughtful, but in the Tiger year there will be times when he will need to tread warily. This applies to domestic, social and work situations. Difficult moments should be handled sensitively.

However, while it is important that the Snake remains aware of the cautionary aspects of the year, there will still be a lot to enjoy in his relations with others. He should aim to keep in regular contact with friends as well as go to social events that appeal to him. For some Snakes these could include exhibitions, shows or events related to their interests. In this busy year it is important that the Snake allows himself the time to enjoy his social life. March, July, September and December will see the most social activity.

The Snake will also enjoy many aspects of his home life. This is very much a year for sharing with others. By discussing plans and tackling them with those around him, the Snake will not only derive much pleasure from some of the occasions that take place but also great satisfaction from what is accomplished. Also, throughout the year he should listen to the words of his loved ones. Although he may not always agree with what is said, they do speak with his interests at heart and he would do well to bear their views in mind. This is not a year for being too independent in approach.

Overall, the Tiger year will be a mixed one for the Snake. The pace may be hectic and he will sometimes feel uneasy about the events taking place. However, important possibilities can open up for him. This is a time of change and learning and by making the most of it the Snake will be able to gain experience he can build on in the future.

And by being mindful in his relations with others, he can also look forward to some very rewarding occasions.

The Metal Snake

The Year of the Tiger can be an erratic one. Some months may be quiet, with activities proceeding well, while others could see a frenzy of activity and plans disrupted. And although there will be much that will be positive for the Metal Snake, there will also be times that will be unsettling. He will need to keep his wits about him. The Tiger year is not one for him to relax his usually careful guard.

In view of the prevailing aspects, the Metal Snake can do a lot to help his situation over the year by being open about his ideas or plans. That way he can benefit from the advice of others as well as from their support. Although, like many Snakes, he does have a tendency to keep his thoughts to himself, in the Tiger year this is something he really would do well to watch.

Some projects the Metal Snake will tackle over the year will concern his home and this could well include sorting through accumulated items. Although this 'spring clean' may take longer than anticipated, the Metal Snake will be pleased by how much neater and better organized some areas of his home become as a result. And if he can encourage others to join him in the clear out, this can help speed the process along.

Over the year the Metal Snake may also decide to buy some new equipment for his home, either to replace broken or outmoded items or help make certain tasks easier. Here again he should involve others as well as take the time to consider different possibilities and the costs involved. Greater flexibility can alert him to more suitable purchases.

The Metal Snake will also follow the activities of family members with great fondness and will appreciate some of the more spontaneous activities of the year, possibly a trip to somewhere special or a break at short notice. Again, by being flexible he will find that some very positive times can be had.

However, while a lot can go well, as with any year, problems can surface. When they do, the Metal Snake should be prepared to talk them through and so help defuse them. Similarly, if he himself has any concerns or worries, he should talk them over rather than leave them unaddressed.

With financial matters, he will need to be his thorough self. When making major purchases he should check the terms and any obligations he is taking on, and with correspondence and forms, he should be thorough and vigilant. If anything is unclear it would be worth him seeking clarification. The Tiger year is not one for risks or taking decisions without checking all the implications.

A more encouraging area concerns the Metal Snake's personal interests and over the year he should make full use of the knowledge and experience he has built up. For some this could be through writing while others may enjoy meeting other enthusiasts. Many Metal Snakes will not only find sharing their insights personally rewarding but also that others are appreciative. This is a year for sharing with others rather than being too independent. It also favours the new, so if there is a local course or event that appeals to him, the Metal Snake should follow it up.

Personal interests can be especially satisfying this year and will often be made all the more rewarding by the social opportunities they bring and, for some, the new friendships that result.

Overall, the Tiger year will be an active one, with the Metal Snake sometimes taken aback by the speed at which events unfold. He may not always have the luxury of the planning and preparation he so favours. However, by being flexible and liaising with others, he can accomplish a great deal.

TIP FOR THE YEAR
Be adaptable and remain mindful of others. This way you will be able to gain far more from the present time.

The Water Snake

The Water Snake is not one who likes to be hurried. He has a careful nature and takes his time in setting about his plans. However, in the Tiger year he could find himself caught up in some fast-moving events. Nevertheless, by being prepared to act on the opportunities that open up, he stands to benefit.

At work this can be an important but volatile time. Whether through the restructuring of their place of work or the introduction of new procedures, schedules or rotas, few Water Snakes will remain unaffected by change. However, as has so often been shown, change can usher in opportunity, and the Water Snake could find some significant chances opening up for him. For some there could be the opportunity to take on a greater role and develop their skills in a new area or to focus on more specific tasks with interesting new objectives. For the Water Snake, this is very much a year to adapt and make the most of emerging situations.

Some Water Snakes will decide to move from where they are, perhaps feeling the time has come to try something different. For these Water Snakes, as well as those seeking work, the Tiger year can be significant. These Water Snakes should be prepared to widen the scope of what they are prepared to consider as well as register with various agencies. By being active and persistent, they will see some interesting possibilities opening up. February, March, June and November could see a lot of activity, but such is the nature of the year that opportunities could arise at any time and the Water Snake should be prepared to act quickly.

For Water Snakes who are self-employed, as well as those whose work is in any way creative, the Tiger year can again be significant. Over the year the Water Snake could develop some interesting thoughts or benefit from some new possibilities. However, he should not abandon his normally careful stance. Ideas and opportunities do need to be thought through and their implications carefully considered. This is a year for the Water Snake to be open to possibility but also to remain aware and be guided by his often reliable instinct.

The Tiger year can also be an encouraging one as far as the Water Snake's interests are concerned. Those who enjoy more creative pursuits could find some projects they set themselves especially satisfying. For Water Snakes who have let their interests lapse, would welcome a new challenge or have thought of learning a new subject or skill, this would be a good time to find out more.

The Water Snake will also find that the Tiger year can bring some good travel opportunities, and if he is able to connect these to a personal interest or event that is taking place, this can often make his time away all the more special. There could be some additional chances to travel towards the end of the year.

The Water Snake often prefers to be selective in the social events he attends and to keep his social circle relatively small. However, over the year, his work, interests and travels can all bring him into contact with new people, some of whom he will get on with especially well. For the lonely and unattached, this can be a year of pleasing developments, with important new friendships and the possibility of romance. March, July, September and December are likely to be the busiest months socially.

The Water Snake's domestic life will also see much activity. With all the various commitments, schedules, activities and ideas of the household, good planning and a certain flexibility will be very much the order of the day. Also, if embarking on any home improvements, the Water Snake should be aware that these could entail more disruption and cost than initially anticipated. Water Snakes, do take note and plan carefully.

However, while the Tiger year will contain its pressures, there will be occasions which will particularly delight the Water Snake. These could include the birth of a grandchild or the recognition of the talents of a younger relation. Shared interests and projects can also bring much pleasure as well as be helpful in terms of general understanding. In this busy year it is important that quality time is preserved for family life.

The Water Snake is generally careful in his handling of money matters, but he would do well to keep a close watch on his outgoings and, when possible, make advance provision for any large expenses. This is a year for good financial management and control.

Generally, the Tiger year will be an eventful one for the Water Snake. By making the most of the changes taking place, he can learn a great deal and often benefit both now and in the future. This is a year for flexibility, awareness and being willing to take on new challenges.

TIP FOR THE YEAR
With change often comes the chance to prove yourself and use your skills in new ways. Be open to this. Positive action can make this a significant time. Also, preserve quality time for those who are important to you and be open and communicative.

The Wood Snake

The Wood Snake is blessed with a perceptive nature and his talents will serve him well this year. By keeping abreast of developments, he will not only be able to turn situations to his advantage but also make some useful strides. The Tiger year may be a demanding one, but it can be constructive *and* illuminating.

Another of the Wood Snake's advantages is his ability to get on well with others. Unlike some Snakes, Wood Snakes tend to be fairly outgoing and over the year will not only establish some helpful contacts but also benefit from the support that others can give. Throughout the year the

Wood Snake should make the most of his opportunities to meet others. By becoming better known, he can benefit in many ways.

As far as his work prospects are concerned, this will be a year of change. For those Wood Snakes who are keen to build on their present position, opportunities could suddenly arise as colleagues move on, creating promotion possibilities. Some Wood Snakes could also be encouraged by more senior colleagues to develop expertise in new areas. Whether undertaking training or taking on greater duties, by making the most of their situation, they can make important progress as well as help their longer-term prospects. The key to success in 2010 is to be adaptable and willing and take advantage of what opens up.

This also applies to those Wood Snakes who decide to move on from where they are or are looking for work. Opportunities in Tiger years can occur in curious ways and it is important that these Wood Snakes remain open, informed and alert. February to early April, June and November could see some interesting developments, but chances do come quickly in the Tiger year, often on the back of disappointment, and the Wood Snake needs to be prepared to act at any time.

The progress the Wood Snake makes at work can lead to a rise in income, but money matters need to be handled with care. The Tiger year does have its awkward aspects and with the possibility of repair and replacement costs and some larger than expected outgoings, the Wood Snake will need to watch his spending and make advance provision for more expensive plans. This is a year for good and prudent financial management.

It is also important the Wood Snake listens to the views of his loved ones during the year. When he has important decisions to take, those close to him could raise points worth considering as well as mention other possibilities worth bearing in mind. Fortunately the Wood Snake is usually very attentive, but to get the best from the year, as well as prevent possible misunderstandings, he does need to consult others and listen carefully to their suggestions.

This also applies to certain domestic decisions, possibly involving choosing items for the home, making day-to-day arrangements or organizing a holiday or family occasion. Openness and a willingness to pool ideas will not only be good for rapport but also lead to more being achieved. In addition, both younger and more senior relations will be grateful for the time and advice the Wood Snake is able to give and his perceptive and empathetic nature will again be valued.

Although the Wood Snake works hard and has many commitments, he also recognizes the need to keep a balance in his lifestyle and many Wood Snakes maintain several different interests. Over the year these will continue to give the Wood Snake pleasure as well as bring him into contact with others. Those who would welcome a more fulfilling social life and perhaps new friendships or romance will find their interests can be an excellent way to meet others. March, July, September and December will be particularly busy.

Overall, the Year of the Tiger will be an active and interesting one for the Wood Snake and by following developments closely and seizing opportunities as they arise, he can make important headway. This is a year for him to remain aware, be flexible and use his many strengths to advantage.

TIP FOR THE YEAR

This is a fast-moving year, with some events going your way and some being more problematic. However, do not let any disappointments deter you. Believe in yourself, and your skills, energies and support will often allow you to turn situations to your advantage or lead to new possibilities opening up.

The Fire Snake

Tiger years are busy years and this will be particularly the case for Fire Snakes. Over the year a lot will be happening in different areas of the Fire Snake's life and he will face many demands on his time. However, while it will be a sometimes frenetic year, he can emerge from it with some lessons learned and important gains to his credit. The Tiger year may be demanding, but it will be instructive as well as usher in some important developments.

To get the most from the year it is important that the Fire Snake remains alert to all that is going on around him and does not immerse himself so fully in certain activities that other areas of his life begin to suffer. Busy though the year may be, he does need to keep his lifestyle in balance.

In his home life it is particularly important that he preserves time for sharing with his loved ones. This includes taking an interest in what others are doing as well as making sure that joint interests and activities do not suffer due to the hectic pace of the year. For Fire Snakes who are parents or who become parents this year, the time they spend with their children can be important and special.

Another key aspect of home life is communication, and the Fire Snake should aim to share his thoughts with his loved ones as well as speak openly about any concerns or pressures he may have. This will not only give other people more chance to understand and assist but can also enable the Fire Snake himself to clarify what is on his mind.

The Fire Snake should also make sure he keeps in regular contact with friends over the year. His friendships are an important aspect of his life and he will often feel reassured by the goodwill and support shown him as well as sometimes helped by the advice offered. Also, during the year he will often get the chance to meet others, and some new acquaintances and contacts could be helpful to him. For the unattached, the Tiger year can have some surprises in store, with a chance encounter leading to an unexpected but very special romance. March, July, September and December 2010 and January 2011 could see the most social activity, but as with other areas of his life, it is important that the Fire Snake does not allow his social life or some of his very good friendships to get sidelined due to all his other activities. Fire Snakes, take careful note and do try to keep your lifestyle in balance.

Another feature of the Tiger year is the way opportunities suddenly arise, and this particularly applies to travel. This could be work related, but the Fire Snake could also receive invitations to visit others as well as see offers that particularly appeal to him. By following these up, he can find his travels adding an enjoyable and beneficial element to his year.

As far as work matters are concerned, this is a year of important developments and many Fire Snakes will be involved in change. Some will be particularly keen to widen their experience and move on from their current position, and for these Fire Snakes, as well as those seeking work, events can unfold in curious ways. Although these Fire Snakes may know what they want to do, they should remain open to new possibilities. Some could be alerted to positions that are quite different from what they have in mind but will still allow them to make headway. Some could also be encouraged to consider another role, and while this could involve a considerable learning curve, it could give their career an interesting new impetus. This is very much a year to remain alert to change and be prepared to learn and develop.

Fire Snakes who are content in their present position will often be encouraged to build on their skills and may be set some new and sometimes exacting objectives. Work-wise, the Tiger year can be demanding, but by rising to its challenges and being adaptable and willing, the Fire Snake can learn a lot. February to early April, June and November could see some important developments.

With the aspects as they are, though, the Fire Snake will need to pay careful attention to his relations with colleagues and avoid being drawn into office politics or misled by rumour or the pettiness of another person. In the Tiger year he needs to be on his mettle – alert, careful and aware.

In money matters he will need to keep a close watch on his outgoings and be disciplined in his spending. With his existing commitments, any expensive purchases he may be considering and possible deposits he may put down or be saving towards, this is a time for care and good management.

The Tiger year will certainly be an active one and will bring the opportunity for the Fire Snake to make more of himself. But with so many demands on his time, he does need to keep his lifestyle in balance and, in particular, pay attention to those who are special to him. With care and good time management, however, this can be a rewarding and important year.

TIP FOR THE YEAR

Be open to possibility. You have your ambitions and aspirations, but remember there are many ways these can be reached. Make the most of chances to widen your experience. The positive actions you take now can be to your future benefit. Learn, gain experience and take satisfaction in what you achieve this year, but also, and so importantly, value and give time to those important and dear to you.

The Earth Snake

This will be an eventful year for the Earth Snake and one which will contain moments of great joy and personal happiness but also some disappointments and a few regrets. Over the year the aspects will fluctuate, but out of all this the Earth Snake can gain some valuable experience as well as enjoy some memorable moments. The Tiger year will be full, active *and* potentially significant.

One of the key features of 2010 will be the opportunities that will arise, and by being alert and willing to act, the

Earth Snake can benefit from them. These could be related to his interests, perhaps giving him the chance to try a new skill, take a course or join others on a project or activity, or they could be work related, offering ways of developing his experience and extending his knowledge. Whatever opens up for him, by viewing it positively the Earth Snake can get much value from the present time. The Tiger year is one which favours a 'try it and see' approach and will reward the keen and enterprising, with the experience they get and skills they learn serving them well both now and in the future.

This particularly applies to those Earth Snakes currently studying for qualifications. By making the most of their opportunities to learn, they will not only find this a satisfying time but will also be doing a lot to help their prospects.

The same is true for Earth Snakes in work or seeking work. This is a time to put themselves forward and show willingness and commitment. By doing so they are not only more likely to be noticed but also to be encouraged to train for future development. Although at the start of his career, the Earth Snake knows he is capable of going far, and a solid start now will give him an important base to build on.

However, while those Earth Snakes in education or work can make important headway this year, it will involve effort. Becoming distracted, giving less than their best or being lax in their approach could undermine their situation. This is no time to waste. Also, the Tiger year will not be without its difficult moments. Sometimes work they have been carrying out will not get the response they were hoping for or applications they have put a lot of effort into will not go their way. Over the year there will be setbacks but, while these can be disheartening, rather than give up the Earth Snake should take note of any feedback, learn from any mistakes and be prepared to try again, this time wiser and better prepared. The Tiger year can be instructive and its trials and tribulations can teach the Earth Snake many valuable lessons. Despite the occasional knock and setback – which is an inevitable part of the journey of life – this is very much a time to have faith and persevere.

For work opportunities, February to early April, June and November are particularly favourable months, and with the Tiger year's emphasis on trying things out and gaining experience, if the Earth Snake is offered training, an apprenticeship or another way to broaden his working knowledge, he should give this careful consideration. Positive action now can open up opportunities later on.

As far as financial matters are concerned, this is a year for careful control. With an often active social life, the commitments he has and the items he may be wanting to purchase, the Earth Snake does need to keep track of his spending and budget well. As with so much this year, he also needs to be wary of taking risks or proceeding too hurriedly. Haste or impulse buys could leave him with some regrets. Earth Snakes, do take note.

The Earth Snake's relations with others will be a very important part of his life this year. Many Earth Snakes will find themselves in demand, with friends to meet and, for some, a wonderful romance. The Tiger year can certainly be special and for those who feel alone – and some Earth Snakes can be shy and reserved – a chance meeting and the resulting friendship could be especially meaningful. On a personal level, the Tiger year can be positive and rewarding, with March, July, September and December seeing the most social activity.

However, while there will be times the Earth Snake will very much enjoy, the aspects do call for care. This is no time to take friendships for granted, be tempted into indiscretions or neglect the views and feelings of another. Without sufficient care, differences of opinion could arise and friendships and romances be undermined. The Earth Snake also needs to be wary of rumour or the jealousy or pettiness of some people. The Tiger year does not always make things easy for Snakes and throughout the year the Earth Snake will need to be alert and aware.

This need for care also applies to his domestic life. Here the Earth Snake could find himself at variance with certain people. Views, approaches or indeed lifestyles may clash and during the year there will need to be a willingness to compromise as well as talk through any problems or disagreements. However, despite any awkward moments, by being open and communicative and prepared to contribute to home life, the Earth Snake can still enjoy some good times, with certain family occasions being marked in fine style. With this being his twenty-first year, there could also be some surprises in store, and some generous gestures and marks of affection will mean a great deal to him.

Overall, the Year of the Tiger is one of opportunity for the Earth Snake and what he achieves can be of great value both now and in the near future. The Tiger year may not be an easy or smooth one, but it will be instructive and also contain some special and meaningful times.

With willingness and commitment, you can make good progress and important doors will start to open up for you. This is a year to show others what you are capable of. Despite any setbacks, believe in yourself and persevere. You have much to gain both now and in following years. Good luck.

FAMOUS SNAKES

Muhammad Ali, Ann-Margret, Lord Baden-Powell, Kim Basinger, Ben Bernanke, Björk, Tony Blair, Michael Bloomberg, Michael Bolton, Brahms, Pierce Brosnan, Casanova, Chubby Checker, Jackie Collins, Tom Conti, Alistair Darling, Cecil B. de Mille, Bob Dylan, Sir Edward Elgar, Sir Alex Ferguson, Sir Alexander Fleming, Mahatma Gandhi, Greta Garbo, Art Garfunkel, J. Paul Getty, Dizzy Gillespie, W. E. Gladstone, Johann Wolfgang von Goethe, Princess Grace of Monaco, Stephen Hawking, Audrey Hepburn, Jack Higgins, Liz Hurley, James Joyce, Stacy Keach, Ronan Keating, J. F. Kennedy, Carole King, Cyndi Lauper, Courtney Love, Mao Tse-tung, Chris Martin, Henri Matisse, David Miliband, Robert Mitchum, Piers Morgan, Alfred Nobel, Mike Oldfield, Jacqueline Onassis, Sarah Jessica Parker, Pablo Picasso, Mary Pickford, Daniel Radcliffe, Franklin D. Roosevelt, Mickey Rourke, J. K. Rowling, Jean-Paul Sartre, Franz Schubert, Shakira, Charlie Sheen, Brooke Shields, Paul Simon, Delia Smith, Ben Stiller, Madame Tussaud, Shania Twain, Dionne Warwick, Charlie Watts, Ruby Wax, Kanye West, Oprah Winfrey, Victoria Wood, Virginia Woolf.

11 FEBRUARY 1918 ∼ 31 JANUARY 1919   *Earth Horse*

30 JANUARY 1930 ∼ 16 FEBRUARY 1931   *Metal Horse*

15 FEBRUARY 1942 ∼ 4 FEBRUARY 1943   *Water Horse*

3 FEBRUARY 1954 ∼ 23 JANUARY 1955   *Wood Horse*

21 JANUARY 1966 ∼ 8 FEBRUARY 1967   *Fire Horse*

7 FEBRUARY 1978 ∼ 27 JANUARY 1979   *Earth Horse*

27 JANUARY 1990 ∼ 14 FEBRUARY 1991   *Metal Horse*

12 FEBRUARY 2002 ∼ 31 JANUARY 2003   *Water Horse*

THE
HORSE

THE PERSONALITY OF THE HORSE

There are many worn paths,
but the most rewarding
is the one you decide on and forge yourself.

The Horse is born under the signs of elegance and ardour. He has a most engaging and charming manner and is usually very popular. He loves meeting people and likes attending parties and other large social gatherings.

The Horse is a lively character and enjoys being the centre of attention. He has many leadership qualities and is much admired for his honest and straightforward manner. He is an eloquent and persuasive speaker and has a great love of discussion and debate. He also has a particularly agile mind and can assimilate facts remarkably quickly.

He does, however, have a fiery temper and although his outbursts are usually short-lived, he can often say things that he will later regret. He is also not particularly good at keeping secrets.

The Horse has many interests and involves himself in a wide variety of activities. He can, however, get involved in so much that he can often waste his energies on projects that he never has time to complete. He also has a tendency to change his interests rather frequently and will often get caught up in the latest craze or 'in thing' until something more exciting turns up.

The Horse also likes to have a certain amount of freedom and independence. He hates being bound by petty rules and regulations and as far as possible likes to feel that he is answerable to no one but himself. But despite this spirit of freedom, he still likes to have the support and encouragement of others in his various enterprises.

Due to his many talents and likeable nature, the Horse will often go far in life. He enjoys challenges and is a methodical and tireless worker. However, should things go against him and he fail in any of his enterprises, it will take a long time for him to recover and pick up the pieces again. Success to the Horse means everything. To fail is a disaster and a humiliation.

The Horse likes to have variety in his life and he will try his hand at many different things before he settles down to one particular job. Even then, he will probably remain alert to see whether there are any better opportunities for him to take up. He has a restless nature and can easily get bored. He does, however, excel in any position that allows him sufficient freedom to act on his own initiative or brings him into contact with a lot of people.

Although the Horse is not particularly bothered about accumulating great wealth, he handles his finances with care and will rarely experience any serious financial problems.

The Horse also enjoys travel and loves visiting new and faraway places. At some stage during his life he will be tempted to live abroad for a short period of time and due to his adaptable nature he will find that he will fit in well wherever he goes.

The Horse pays a great deal of attention to his appearance and usually likes to wear smart, colourful and rather distinctive clothes. He is very attractive to others and will often have many romances before he settles down. He is loyal and protective to his partner, but despite his family commitments he still likes to retain a certain measure of independence and have the freedom to carry on with his own interests and hobbies. He will find that he is especially well suited to those born under the signs of the Tiger, Goat, Rooster and Dog. He can also get on well with the Rabbit, Dragon, Snake, Pig and another Horse, but he will find the Ox too serious and intolerant for his liking. He will also have difficulty in getting on with the Monkey and the Rat – the Monkey is very inquisitive and the Rat seeks security, and both will resent the Horse's rather independent ways.

The female Horse is usually most attractive and has a friendly, outgoing personality. She is highly intelligent, has many interests and is alert to everything that is going on around her. She particularly enjoys outdoor pursuits and often likes to take part in sport and keep-fit activities. She also enjoys travel, literature and the arts, and is a very good conversationalist.

Although the Horse can be stubborn and rather self-centred, he does have a considerate nature and is often willing to help others. He has a good sense of humour and will usually make a favourable impression wherever he goes. Provided he can curb his slightly restless nature and keep tight control over his temper, he will go through life making friends, taking part in a multitude of different activities and generally achieving many of his objectives. His life will rarely be dull.

THE FIVE DIFFERENT TYPES OF HORSE

In addition to the 12 signs of the Chinese zodiac there are five elements and these have a strengthening or moderating influence on the signs. The effects of the five elements on the Horse are described below, together with the years in which the elements were exercising their influence. Therefore those Horses born in 1930 and 1990 are Metal Horses, those born in 1942 and 2002 are Water Horses, and so on.

Metal Horse: 1930, 1990

This Horse is bold, confident and forthright. He is ambitious and a great innovator. He loves challenges and takes great delight in sorting out complicated problems. He likes to have a certain amount of independence and resents any outside interference in his affairs. He has charm and a certain charisma, but he can also be very stubborn and rather impulsive. He usually has many friends and enjoys an active social life.

Water Horse: 1942, 2002

The Water Horse has a friendly nature and a good sense of humour and is able to talk intelligently on a wide range of topics. He is astute in business matters and quick to take advantage of any opportunities that arise. He does, however, have a tendency to get easily distracted and can change his interests – and indeed his mind – rather frequently, and this can often work to his detriment. He is nevertheless very talented and can often go far in life. He pays a great deal of attention to his appearance and is usually smart and well turned out. He loves to travel and also enjoys sport and other outdoor activities.

Wood Horse: 1954

The Wood Horse has a most agreeable and amiable nature. He communicates well with others and is able to talk intelligently on many different subjects. He is a hard and conscientious worker and is held in high esteem by his friends and colleagues. His opinions are often sought and, given his imaginative nature, he can often come up with some very original and practical ideas. He is usually widely read and likes to lead a busy social life. He can also be most generous and often holds high moral views.

Fire Horse: 1966

The element of Fire combined with the temperament of the Horse creates one of the most powerful forces in the Chinese zodiac. The Fire Horse is destined to lead an exciting and eventful life and to make his mark in his chosen profession. He has a forceful personality and his intelligence and resolute manner bring him the support and admiration of many. He loves action and excitement and his life will rarely be quiet. He can, however, be rather blunt and forthright in his views and does not take kindly to interference in his own affairs or to obeying orders. He is a flamboyant character, has a good sense of humour and will lead a very active social life.

Earth Horse: 1918, 1978

This Horse is considerate and caring. He is more cautious than some of the other types of Horse, but is wise, perceptive and extremely capable. Although he can be rather indecisive at times, he has considerable business acumen and is very astute in financial matters. He has a quiet, friendly nature and is well thought of by his family and friends.

PROSPECTS FOR THE HORSE IN 2010

The Horse is born under the signs of elegance and ardour, and with the Ox year (26 January 2009 to 13 February 2010) favouring commitment and effort, his industrious nature will stand him in excellent stead. In the remaining months of the year he can look forward to making useful headway as well as enjoying some positive developments.

In his work the Horse could find pressures increase as the Ox year draws to a close. Not only will many Horses face a growing workload but they could also have some additional challenges or targets to meet. However, while many will find this an exacting time, it will give them a good opportunity to use and broaden their skills and help their reputation. September to early October could bring some interesting work developments.

Many Horses can also look forward to some positive financial news, with a possible increase in income or a bonus or gift. In addition the Horse could be fortunate with some purchases he makes at this time. There will also be travel opportunities as the Ox year draws to a close.

The aspects in the Ox year are generally encouraging for the Horse, although in his relations with others he does need to remain attentive and aware of their views. Should he be obtuse, unaware or uncompromising over certain matters, difficulties could arise. He does need to be on his mettle. However, this warning apart, his domestic and social life can see much activity in the closing months of the Ox year, with several fine occasions to look forward to. August and December could be especially busy.

The Tiger year begins on 14 February and with its vitality and opportunities, it can be a favourable one for the Horse. Many Horses will be able to use their experience to advantage and enjoy some personal success.

However, while the aspects are generally encouraging, there is one area in which the Horse will need to exercise particular care: finance. In 2010 he will face many demands on his resources. This could be the result of family commitments, home expenses, deposits he may be required to make and/or some large purchases. His various interests and often busy social life can also result in him spending more over the year and he will need to keep close watch on his outgoings. Without sufficient control, his spending could become greater than anticipated and lead to modifications or economies later on. Also, if he has any concerns about the terms or implications of a transaction he may be considering, it would be worth him seeking advice. Tiger years can be expensive ones and in money matters the Horse needs to be prudent and wary of risk.

A further feature of the year which can bring expense will be the chance to go out and socialize. Many Horses will find themselves in demand, with people to meet or occasions to attend. Some could also join a work-related group or a local society connected with an interest they have. The Tiger year can certainly lead to a considerable increase in the Horse's social circle. Some of the people he meets will, in time, become important friends, and for the unattached the prospects for finding love are especially promising. April, August, November and December could see the most social activity.

With the prevailing aspects, this is also an excellent year for the Horse to make the most of networking opportunities at work. The more people he knows and who know of him, the more he will benefit from the opportunities that will arise over the year. This is a time for him to use his considerable social skills to advantage.

This will also be an active year as far as the Horse's domestic life is concerned, with several changes taking place. For some this could involve a relation moving away, perhaps for work or education. With all the activity of the year, there will need to be close co-operation and good communication. The better this is – and the Horse does have great organizational skills – the better home life will generally be. Also, if the Horse is under particular pressure or is tired and tense, if he speaks openly about this, those around will be better able to understand and help. If tiredness gives way to irritability, there is a risk this could lead to disagreements and arguments. This is something all Horses need to be mindful of during the year. Generally, though, the Horse's domestic life will be rewarding, with joint activities bringing particular pleasure.

The aspects are also encouraging in work matters, with many Horses now reaping the rewards of their earlier efforts. This is very much a year for progress, with the Horse often being a strong candidate for promotion or successful in moving to a more interesting position elsewhere. Another factor in his favour will be the support he is given, with some colleagues or more senior personnel putting in recommendations on his behalf. This is a year for the Horse to make the most of his strengths and opportunities. March, April, June and September could see some interesting developments, but with the fast pace of the year, should the Horse see an opening that interests him, he should act quickly.

This is also a favourable year for Horses who are frustrated in their present position and feel they are not making the best use of their abilities. For these Horses, as well as those seeking work, the Tiger year is one for seizing the initiative. By being active, making enquiries and following up vacancies, their initiative and persistence will be noticed and bring results. The positions some obtain will not only give them important experience in another area but also the chance to prove themselves in new ways. Work-wise, the Horse can fare well in the Tiger year.

The Horse always likes to keep himself active and to have things to do, and here the Tiger year will not disappoint. However, amid all the activity, the Horse does need to give some consideration to his well-being, including allowing time for rest and relaxation (too many demanding days and late nights could, after time, sap his energy) as well as making sure he exercises regularly and has a healthy diet. To get the most from this active year, he does need to take good care of himself.

The Year of the Tiger has considerable promise for the Horse and will give him the chance to make more of his skills. Work-wise, this is a positive and encouraging year. The Horse will also find himself in demand on a personal level, with opportunities to get to know others. He will need to keep a close watch on his financial situation and, at times of pressure or tiredness, remain mindful of others. But overall this is a promising and progressive year and with his enterprising and personable nature, the Horse is set to do well.

The Metal Horse

This year marks the start of a new decade in the Metal Horse's life and it promises to get off to a lively start. The energy and pace that so characterize Tiger years combined with the enthusiasm of the Metal Horse can make this a memorable year.

Almost all areas of the Metal Horse's life will see activity, and by seizing his opportunities and working towards his aims, he can do particularly well. As the Chinese proverb reminds us, 'Diligence leads to riches,' and for the Metal Horse, diligence this year will not only lead to progress but also increase the number of possibilities open to him.

For the many Metal Horses studying for qualifications, this can be an important year. By concentrating on their studies and remaining disciplined (with personal interests and social opportunities, the Tiger year can bring its distractions), many can look forward to some good results, with their efforts and commitment being noticed and rewarded.

This also applies to Metal Horses in work or seeking work. Although at the start of their working lives, they can gain experience they can build on in the future. Even if their current work is routine, it is a start, and once established on the employment ladder, they will find that advancement can quickly follow. This is a fast-moving year and the Metal Horse should keep alert. As he recognizes, his progress rests with him, and by being willing to put himself forward, he will often benefit from some of the year's very good opportunities. This is very much a time to be active, alert *and* prepared to venture. Late February to April, June and September will see some interesting developments, but when opportunities arise they do need to be grasped.

Another important feature in the Metal Horse's favour will be the many opportunities he will have to get to know others. Some of these, particularly in his work or where he is studying, could become close friends. In addition, in work situations more senior colleagues could be impressed by his commitment and be keen to guide and encourage him. Over the year the Metal Horse can really benefit from his friendships and the support he is given.

He can also look forward to an active social life and by pursuing his interests and going to events that appeal to him, he can have a lot of fun. Any Metal Horses who move to a new location, are on their own or feel lonely will find the Tiger year can bring an important change in their situation. April, August and November to early January could see the most social opportunities and for quite a few Metal Horses, affairs of the heart can add extra excitement and sparkle to the year.

With his socializing, the commitments he has and the items he wants to buy, the Metal Horse will have many outgoings. As a result he does need to keep a close watch on his spending and be careful if tempted by too many impulse purchases. To do all he wants he does need to keep sensible control over his financial situation.

The Tiger year also has a strong spirit of adventure and quite a few Metal Horses will be keen to travel. The more they can prepare, plan and save in advance the better. Not only will this allow them to do more while away but it can also prevent last-minute problems or them leaving ill prepared. The Tiger year can give rise to some great experiences, but it is one for diligence and thoroughness.

As far as the Metal Horse's domestic life is concerned, he will often be grateful for the assistance and encouragement he is given. However he does have an independent streak and sometimes may be reluctant to talk over his ideas, hopes or current situation. Although others, particularly senior relations, respect this, the Metal Horse would benefit from being more forthcoming. By letting others know what he is doing or is hoping for, he will be able to gain better support and advice. In his domestic life this is a year for openness as well as willingness to participate. Also, some Metal Horses could leave home over the year due to work, education or a change in personal circumstances, and if they are willing to let others help and be involved, this important stage of their life can be made easier and smoother.

The Metal Horse's twentieth year can be an important one but, as with any year, problems can still arise. In the Tiger year the Metal Horse does need to be particularly careful in any difficult or fraught situation. To lose his temper, be indiscreet or say or do things he may later regret can undermine rapport. Also, he does need to be careful not to allow any minor difficulties to get out of proportion. While his relations with others can often be special, for the unwary, sudden problems can risk spoiling parts of an otherwise good year. Metal Horses, do take careful note.

Generally, though, the aspects are very much on the Metal Horse's side, and with the willingness to make the most of his opportunities to learn, he will not only make important headway but also prepare the way for the exciting prospects that lie ahead.

TIP FOR THE YEAR
Believe in yourself and be committed, whether studying, working or seeking a position. With determination and the good use of opportunities, you can accomplish a lot that will have far-reaching value. Use this time to invest in yourself and so get this new decade in your life off to a positive start.

The Water Horse
The Water Horse has an inquisitive nature and keeps himself informed. And over the year he will derive considerable satisfaction from the interests he pursues and the ways in which he can use his knowledge.

To get the most from the year the Water Horse should give some thought to what he would like to accomplish over the next 12 months. He could be keen to carry out projects, learn or practise skills or find out more about certain subjects. He may feel there are gaps in his knowledge that he would like to fill or that it would be helpful to become more proficient in certain computer skills or another practical area. By giving himself some aims, he will find he is able to accomplish far more. In addition he should keep alert for the opportunities the Tiger year can suddenly produce. These could include an offer by a relation or friend to share in or start a pursuit together, a course that appeals or an event that he would like to attend. Some Water Horses have a talent for writing and over the year could find this a satisfying activity. A key feature in the Tiger year is to be willing and make the most of ideas and opportunities.

The Water Horse will also be grateful for the encouragement he receives and, whenever possible, should try to discuss his ideas and thoughts with those close to him. This way he can benefit from their suggestions. In addition some of his activities will have a positive social element which he will value.

Many Water Horses will also have the opportunity to travel during the year and if there is a particular destination they would like to visit or they see an attractive offer they should follow this up. Some may delight in travelling more locally, possibly to places they have often considered visiting as well as to specific events and attractions. The Tiger year can have a strong cultural edge to it which will often satisfy the Water Horse's desire to learn. And the involvement of others can add to the fun.

With travel possibilities, personal interests and other commitments, the Water Horse does, however, need to keep a close watch on his outgoings. With sensible control of his budget he will be able to go ahead with many of his plans, but if he is tempted to take risks or proceed on too much of an ad hoc basis, he may find he has to make economies or cut back on certain activities. He also needs to be thorough when dealing with any financially related forms he has to complete. A delay or mistake could result in onerous correspondence. Water Horses, do take careful note.

With his interests, practical ideas and the activities of his loved ones, the Water Horse will nearly always have something to do or look forward to in his domestic life, and generally this will be very satisfying. However, as with every year, problems can sometimes arise and the Water Horse needs to be careful these do not get out of proportion. A willingness to talk through any differences of opinion and seek agreement will be far better than allowing tensions to linger. Fortunately such times will be few, but there can be a certain volatility to the Tiger year which the Water Horse does need to watch.

While there is this need for care, the Tiger year can still bring some special family moments, with the Water Horse taking particular pleasure in following the activities of younger relations as well as advising others and playing a full part in a gathering or occasion that takes place, possibly in late summer. For many, this year will be another active and full one.

Overall, the Tiger year is encouragingly aspected for the Water Horse and with his wide interests and keen nature, he will often get much pleasure from the great mix of things he will be able to do.

Seize your opportunities and build on your interests. By setting yourself some interesting aims and projects, you can make this a personally satisfying time. Also, involve others, as this will enable you to do more. The support and camaraderie of those around you can be an important and encouraging factor in your progress.

The Wood Horse

This will be a busy year for the Wood Horse and during it he will face many demands on his time. There will be a myriad of matters to deal with and there will be occasions when the Wood Horse will feel in a whirl, wondering how best to divide his time. However, amid all the activity, there will be some very good opportunities and some special occasions.

The Tiger year is likely to be hectic from the start and many Wood Horses will find events happening quickly in their work. Changes can suddenly be introduced, new practices implemented and offers unexpectedly arise. Few Wood Horses will remain unaffected by the events of the year and it is very much a case of remaining alert and being prepared to adapt. For quite a few Wood Horses there will be the opportunity to take on different duties and while these may not quite be what the Wood Horse had in mind, especially as many will have been content in their existing role, what happens can give them an interesting new challenge. March, April, June and September to mid-October could see some key developments.

For Wood Horses who decide to move on from where they are, as well as those seeking work, again the Tiger year can be eventful. Obtaining a position will not be easy and the Wood Horse will need to widen the scope of what he is prepared to consider and maybe take up the chance to retrain. However, a key feature of the year is that it can open new doors and many Wood Horses will be offered positions quite different from what they have done before. With any new job there could be a lot of learning involved, but many Wood Horses will settle into their new role and feel invigorated by the challenge. As so many will find, results will need to be worked for, but when they come, they can be doubly satisfying.

With his wide interests and good communication skills, the Wood Horse is able to get on well with many people and throughout the year he should pay particular attention to his relations with his colleagues. By liaising well with others, he will not only be better informed but also able to benefit from the support and advice given. In addition he should make the most of his opportunities to network. Being active and using his good people skills will be helpful in his present situation and also lead to some good advice should he embark on change. However, while relations with his colleagues will for the most part be constructive, the Wood Horse should be careful if he finds himself in a volatile, contentious or pressured situation. A loss of temper or misplaced comment could cause problems and the Wood Horse does need to be on his guard.

A further feature of the Tiger year will be the increased social opportunities that arise, often as a result of changes in Wood Horse's work or the different interests he pursues. Late March, April, August and November to early January will see the most social activity and for those who would welcome a fuller and more meaningful social life, the Tiger year can see a noticeable improvement, including, for some, the excitement of romance.

With the increased opportunities to go out and the other expenses he will have, the Wood Horse does, though, need to keep close watch on his financial situation. Over the year his outgoings could creep up and without care result in him having to make economies later. This is a year to keep sensible control over his purse-strings and think carefully if tempted by impulse purchases.

Also, with the pressure and activity of the year, the Wood Horse would do well to try and make provision for a holiday at some time. A break from routine and the opportunity to relax and unwind can do him a lot of good.

It is also important that he gives quality time to his loved ones and plays his usual full part in home life. Sometimes, with work commitments and all the other demands on his time, he will feel drawn in many different directions, but he does need to preserve time both for himself and for his loved ones. This can make a great difference to his home life. Some of the assistance and advice he is able to give will also be important. His domestic life is very special to him and, with care, can be particularly rewarding.

With the activity of the year, the Wood Horse should also aim to give consideration to his own well-being, including maintaining his interests and ensuring he has a good diet and level of exercise. In this busy year this can be very much to his advantage.

Overall, 2010 will be an active year for the Wood Horse. Although there will be occasions when he will despair of all he has to do, by being prepared to adapt and seize opportunities as they arise, he will be given the chance to make progress and will take much personal satisfaction in his achievements.

TIP FOR THE YEAR
Pay attention to your relations with others. In your home life, be involved, and in work situations, communicate well and be aware of the views of others. With care and mindfulness, you will be well supported. Treasure those who are important to you.

The Fire Horse

With the considerable energy of the Fire element combined with the Horse's already eager nature, the Fire Horse is poised to make important strides this year. This is a time for progress and many Fire Horses will be feeling ready to make more of their considerable selves.

In order to benefit from the prevailing aspects the Fire Horse should give some thought to what he would like to achieve over the next 12 months. By having some ideas he is not only likely to benefit from some moments of synchronicity and good fortune but also to direct his energies in a more purposeful way. Plans made early in 2010 can be significant.

One of the most active areas of the year will be work, and here almost all Fire Horses will be involved in change. Many will be keen to build on their recent achievements and move their career forward. With the active nature of the Tiger year, if they keep alert and make enquiries, interesting possibilities can arise. Sometimes these could be in their present place of work, with some Fire Horses being recommended for a particular role or benefiting from in-house opportunities. For those who feel they would be better off elsewhere, once they make the decision to move on and start to make enquiries, opportunities can begin to open up. The Fire Horse will often be well placed to benefit from these fast-moving times.

This also applies to Fire Horses seeking work, either at the start of the year or during it. By remaining active and persistent, many will secure a position which will give them experience in a different type of work and be something they can build on in the future. Overall, this is a year of very good opportunities, and with willingness, the Fire Horse can achieve a lot. March, April, June and September to mid-October could see some important work developments.

Another of the Fire Horse's strengths is his ability to relate to others, and by talking to colleagues, he will often impress and be able to move his situation forward. However, while a lot of good can come from networking and being proactive, as with all Horses this year, if the Fire Horse finds himself in a fraught or volatile situation, he needs to be careful. Heated exchanges could undermine his progress and in potentially difficult moments he needs to think before he speaks. Fire Horses, do take note. Do not jeopardize your good work by a momentary slip.

The progress the Fire Horse makes in his work can lead to an increase in his income, but over the year he will face many demands on his resources, possibly including additional commuting and travel costs, repairing or replacing items, and family and recreational costs. As a result he will need to keep a close watch on his outgoings and budget carefully for certain plans. If he does not do so already, he could find keeping a set of accounts would enable him to keep better track of his position. This is a year for good financial control.

With the active nature of the Tiger year, the Fire Horse could also see some important changes in his home life. For some, this could involve a family member moving out for the purpose of education or work or due to another change in their situation. Home life will often be conducted at a fast pace and there will need to be good communication and co-operation and a willingness to share domestic chores. However, with mutual support and encouragement, this can be a special year, with some notable achievements to mark. And by preserving time for more pleasurable occasions, including some local outings, the Fire Horse can add special meaning and richness to the year.

His social life is also set to become busier this year, with invitations to take up and events to attend. By making the most of these, the Fire Horse will derive a lot of value from them. Some good contacts can be made and, for the unattached, a chance encounter could develop into a significant romance. The Tiger year will certainly keep the Fire Horse active and can reward him in many different ways. Mid-March to April, August and November to early January will see the most social activity.

With the Fire Horse's busy lifestyle it is also important that he takes good care of himself, including having sufficient rest after busy or stressful times. He should also preserve time for recreational pursuits and, as the Tiger year favours trying out the new, a fresh interest or skill could be particularly rewarding.

Generally, the Tiger year is a promising one for the Fire Horse and by deciding on his aims, remaining focused and liaising well with his loved ones, he can make this a constructive and positive time.

TIP FOR THE YEAR

With awareness backed by your own desire to move forward, you can enjoy an eventful and progressive year. Be alert for opportunities and draw on the assistance and goodwill of those around you. You have a lot to gain.

The Earth Horse

The element of Earth can make the Horse more focused. Rather than going off on tangents or spreading his energies too widely, the Earth Horse likes to plan ahead and think his actions through, and is generally more cautious in approach. However, the Tiger year is one of change. Some parts of it may be unsettling for the Earth Horse, but by being flexible and adapting to the situations that arise, he can benefit in ways that can be considerable *and* far-reaching.

Several areas of his life will see considerable activity, but one in particular will be his social life. Sometimes this could be the result of his interests, with him going to gatherings, events or exhibitions which particularly appeal to him. Some Earth Horses may also join local groups of enthusiasts or enrol on courses. Over the year many will find their interests having a strong social element and they will enjoy the chance to meet others who are like-minded. Any Earth Horses who are alone, move to a new area or have had some recent personal difficulty will find their interests can add greatly to their year and, for some, lead to important new friendships or romance. In addition the Earth Horse's work situation can often give him the opportunity to go out more, with excellent chances to network and meet others. Mid-March to April, August, November and December could see the most activity, but with the aspects as they are, invitations and social opportunities can appear quickly and at almost any time. The Tiger year is not always a respecter of planning and the year will have a great deal of spontaneity to it.

It could also be to the Earth Horse's benefit to develop his existing interests or consider trying something new. For the keen and enterprising, the Tiger year can be personally rewarding, and in view of all the activity of the year, the Earth Horse's interests can also be a good way to keep his lifestyle in balance, get additional exercise or just rest and unwind.

The Earth Horse's domestic life will also see considerable activity, with him doing a lot to help and support others, including both younger and more senior relations. Here his words, time and encouragement will often be of more value than he realizes.

With the hectic and unpredictable nature of the year, the Earth Horse should, though, be more flexible than usual with some of his planning. This includes home projects as well as possible purchases. To stick to a rigid timetable or rush activities could bring about problems, tension and less satisfactory outcomes. Although it may not always fit in with the Earth Horse's style and approach, he should do what he can *when he can*. To do otherwise can only add to the pressure of this already busy year.

Despite this, the Earth Horse can look forward to some very special times with his loved ones, with some spur-of-the-moment occasions being especially appreciated. Whenever the Earth Horse has an idea he thinks others may enjoy, whether a family activity, trip out or other treat, he should put it forward. Over the year his input will be valued.

However, while the Earth Horse's relations with others will be mostly positive, they do require care. With his busy lifestyle, there will be times when the Earth Horse will be tired and tense and will need to be careful not to take his irritations out on others. In any fraught or pressured situation, he should also watch his words. In the Tiger year there is the potential danger for all Horses to undermine their position and damage their relationships by losing their temper or saying things they later regret. Earth Horses, do take careful note.

This will be an eventful year as far as work is concerned, with the chance for many Earth Horses to move their career forward. For some there will be good promotion opportunities in their current place of employment and although these may offer different duties than the Earth Horse is used to and may involve some learning and adjustments, by being willing and adaptable, the Earth Horse can make headway and gain experience that can widen his options later on.

The prospects are also promising for those Earth Horses who are keen to move on from where they are or are seeking work. The Tiger year favours those who are prepared to take the initiative, and by making enquiries and widening the range of possibilities they are prepared to consider, these Earth Horses can find their commitment and drive rewarded. March, April, June and September could see some important career developments, but opportunities can arise quickly and to benefit the Earth Horse will need to act quickly.

The progress many Earth Horses make at work will often lead to an increase in income, although, with their often active lifestyle, this could be matched by an increase in outgoings. Over the year the Earth Horse will need to keep a watchful eye on his spending and make allowance for any large expenses. The Tiger year does call for good financial discipline.

Overall, the Earth Horse can fare well in the Tiger year and achieve a great deal. However, to benefit from the opportunities it will bring he will need to be flexible and make the most of situations as they arise. It is also important, in view of the many demands on his time, that he keeps his lifestyle in balance and allows time for recreation as well as preserves quality time for those who are special to him. This can be a successful and progressive year, but the Earth Horse does need to strike a good balance in all he does.

TIP FOR THE YEAR
Go with the flow of the year. Adapt to unfolding situations, take advantage of opportunities and be prepared to move

forward. Whether in your work or your personal interests, look to advance your skills and knowledge and possibly take up something new. With a willingness to learn, you can make this a positive and rewarding year. Also, value your relations with those around you. These are precious and the time and attention you give will often be more important than you will realize.

FAMOUS HORSES

Roman Abramovich, Neil Armstrong, Rowan Atkinson, Samuel Beckett, Ingmar Bergman, Leonard Bernstein, Joe Biden, Helena Bonham Carter, James Blunt, David Cameron, James Cameron, Jackie Chan, Ray Charles, Chopin, Sir Sean Connery, Billy Connolly, Catherine Cookson, Elvis Costello, Kevin Costner, Cindy Crawford, James Dean, Clint Eastwood, Thomas Alva Edison, Harrison Ford, Aretha Franklin, Bob Geldof, Samuel Goldwyn, Billy Graham, Gene Hackman, Rolf Harris, Rita Hayworth, Jimi Hendrix, Janet Jackson, Calvin Klein, Lenin, Annie Lennox, Sir Paul McCartney, Nelson Mandela, Angela Merkel, Michael Moore, Ben Murphy, Sir Isaac Newton, Louis Pasteur, Katie Price (Jordan), Gordon Ramsay, Lou Reed, Rembrandt, Ruth Rendell, Jean Renoir, Condoleezza Rice, Theodore Roosevelt, Helena Rubenstein, David Schwimmer, Martin Scorsese, Barbra Streisand, Kiefer Sutherland, Patrick Swayze, John Travolta, Kathleen Turner, Vivaldi, Robert Wagner, Denzil Washington, Billy Wilder, Andy Williams, Brian Wilson, the Duke of Windsor, Will Young.

1 FEBRUARY 1919 ～ 19 FEBRUARY 1920   *Earth Goat*

17 FEBRUARY 1931 ～ 5 FEBRUARY 1932   *Metal Goat*

5 FEBRUARY 1943 ～ 24 JANUARY 1944   *Water Goat*

24 JANUARY 1955 ～ 11 FEBRUARY 1956   *Wood Goat*

9 FEBRUARY 1967 ～ 29 JANUARY 1968   *Fire Goat*

28 JANUARY 1979 ～ 15 FEBRUARY 1980   *Earth Goat*

15 FEBRUARY 1991 ～ 3 FEBRUARY 1992   *Metal Goat*

1 FEBRUARY 2003 ～ 21 JANUARY 2004   *Water Goat*

THE
GOAT

THE PERSONALITY OF THE GOAT

Amid the complexities of life,
it is the ability to appreciate that is so special.

The Goat is born under the sign of art. He is imaginative, creative and has a good appreciation of the finer things in life. He has an easy-going nature and prefers to live in a relaxed and pressure-free environment. He hates any sort of discord or unpleasantness and does not like to be bound by a strict routine or rigid timetable. He is not one to be hurried against his will, but despite his seemingly relaxed approach to life, he is something of a perfectionist and when he starts work on a project he is certain to give his best.

The Goat usually prefers to work in a team rather than on his own. He likes to have the support and encouragement of others and if left to deal with matters on his own he can get very worried and tend to view things rather pessimistically. Wherever possible he will leave major decision-making to others while he concentrates on his own pursuits. If, however, he feels particularly strongly about a certain matter or has to defend his position in any way, he will act with great fortitude and precision.

The Goat has a very persuasive nature and often uses his considerable charm to get his own way. He can, however, be rather hesitant about letting his true feelings be known and if he were prepared to be more forthright he would do much better as a result.

The Goat tends to have a quiet, somewhat reserved nature, but when he is in company he likes he can often become the centre of attention. He can be highly amusing, a marvellous host at parties and a superb entertainer. Whenever the spotlight falls on him, his adrenaline starts to flow and he can be assured of giving a sparkling performance, particularly if he is allowed to use his creative skills in any way.

Of all the signs in the Chinese zodiac, the Goat is probably the most gifted artistically. Whether it is in the theatre, literature, music or art, he is certain to make a lasting impression. He is a born creator and is rarely happier than when occupied in some artistic pursuit. But even in this the Goat does well to work with others rather than on his own. He needs inspiration and a guiding influence, but when he has found his true *métier*, he can often receive widespread acclaim and recognition.

In addition to his liking for the arts, the Goat is usually quite religious and often has a deep interest in nature, animals and the countryside. He is also fairly athletic and there are many Goats who have excelled in some form of sporting activity or who have a great interest in sport.

Although the Goat is not particularly materialistic or concerned about finance, he will find that he will usually be lucky in financial matters and will rarely be short of the necessary funds to tide himself over. He is, however, rather self-indulgent and tends to spend his money as soon as he receives it rather than make provision for the future.

The Goat usually leaves home when he is young but he will always maintain strong links with his parents and the other members of his family. He is also rather nostalgic and is well known for keeping mementoes of his childhood and souvenirs of places that he has visited. His home will not be particularly tidy, but he knows where everything is and it will be scrupulously clean.

Affairs of the heart are particularly important to the Goat and he will often have many romances before he finally settles down. Although he is fairly adaptable, he prefers to live in a secure and stable environment and he will find that he is best suited to those born under the signs of the Tiger, Horse, Monkey, Pig and Rabbit. He can also establish a good relationship with the Dragon, Snake, Rooster and another Goat, but he may find the Ox and Dog a little too serious for his liking. Neither will he care particularly for the Rat's rather thrifty ways.

The female Goat devotes all her time and energy to the needs of her family. She has excellent taste in home furnishings and often uses her considerable artistic skills to make clothes for herself and her children. She takes great care over her appearance and can be most attractive to others. Although she is not the most organized of people, her engaging manner and delightful sense of humour create a favourable impression wherever she goes. She is also a good cook and usually derives much pleasure from gardening and outdoor pursuits.

The Goat can win friends easily and people generally feel relaxed in his company. He has a kind and under-standing nature and although he can occasionally be stub-born, he can, with the right support and encouragement, live a happy and very satisfying life. And the more he can use his creative skills, the happier he will be.

THE FIVE DIFFERENT TYPES OF GOAT

In addition to the 12 signs of the Chinese zodiac there are five elements and these have a strengthening or moderating influence on the signs. The effects of the five elements on the Goat are described below, together with the years in which the elements were exercising their influence. Therefore those Goats born in 1931 and 1991 are Metal Goats, those born in 1943 and 2003 are Water Goats, and so on.

Metal Goat: 1931, 1991

This Goat is thorough and conscientious in all that he does and is capable of doing very well in his chosen profession. Despite his confident manner, he can be a great worrier and he would find it helpful to discuss his concerns with others rather than keep them to himself. He is loyal to his family and employers and will have a small group of particularly close friends. He has good taste and is usually highly skilled in some of aspect of the arts. He is often a collector of antiques and his home will be very tastefully furnished.

Water Goat: 1943, 2003

The Water Goat is very popular and makes friends with remarkable ease. He is good at spotting opportunities but does not always have the necessary confidence to follow them through. He likes to have security both in his home life and work and does not take kindly to change. He is articulate, has a good sense of humour and is usually very good with children.

Wood Goat: 1955

This Goat is generous, kind-hearted and always eager to please. He usually has a large circle of friends and involves himself in a wide variety of activities. He has a very trusting nature but he can sometimes give in to the demands of others a little too easily and it would be in his interests if he were to stand his ground more often. He is usually lucky in financial matters and, like the Water Goat, is very good with children.

Fire Goat: 1967

This Goat usually knows what he wants in life and often uses his considerable charm and persuasive personality to achieve his aims. He can sometimes let his imagination run away with him and has a tendency to ignore matters that are not to his liking. He is rather extravagant in his spending and would do well to exercise a little more care when dealing with financial matters. He has a lively personality, many friends, and loves attending parties and social occasions.

Earth Goat: 1919, 1979

This Goat has a considerate and caring nature. He is particularly loyal to his family and friends and invariably creates a favourable impression wherever he goes. He is reliable and conscientious in his work but sometimes finds it difficult to save and never likes to deprive himself of any little luxury he might fancy. He has numerous interests and is often very well read. He usually derives much pleasure from following the activities of the various members of his family.

PROSPECTS FOR THE GOAT IN 2010

The Year of the Ox (26 January 2009 to 13 February 2010) can be a challenging one for the Goat. The closing months will see increased activity and he may frequently despair over all he has to do. To help, he would do well to remember the words of the Chinese proverb: 'You won't get lost if you frequently ask for directions.' At times of pressure or decision, it is important that the Goat is forthcoming and asks, whether for advice or more assistance.

In his work this is a time for focus and concentrating on what he has to do. While his workload will often be great, with good use of time and skills, this can be a productive period. October could see some interesting developments, particularly for those Goats keen to progress in their career or seeking a position.

The Goat's domestic life can also see much activity, and with so much to fit in, the more that can be agreed in advance, the better. With all his pressures and commitments, it is also important that the Goat talks to others about any concerns he may have. The more open he is and, again, the more he asks for directions, the more those around him will be able to help and advise.

Towards the end of the year many Goats will also have the chance to spend time with relations or close friends they do not often see, and they will especially appreciate this. September and the closing weeks of 2009 can be a busy and personally rewarding time.

The Goat likes to keep his life on an even keel. He does not like turbulence or sudden change, but such is the way of the Year of the Tiger. Few Goats will remain unaffected by the events of the next 12 months, but while this can be an unsettling time, out of change can come important opportunities and new pathways. This is a year which can have far-reaching significance.

The Year of the Tiger begins on 14 February and to make the best of it the Goat will need to remain aware and open in his approach. This is no time to close his mind to unfolding situations if they are not to his liking or remain wedded to one particular plan or course of action. Instead this is a year for venturing out – sometimes being forced out – of his comfort zone and facing up to new situations. If he is willing to do his best, the Tiger year can be an illuminating one as well as give him the opportunity to discover new strengths.

At work this can be a time of considerable activity. Many Goats will find that work they have recently been engaged in or pressures that they have dealt with will not only have given them useful experience but also brought their qualities to the attention of others. When opportunities arise or staff are required for particular duties, many will be well placed to benefit and will be encouraged to take their career further. Although taking on new responsibilities will often involve a steep learning curve, this is very much a year to be open to possibility. Also, if the Goat is offered training, he should take it up. By showing willing, he will again be helping his prospects.

This also applies to Goats who are feeling staid or dissatisfied in their present position, or are seeking work. By taking the initiative and actively looking for opportunities, they could uncover some interesting possibilities. Those who have been seeking work for some time or are keen on more substantial change could find it worth investigating training opportunities or refresher courses. By not being too narrow in what they consider, many will be successful in gaining an important new opportunity. April, July, September and November could see some interesting developments.

The changes of the year will also bring the Goat into contact with many new people, and with his ability to relate well to others, he will welcome the chance to add to his social circle. Some of those he meets this year could become firm friends. Social opportunities can occur throughout the year, with May to August and December seeing the most activity.

Another positive area will be the Goat's interests, and for the creative, this is a time to enjoy and explore their ideas as well as consider putting forward anything they wish to promote. With the year favouring originality, some Goats could find their creative talents greatly encouraged and in some cases bringing further reward. All Goats can derive much satisfaction this year by furthering their knowledge, and whether reading, studying or trying out new activities, they will often benefit from what they do. This is very much a year for acting on ideas and opportunities.

With the busy nature of the year the Goat will have many outgoings and while he will take pleasure in a lot of what he spends his money on, he should be careful not to succumb to too many impulse purchases or be rushed into quick decisions. Without care he could find he is spending more than he allowed for or that with more consideration he could have made a better choice. This is a year for firm control. He should also be wary of risk and if he has doubts over any financial matter, he should seek advice.

The Goat's home life will see much activity and he will often have ideas he is keen to share or projects he wants to get underway. However, with the pressures of the year, he will need to be flexible with his plans and prepared to compromise. The Tiger year is no respecter of rigid timetables, and arrangements are often liable to change. But provided the Goat is prepared to accept this and carry through his plans when convenient, he will appreciate what he manages to get done. If possible, he should also try to take a holiday with his loved ones over the year. Even if he does not travel too far, a rest from routine can do everyone good. Domestically, this can be a rewarding year, but there will need to be flexibility, co-operation and a willingness for everyone in the household to do their fair share.

Overall, this will be a busy year for the Goat, and by being prepared to make the most of the changes that take place, he can make satisfying headway and gain valuable new experience as well as take pleasure in what he achieves. The year may ask a lot of him, but it can be instructive and prepare the way for future success.

The Metal Goat

This will be a lively and significant year for the Metal Goat, and one which can also bring considerable change. Although the Metal Goat may sometimes feel daunted by the challenges he faces or anxious over certain decisions, with support and the careful consideration of his options, he can emerge from the year with some solid gains to his credit as well as more confidence. The experiences of the Tiger year will be instructive in many respects.

One feature of the Tiger year is its high level of activity. Throughout there will be many competing demands on the Metal Goat's time and he does need to be careful not to get distracted from his aims or squander his energies. Whether in education or work, he should concentrate on his priorities. With discipline, he can achieve some good results this year, but if he is half-hearted, there could be disappointments in store. The Tiger year is very much one for application.

The year can be particularly important for those Metal Goats in education, especially as many will be starting new courses or moving on to more specialized work. Putting in the effort now will not only give these Metal Goats a good foundation to build on but can also make their subsequent work more interesting. As the Chinese proverb reminds us, 'Well begun is half done,' and the Metal Goat will find this particularly true this year. To help stay motivated, he would do well to keep in mind the benefits that certain qualifications can bring. The rewards of this year can be far-reaching.

The Tiger year can also open up some interesting opportunities for the Metal Goat. For those in education there could be chances to vary their course or perhaps try out some of the facilities available in their place of study. By taking up the opportunities available to them, these Metal Goats will be able to get far more out of the present time as well as gain experience and skills they will often be keen to take further in the future.

For those who are keen to make more of their creative talents, this is again an excellent year for exploring and developing their skills. The Metal Goat often has an innovative approach, and with self-belief and the support of others, he can look forward to making encouraging headway. The Tiger year has a vitality about it, and creative Metal Goats could find their talents being noticed and appreciated.

This will also be an important year as far as the Metal Goat's work situation is concerned. For those already in work, there will be significant developments in store. If they are happy with their choice of career, they could find themselves encouraged to undertake further training, develop particular skills or take on other responsibilities with a view to later progression. Some of this could be daunting, but this is a time for the Metal Goat to rise to the challenge. With focus and willingness, he can see important opportunities opening up this year.

For those Metal Goats who feel unfulfilled in their current position, this can also be a significant time. Rather than remain in an unsatisfactory situation, these Metal Goats should give serious thought to what it is they want to do and where their main strengths lie. By considering this and contacting those able to advise, they could be alerted to other ways in which they could use their skills or a possible course or qualification that could help. This is a year favouring action and initiative.

This also applies to those Metal Goats seeking work. By getting advice and giving serious consideration to the sort of work they want to do, they can find their commitment and determination leading to an opening they can build on in the future. April, July, September and November could see some key developments.

In financial matters, however, the Metal Goat will need to remain disciplined. With an active social life and all his interests and commitments, he does need to watch his spending and be wary about buying too much on impulse. This is a year for good financial control and the avoidance of risk. If the Metal Goat has any concerns over a financial matter, it would be worth him seeking advice.

He can look forward to a full and active social life, however, and, whether through his work or interests, will often have the chance to meet those in a similar position to his own, some of whom will become long-standing friends. Mid-April to August and December could see the most social activity, as well as be very good times for getting to know others.

Another feature of the year will be the camaraderie the Metal Goat enjoys with others, and not only will he welcome the support he receives but if he has any worries or is anxious over certain decisions, it is important that he is forthcoming. Family members and close friends could be particularly helpful. Also, although the Metal Goat will often be kept busy with his various activities, he should make the time to contribute to domestic life as well as help out with certain tasks. His involvement and thoughtfulness will be appreciated and may mean more than he realizes.

The Tiger year will be a busy one for the Metal Goat and will bring some excellent chances to further his experience. However, he does need to make the most of them. If he concentrates on his priorities, his efforts this year will not only bring rewards now but be something he can build on in following years. For the determined and keen, this can be a valuable and potentially important year.

TIP FOR THE YEAR
Enjoy the many strands of your life. Pursue and develop your interests, make the most of your opportunities to study and use any chances you have to add to your work skills. There will be a lot to do this year and a lot you can ultimately benefit from. Use your time well.

The Water Goat

The Tiger year will be a busy one and while much of it will be pleasant and generally constructive for the Water Goat, certain weeks will be fraught with activity and he may be in despair over all the pressure and disruption. Also, as is the way sometimes, everything will tend to happen at once. At particularly busy times it is important that the Water Goat remembers he is not alone and his friends and relations are keen to assist. He should also show increased flexibility over the year. If it is not convenient for certain plans to go ahead when he wants them to, he should see if they can be rearranged. Similarly, if others have misgivings about actions he may be considering, it is important that he listens closely to their views, remembering that they speak with his interests at heart. This is no year for intransigence or sticking too rigidly to plans when delays occur or situations change. Water Goats, take note and over the year do be accommodating in approach.

One of the trickiest areas of the year will concern paperwork and although the Water Goat may be tempted to put forms and official letters to one side, it is important that these are dealt with properly and promptly, otherwise the Water Goat could find himself disadvantaged, maybe remaining unaware of benefits he is eligible for or of changes which could have important implications for him. Should he have concerns over any bureaucratic matter, he should seek advice.

This need for care also applies to any large transactions the Water Goat may be involved in. He needs to allow time to assess the suitability of his purchases and compare costs as well as check the terms and implications of any agreement he may enter into. While he is usually careful, he also needs to make sure policies, guarantees and receipts are kept safely. To lose or misplace important paperwork could be to his detriment. This is a time for extra care and vigilance.

A particular feature of the Tiger year will be the opportunities that can suddenly arise. These can include the chance to travel or visit others at relatively short notice. Although this may involve rearranging existing plans, by taking advantage of such opportunities, the Water Goat will enjoy many of the interesting places he gets to visit. Again, this is a year for flexibility. In addition many Water Goats will have the chance to go away in the closing weeks of the year and this may be something they very much look forward to.

The year can also see some positive developments as far as the Water Goat's interests are concerned. These could include chances to try out new activities, enrol on courses, develop an existing skill or start a creative project. By being ready to try something new, the Water Goat can benefit a great deal.

Some of his interests can also have a pleasing social element and over the year it will do him a lot of good to spend time with others as well as to get to meet new people. This is no year for keeping himself to himself. For some Water Goats, joining a local group could be well worth considering. April to August and December could see the most social activity.

As far as the Water Goat's domestic life is concerned, this will be a busy year and here again he will need to show some flexibility. When making plans, he will need to discuss them fully with those around him, taking into account their existing commitments and any suggestions they may have. If problems or delays occur, as they are apt to do in Tiger years, he should look at ways around these and again draw on the advice of others. Over the year, many Water Goats could have the additional burden of some home repairs or need to replace some equipment. Again this can cause inconvenience, but by getting good advice, they can make changes or purchases that can be a great improvement on what they had before.

Domestically, while there be some pressured and awkward weeks for the Water Goat, much of the year will go well for him and co-operating with others can lead to some good decisions and pleasing occasions. Towards the end of the year many Water Goats can also look forward to a key family event, often involving travel.

In general, this will be an active year for the Water Goat and while there will be times of pressure and disruption, with support and good advice, he will fare well. During the Tiger year it is very much a case of being flexible, liaising closely with others and acting on opportunities.

TIP FOR THE YEAR

Consult those you trust and who know you well. With their support, some of the pressures and decisions of the year can be made much easier. Also, embrace the innovative spirit of the Tiger year and be willing to try something different or set yourself a new personal challenge, ideally one that suits your creative talents. It can give rise to some interesting times as well as bring personal satisfaction.

The Wood Goat

During some parts of the Tiger year the Wood Goat will feel he is putting in a lot of energy just to keep up with events, let alone make any progress. The Tiger year *will* be busy and sometimes pressured. However, while there will be times when the Wood Goat will despair of all that is being asked of him, when he later looks back at all he has done, he will be surprised at how much he has achieved.

This will be an active year, with key developments in several areas of his life.

At home, some Wood Goats could see a family member move out for the purposes of education, work or some other change in circumstances, and while this may cause the caring Wood Goat some anxiety, if he is willing to be supportive and share any concerns, he will find his assistance will be truly appreciated. Throughout the year he will be closely involved in the activities of many around him and here his ability to empathize and willingness to give his time will be of great value. In the Tiger year he will certainly play a pivotal role in the running of his home life and a lot more besides.

As the year will be busy, he will, though, need to show some flexibility in his planning. Practical projects and home purchases should not be rushed and will be best fitted in when time allows. The Tiger year possesses a certain spontaneity and should the Wood Goat have the opportunity to go away for a break at short notice, he should seize the chance. This is very much a year for making the most of situations as they arise.

Another area which can give the Wood Goat much satisfaction is his interests, and if he can join other enthusiasts this can not only add to the meaning and pleasure of what he does but often lead to him doing more. The Tiger year favours new activities and if the Wood Goat has the opportunity to try something different or is intrigued by a recreational pursuit or self-improvement course, it would be worth him following it up. It could mark the beginning of an important new activity which he will enjoy developing in following years.

Some Wood Goats will also decide to pay greater attention to their well-being this year, particularly their diet and level of exercise. Before making any change they should seek medical advice on the most appropriate way to proceed, but the care and attention they give themselves can, over time, make a difference.

The Wood Goat will very much appreciate his social life over the year and opportunities to go out will often arise suddenly. Many Wood Goats will find that new interests or activities they become involved in are good ways to meet others and make some new friends. Late April to August and December could see the most social activity.

As far as work matters are concerned, this will be a demanding year with many Wood Goats facing a heavy workload and certain tasks proving more problematic than they should be. The Tiger year can be exacting and may not be made any easier by the pettiness of other people or the slow workings of bureaucracy. There will be times during the year which will frustrate the Wood Goat and it is very much a case of him doing his best in the situations in which he finds himself. Also, if any new practices are introduced, he will need to adapt and be prepared to learn what is required. Although there will be times when he will feel he is putting in a lot of effort for little return, his commitment *will* be noticed and in time prevail.

For Wood Goats who are keen to move on in their career or switch to something different, as well as those seeking work, the Tiger year can have some important developments in store. Securing a new position will not be easy and there will be disappointments in the Wood Goat's quest but, almost as if fate were intervening, opportunities will suddenly open up and give many Wood Goats the chance to develop their skills in a new way. The Tiger year can work in curious ways and by widening the scope of what they are prepared to consider, these Wood Goats can be well rewarded. April, July, September and November could see some important work developments.

With his active lifestyle and home and family commitments, as well as some of the plans he has, the Wood Goat will need to be careful in financial matters. He does need to watch his spending in the Tiger year and make allowance for specific purchases and plans. With good control, he will be pleased with what he is able to do, but this is no time for taking risks, rushing purchases or proceeding on an ad hoc basis. And, as with other Goats, he needs to be attentive and prompt when dealing with financially related correspondence.

Overall, the Year of the Tiger will be an active one for the Wood Goat, with some important changes taking place. While parts will be demanding, by doing his best and what he feels to be right, he will accomplish and learn a great deal over the year. It may not be an easy one, but it can be constructive. And amid all the activity there will be times with loved ones and friends which will bring real pleasure.

TIP FOR THE YEAR

Keep alert. With willingness, determination and the support of others, you can do a lot this year. It may not always feel as though you are making progress, but your efforts will be appreciated and in time lead to some important opportunities. Self-belief and perseverance will pay off.

The Fire Goat

Tiger years are fast-paced and throughout this one the Fire Goat will need to keep alert and act quickly when the situation requires.

This is particularly the case in his work. With the considerable experience he has built up, he may well find himself with the chance to take on a greater role this year. This could be through promotion, the chance to train and supervise others or being involved in more specialist duties. Although it may not always be apparent at the time, these new responsibilities can often be the preparation necessary for further advancement. However, to benefit, the Fire Goat does need to put himself forward. This is very much a year for action and involvement.

Apart from this, in the course of their everyday work many Fire Goats will face new pressures. Although these can be demanding and cause the Fire Goat some anxiety (he is, after all, very conscientious), they will give him the chance to test his abilities as well as learn more about different aspects of his work. The pressures of the Tiger year may not always make situations easy, but these are instructive and important times.

For Fire Goats who feel unfulfilled in their current position, as well as those seeking work, the Tiger year can usher in some interesting possibilities. Tiger years favour innovation and for quite a few of these Fire Goats there will be the chance to switch to a very different type of work. They should not be too restrictive in what they are considering and if a change appeals to them, should seek guidance. Sometimes employment agencies or professional bodies could make constructive suggestions. The Tiger year is a time to be open to possibility. April, July, September and mid-October to November could see important developments. Also, when taking on a new position, the Fire Goat will find his enthusiasm will be noted and encouraged, and sometimes lead to swift advancement.

The progress many Fire Goats enjoy in their work will often bring an increase in income. Although this will be welcome, to do all he wants, the Fire Goat does still need to keep control of his spending. With discipline, he will be able to reap the rewards of his good work, but if he is more lax, then it could be that some plans have to be shelved. Also, as with all Goats this year, the Fire Goat needs to be careful when dealing with important paperwork. Delay or carelessness could leave him at a disadvantage. Fire Goats, take note.

With the many demands on the Fire Goat's time it is also important that he keeps his lifestyle in balance. This not only includes preserving quality time for his loved ones but also giving himself the chance to relax and unwind and enjoy recreational pursuits. With the Tiger year favouring new activities, he would do well to consider taking up a different hobby. Similarly, those Fire Goats who do not get much regular exercise should consider ways of correcting this and take medical advice on how best to proceed.

Another feature of the year will be the chances the Fire Goat has to meet others. This could be through his work, his friends or interests he pursues, but some of those he meets this year can not only become good friends but also be useful in offering support or advice. The Fire Goat will also enjoy many of the social occasions he goes to, with some occurring at short notice. April to early September and December could be busy and special months socially.

The Fire Goat's domestic life will also see much activity, and to cope with the many and sometimes competing demands on his time there will need to be good co-operation between everyone in his household. The Fire Goat should aim to set time aside for joint activities and if he has ideas he feels others may enjoy, he should put these forward. His thoughtfulness and the time he gives to others will be an important factor in his home life. In turn, whenever he is under pressure or has decisions preying on his mind, it is important that he speaks of these so that others are not only made more aware of them but can also do more to assist and advise.

In general, the Tiger year will be a demanding one for the Fire Goat, with a lot happening and being expected of him. However, by rising to the challenges, he can not only make important progress but also develop new strengths which can often be to his benefit in the future. If he makes sure his lifestyle has balance and preserves time for his loved ones and personal interests, he will find the Tiger year will reward him well for all his effort and commitment.

TIP FOR THE YEAR

Look to move forward. So much can now open up for you. Also, draw on the support of others. There will be many who believe in you and are keen for you to make more of yourself. With faith, commitment and goodwill, you can make this a busy and positive year.

The Earth Goat

This will be a demanding year for the Earth Goat but it will not be without its successes or personal triumphs.

In his work the Tiger year can be a time of considerable change. For some Earth Goats, particularly those well established in a company or certain type of work, there will be the opportunity to take on new responsibilities. However, while this may be welcome, the Earth Goat could face a steep learning curve or find the nature of his work is very different from what he has been used to. Work-wise, this can be an exacting time, but it will allow him to develop strengths he can subsequently build on. It is often during the more challenging times that the greatest learning opportunities occur, and so it will be in 2010.

Some Earth Goats will decide to further their experience by moving on from where they are, and for these Earth Goats, as well as those looking for work, the Tiger year can move in curious ways. Obtaining a new position will not be easy, but a key feature of the year is that it is one to explore possibilities, so by looking at different ways in which they can use their skills, they will find chances will begin to open up. For many, these can be an important springboard to later progress, especially in the following and favourably aspected Year of the Rabbit.

Another encouraging feature of the Tiger year is the opportunity the Earth Goat will have to work with other colleagues. With his excellent people skills and often enter-prising manner, he will not only impress others but also have the chance to make new contacts. In addition, at times of pressure, or if looking for a position, he should seek the advice of those who are able to advise. April, July,

September and November could see some important work developments, but in this fast-moving year the Earth Goat needs to keep alert and act swiftly.

With the emphasis this year on moving forward, he should also consider ways in which he can make more of his interests. If he is expert in a certain hobby or skill, he may be able to promote what he does or share his knowledge with others. For creative Earth Goats this can be an exciting and potentially rewarding year. In addition, if a new subject appeals to the Earth Goat, he should find out more. By venturing forth and trying things out, he can gain a lot from the year.

The Tiger year can also bring travel opportunities. Sometimes these could arise suddenly and possibly alter existing plans, but by being flexible the Earth Goat will appreciate visiting some interesting new places.

In money matters, however, he will need to be thorough and disciplined. He should aim to keep a close watch on his spending and be wary of making decisions or purchases too hurriedly. Sometimes the pace of the Tiger year can tempt Earth Goats (and others) into making snap judgements, but more time spent considering their options will often result in better decisions. Also, if the Earth Goat has any doubts or problems over a financial matter, he should seek advice.

Although he will often have a lot to do this year, he should also try to make sure his various commitments do not make too many incursions into his social life. Over the year he can get much pleasure from keeping in contact with his friends as well as from going to social events. Late April to August and December could see the most social activity.

This will also be a busy year as far as the Earth Goat's domestic life is concerned. He will often be in demand and whether assisting his partner, attending to the needs of babies or children or helping more senior relations, he may find his time and attention being drawn in several different directions. However, while some of the Tiger year will be demanding (sometimes with the added complication of plans changing or being disrupted), by doing what he can when he can and concentrating on his priorities, the Earth Goat will not only cope with a lot but also take pleasure in what is achieved. It will help, too, if there is good communication and co-operation between all in his household. Even if sometimes views may clash, with a willingness to talk matters through, differences of opinion can often be settled quickly and will not detract from the many pleasures the Tiger year can bring.

Generally, in 2010 the Earth Goat will need to keep his wits about him and be prepared to adapt as necessary. However, by rising to the year's challenges and doing his best, he can learn and accomplish a great deal. Some of the year may be a struggle, but what the Earth Goat takes from it can be significant.

TIP FOR THE YEAR

In this busy year, use your people skills well and value your relations with others. Spend time with those who are important to you and seize your opportunities to meet others. With support, encouragement and good advice, you will find the year will become easier and more rewarding.

FAMOUS GOATS

Pamela Anderson, Jane Austen, Daniel Bedingfield, Lord Byron, Coco Chanel, Mary Higgins Clark, Nat 'King' Cole, Jamie Cullum, Robert de Niro, Catherine Deneuve, Charles Dickens, Ken Dodd, Sir Arthur Conan Doyle, Umberto Eco, Douglas Fairbanks, Will Ferrell, Dame Margot Fonteyn, Jamie Foxx, Noel Gallagher, Bill Gates, Mel Gibson, Whoopi Goldberg, Mikhail Gorbachev, John Grisham, Oscar Hammerstein, George Harrison, Billy Idol, Julio Iglesias, Sir Mick Jagger, Norah Jones, Nicole Kidman, Sir Ben Kingsley, Matt le Blanc, John le Carré, Doris Lessing, Franz Liszt, Sir John Major, James McAvoy, Michelangelo, Joni Mitchell, Rupert Murdoch, Randy Newman, Des O'Connor, Sinead O'Connor, Michael Palin, Eva Peron, Marcel Proust, Keith Richards, Julia Roberts, Nicolas Sarkozy, William Shatner, Gary Sinise, Jerry Springer, Lana Turner, Mark Twain, Rudolph Valentino, Vangelis, Barbara Walters, John Wayne, Fay Weldon, Bruce Willis.

20 FEBRUARY 1920 ～ 7 FEBRUARY 1921   *Metal Monkey*

6 FEBRUARY 1932 ～ 25 JANUARY 1933   *Water Monkey*

25 JANUARY 1944 ～ 12 FEBRUARY 1945   *Wood Monkey*

12 FEBRUARY 1956 ～ 30 JANUARY 1957   *Fire Monkey*

30 JANUARY 1968 ～ 16 FEBRUARY 1969   *Earth Monkey*

16 FEBRUARY 1980 ～ 4 FEBRUARY 1981   *Metal Monkey*

4 FEBRUARY 1992 ～ 22 JANUARY 1993   *Water Monkey*

22 JANUARY 2004 ～ 8 FEBRUARY 2005   *Wood Monkey*

THE
MONKEY

THE PERSONALITY OF THE MONKEY

The more open to possibility,
the more possibilities open.

The Monkey is born under the sign of fantasy. He is imaginative, inquisitive and loves to keep an eye on everything that is going on around him. He is never backward in offering advice or trying to sort out the problems of others. He likes to be helpful and his advice is invariably sensible and reliable.

The Monkey is intelligent, well read and always eager to learn. He has an extremely good memory and there are many Monkeys who have made particularly good linguists. The Monkey is also a convincing talker and enjoys taking part in discussions and debates. His friendly, self-assured manner can be very persuasive and he usually has little trouble in winning people round to his way of thinking. It is for this reason that he often excels in politics and public speaking. He is also particularly adept in PR work, teaching and any job that involves selling.

The Monkey can, however, be crafty, cunning and occasionally dishonest, and he will seize on any opportunity to make a quick profit or outsmart his opponents. He has so much charm and guile that people often don't realize what he is up to until it is too late. But despite his resourceful nature, he does run the risk of outsmarting even himself. He has so much confidence in his abilities that he rarely listens to advice or is prepared to accept help from anyone. He likes to help others but prefers to rely on his own judgement when dealing with his own affairs.

Another characteristic of the Monkey is that he is extremely good at solving problems and has a happy knack of extricating himself (and others) from the most hopeless of positions. He is the master of self-preservation.

With so many diverse talents the Monkey is usually able to make considerable sums of money, but he does like to enjoy life and will think nothing of spending his money on some exotic holiday or luxury he has had his eye on. He can, however, become very envious if someone else has what he wants.

The Monkey is an original thinker and despite his love of company, he cherishes his independence. He has to have the freedom to act as he wants and any Monkey who feels hemmed in or bound by too many restrictions will soon become unhappy. Likewise, if anything becomes too boring or monotonous, the Monkey will soon lose interest and turn his attention to something else. He lacks persistence and this can often hamper his progress. He is also easily distracted, a tendency that he should try to overcome. By concentrating on one thing at a time, he will almost certainly achieve more in the long run.

The Monkey is a good organizer and even though he may behave slightly erratically at times, he will invariably have a plan at the back of his mind. On the odd occasion when his plans do not work out, he is usually quite happy to shrug his shoulders and put it down to experience. He will rarely make the same mistake twice and throughout his life he will try his hand at many different things.

The Monkey likes to impress and is rarely without followers or admirers. Many are attracted by his good looks, his sense of humour, or simply because he instils so much confidence.

Monkeys usually marry young and for it to be a success their partner must allow them time to pursue their many interests and indulge their love of travel. The Monkey has to have variety in his life and is especially well suited to those born under the sociable and outgoing signs of the Rat, Dragon, Pig and Goat. The Ox, Rabbit, Snake and Dog will also be enchanted by the Monkey's resourceful and outgoing nature, but he is likely to exasperate the Rooster and Horse, and the Tiger will have little patience with his tricks. A relationship between two Monkeys will work well – they will understand each other and be able to assist each other in their various enterprises.

The female Monkey is intelligent, extremely observant and a shrewd judge of character. Her opinions are often highly valued and, having such a persuasive nature, she invariably gets her own way. She has many interests and involves herself in a wide variety of activities. She pays great attention to her appearance, is an elegant dresser and likes to take particular care over her hair. She can be a doting parent and will have many good and loyal friends.

Provided the Monkey can curb his desire to take part in everything that is going on around him and concentrate on one thing at a time, he can usually achieve what he wants in life. Should he suffer any disappointment, he is bound to bounce back. He is a survivor and his life is usually both colourful and eventful.

THE FIVE DIFFERENT TYPES OF MONKEY

In addition to the 12 signs of the Chinese zodiac there are five elements and these have a strengthening or moderating influence on the signs. The effects of the five elements on the Monkey are described below, together with the years in which the elements were exercising their influence. Therefore those Monkeys born in 1920 and 1980 are Metal Monkeys, those born in 1932 and 1992 are Water Monkeys, and so on.

Metal Monkey: 1920, 1980
The Metal Monkey is very strong-willed. He sets about everything he does with dogged determination and often prefers to work independently rather than with others. He is ambitious, wise and confident, and is certainly not afraid of hard work. He is very astute in financial matters and usually chooses his investments well. Despite his somewhat independent nature, he enjoys attending parties and social occasions and is particularly warm and caring towards his loved ones.

Water Monkey: 1932, 1992
The Water Monkey is versatile, determined and perceptive. He also has more discipline than some of the other Monkeys and is prepared to work towards a particular goal

rather than be distracted by something else. He is not always open about his true intentions and when questioned can be particularly evasive. He can be sensitive to criticism but also very persuasive and usually has little trouble in getting others to fall in with his plans. He has a very good understanding of human nature and relates well to others.

Wood Monkey: 1944, 2004

This Monkey is efficient, methodical and extremely conscientious. He is also highly imaginative and is always trying to capitalize on new ideas or learn new skills. Occasionally his enthusiasm can get the better of him and he can get very agitated when things do not quite work out as he had hoped. He does, however, have a very adventurous streak and is not afraid of taking risks. He also loves travel. He is usually held in great esteem by his friends and colleagues.

Fire Monkey: 1956

The Fire Monkey is intelligent, full of vitality and has no trouble in commanding the respect of others. He is imaginative and has wide interests, although sometimes these can distract him from more useful and profitable work. He is very competitive and always likes to be involved in everything that is going on. He can be stubborn if he does not get his own way and he sometimes tries to indoctrinate those who are less strong-willed than himself. He is a lively character, attractive to others and most loyal to his partner.

Earth Monkey: 1968

The Earth Monkey tends to be studious and well read, and can become quite distinguished in his chosen line of work. He is less outgoing than some of the other types of Monkey and prefers quieter and more solid pursuits. He has high principles, a very caring nature and can be most generous to those less fortunate than himself. He is usually successful in handling financial matters and can become very wealthy in old age. He has a calming influence on those around him and is respected and well liked. He is, however, especially careful about whom he lets into his confidence.

PROSPECTS FOR THE MONKEY IN 2010

The Monkey has a great knack of making the best of situations and while the Year of the Ox (26 January 2009 to 13 February 2010) may not have been the smoothest of years for him, his resourceful nature will still have allowed him to accomplish a great deal. As Monkeys recognize, to do well in Ox years means putting in the effort and many will have done so and will continue to do so successfully in the remaining months of the year.

In their work many Monkeys will have had a lot to deal with and in the process added considerably to their skills. As the Ox year draws to a close the Monkey should take advantage of any chances he has to broaden his role, including any training opportunities that become available. The final quarter of the Ox year can be constructive, with

September and November seeing encouraging developments.

The Ox year can also give rise to some good travel opportunities and quite a few Monkeys will be visiting relations and/or some interesting destinations in the closing months. However, with the likelihood of travel, as well as the commitments he has and purchases he may be considering, the Monkey does need to remain disciplined in money matters. The latter part of the Ox year can be expensive for him.

With his widespread interests and many friends he can however, look forward to some pleasing social occasions. December and early January could be particularly active and, for some Monkeys, affairs of the heart can make this a special time.

The Monkey's home life will also see increased activity and here his organizational ability will be much appreciated and lead to some often meaningful times. The end of 2009 and start of 2010 promise to be busy.

Tiger years are often active and few signs will remain unaffected by the changes this year will bring. But the Monkey, who himself favours action, will need to be careful. This is no time for risks or being overly ambitious in what he sets out to do. Progress can be made, but plans do need to be carefully thought through.

The Tiger year begins on 14 February and almost as soon as it starts quite a few Monkeys will get a taste of some of the changes it can bring. For many, these will be in their work, with new staff, different working practices or a change in their role or objectives. What happens early on in the

Tiger year could concern many Monkeys and be far from ideal, but it is a case of adapting and adjusting as required.

Also, while the Monkey usually has excellent people skills, he needs to pay careful attention to his relations with his colleagues during the Tiger year. Failure to do so could leave him isolated or undermine his position or recent good work. In this exacting year, he will need to keep his wits about him. Also, while it may not always suit his style, it would sometimes be prudent for him to keep a low profile and avoid exacerbating any difficult or volatile situations. The early months of the year in particular will require many Monkeys to tread warily *and* carefully.

However, while the Tiger year may get off to a demanding start, it does offer considerable scope to the Monkey. Tiger years do favour ideas and input, and with the Monkey's ability to come up with solutions or consider problems from different perspectives, whenever he feels able to make constructive suggestions he should put these forward. Similarly, if he sees an opportunity that appeals to him, he should act. Provided he thinks through his actions he can fare reasonably well, but should he take risks or act without sufficient thought, problems are likely to arise. Tiger years do require Monkeys to be on their mettle!

For Monkeys who are interested in furthering their career, the second half of the year could see the best chances, notably July and the months from September to November. However, such is the nature of the Tiger year that opportunities can arise suddenly and often when the Monkey least expects them.

This also applies to those Monkeys who are keen to move on from where they currently are or are seeking work. Whenever they see vacancies that appeal to them, they do need to act quickly and, to help strengthen their application, find out more about the company and duties involved. With initiative, many can secure a new and potentially rewarding position. These Monkeys will generally fare best by looking for positions for which they have the necessary knowledge and experience rather than embarking on more major and potentially riskier change. They will be helped by emphasizing their experience and their prospects will generally be more favourable in the second half of the year.

Financial matters, however, will need care. The Monkey will need to remain disciplined and be wary of making impulse purchases. Without sufficient control, his outgoings could creep up. Here again he must be careful not to get caught up in the speed and frenzy of the year and act hurriedly or without sufficient thought. In addition, if he is tempted to take any risks or become involved in more speculative ventures, he needs to check the implications and get good advice. This is a year for caution.

Although the Monkey usually keeps himself active it would also be to his benefit to give some consideration to his well-being. With the pressures and strains of the year and, for some, long hours at work, it is important that the Monkey takes regular and appropriate exercise as well as has a nutritious and balanced diet. If he has any concerns or decides to make some changes, he should seek advice. In addition all Monkeys should try to go away during the year. A break from their routine can do them a lot of good.

With all the activity of the year, the Monkey should also take care that his social life does not get sidelined. He should aim to keep in regular contact with friends and even if it is not always possible to meet up, a phone call or e-mail could still be appreciated. If he has invitations or sees events that appeal to him, he should try to follow these up. His social life can help balance his lifestyle and do him good. The only thing to be aware of is that should he find himself in a difficult, delicate or inflammatory situation, he does need to be wary and discreet. Throughout the Tiger year he needs to keep his wits about him.

His domestic life will also see considerable activity and while the Monkey is usually expert at juggling with many things at once, even he could have problems keeping tabs on everything. This will be a busy year and everyone in the household will need to pool together and help one another. Certain plans may have to be altered and the Monkey will need to be accommodating and flexible. However, while the Tiger year can be a highly active one, it can also contain a great many pleasures. There will be achievements to mark, a possible family surprise and some pleasing times for the Monkey to enjoy. His talent for coming up with suggestions will be appreciated and if he has ideas for activities or treats or there are interests and projects that everyone can carry out together, this can add a richness to his home life. Spending quality time with his loved ones really will reward the Monkey well this year.

The Monkey likes activity and to keep himself occupied, but the pressures, changes and unsettling events of the Tiger year can make this a testing time. However, the Monkey is also resourceful and ready for challenge, and by keeping alert and being flexible in approach, he can gain a lot from the year. And amid all the activity it will contain some particularly satisfying times.

The Metal Monkey

The Metal Monkey has ambition and a strong will. And as he enters a new decade in his life, he will be keen to get his thirties off to a positive start and make headway. Over the year a lot can open up for him, but throughout he will need be careful and wary. To become complacent, take risks or pursue aims without sufficient thought or preparation can lead to disappointment. This is a year for vigilance and a certain flexibility.

The Tiger year is often characterized by change and during it the Metal Monkey will need to keep aware of the developments going on around him and the plans under consideration. This way he will be better able to adapt as well as benefit from some of the situations that arise. He is likely to see a lot happen over the year, particularly in his work, including changes of personnel, new working methods or alterations to his duties. Although some of these developments may concern him, by rising to the challenges and using any opportunities to add to his skills, he can do his standing and prospects a lot of good. This is very much a year for making the most of situations, even if they are not exactly as the Metal Monkey would want.

Another aspect of the year is that many Metal Monkeys could face additional obstacles. These could include delays, developments outside their control or the difficult attitude of some of the people they are working with. However, by doing what they can and dealing with problems as they arise, these Metal Monkeys can emerge with much to their credit and some valuable experience behind them. Work-wise, this may be a challenging time, but it can be instructive and often helpful in the future.

While the aspects may be mixed, there will still be opportunities for quite a few Metal Monkeys to take on a greater role, whether through promotion or being offered new duties. Tiger years are progressive and will allow many Metal Monkeys to make headway. The second half of the year will generally be more favourable, with July and September to November seeing possible opportunities to move forward.

For Metal Monkeys who feel their prospects are limited where they are or are seeking work, the Tiger year can be important. Securing a new position will not be easy and this is why it is so important that the Metal Monkey remains aware of what is going on around him. Sometimes a chance remark or something he reads could alert him to a possibility worth following up. If he remains active, keeps in regular contact with employment agencies and gets appropriate advice, his keen and persistent nature will prevail, sometimes in an unusual and almost fortuitous way. Progress does not always come easily in Tiger years, but the Metal Monkey is resourceful and resilient and these two attributes will serve him well.

Although the progress many Metal Monkeys make at work will bring an increase in income, they will still need to manage their financial situation well. The Metal Monkey should watch his spending and to prevent mistakes or misjudgements, he should be wary of risk or acting in haste. This is a year for discipline and control.

Also, should the Metal Monkey have any financial concerns, it would be worth him seeking advice rather than letting any problems continue or possibly worsen. Metal Monkeys take note and, when necessary, do consult those with the knowledge to help.

With his work, interests and many friends, there will be some good social opportunities for the Metal Monkey over the year, as well as chances to meet new people. For the most part he will enjoy his socializing, but here again this is a year for care. An inadvertent comment, petty jealousy or a clash of views could cause difficult moments and the Metal Monkey will need to be aware of this risk and careful not to exacerbate any tensions. Awareness will be so important throughout the year. March, June, August and September could see the most social activity, and for the unattached, the Tiger year could produce some interesting and almost fortuitous romantic opportunities which can, with care, develop well.

This need for awareness also applies to the Metal Monkey's domestic life. With all his own activities and an often increased workload, there will be times when he may be tired and tense. This may not always be helped by those who are parents or who become parents this year having to cope with disturbed nights. However, by sharing household activities, helping and supporting each other and communicating well, they can still make these special times. Also, some loved ones could have surprises in store to mark the Metal Monkey's thirtieth year and may also be able to encourage him in some unexpected ways. Those close to him, whether his partner, children or more senior relations, will certainly mean a great deal to him this year.

There will also be some good travel opportunities during the year and all Metal Monkeys should try to go away at some time, as they will enjoy the rest this brings and the chance to visit somewhere new. Some may be tempted to mark their thirtieth year with a special trip and if they plan ahead, it could turn out to be a very special occasion.

The Tiger year will certainly be an eventful one for the Metal Monkey and, while he will need to remain alert and adapt to the situations that arise, he will be able to make headway as well as learn much of value. And despite the year's pressures and more testing times, it can prepare the way for some of the more substantial progress the Metal Monkey will enjoy in following years.

TIP FOR THE YEAR
Build on your skills and talents. That way you will be investing in yourself *and* your future. Also, keep alert. By remaining aware of what is going on around you, you will not only be better able to adapt to certain situations but also identify some opportunities worth developing.

The Water Monkey
The Water Monkey likes to keep himself active and his vitality and enthusiasm will help to open many doors this year.

During the year many Water Monkeys will be giving considerable thought to their future and to some of the decisions they will need to make. These could involve ways in which they could further their studies, courses they could take, types of work to pursue or, for those reaching the end of their current courses, whether to take a gap year and temporary break from their education. Although the Water Monkey may already have some ideas about what he wants to do, it is important that he is forthcoming and prepared to discuss his options with those close to him. With advice from those who know him well, some of his decisions will be made easier and the choices made will be right for him.

However, while the Water Monkey will be considering his future, he also needs to concentrate on the present. Many Water Monkeys will be preparing for exams and will need to remain focused and disciplined. With all its activity, the Tiger year can be full of distractions and these Water Monkeys will need to be careful not to get diverted from their studying. The good solid effort they put in now will produce results and help in what they subsequently choose to do.

For Water Monkeys who start new courses or subjects over the year, often at a new place of study, this can be a daunting time. Not only will many be in an unfamiliar environment, but they could have concerns over their work or course. However, again it is a case of focus and adjusting. As they will soon find, many around them have similar anxieties, and by allowing themselves time, these Water Monkeys will begin to feel more settled as well as better able to rise to the challenge before them. The Tiger year may be demanding but will give the Water Monkey an excellent chance to further his skills and develop greater confidence.

For Water Monkeys seeking work the Tiger year can again bring some interesting possibilities. However, to fully benefit they should seek advice from those with the knowledge to help as well as not be too restrictive in what they are prepared to consider. The chief aim this year will be to get a foot on the employment ladder and once they have achieved this and can show what they are capable of, they will find progress much easier. March, July and September to November will see the best chances, but with the year's fast pace openings can arise at almost any time.

For Water Monkeys already in work the Tiger year can again present some interesting opportunities. These could involve taking on a greater role where they are or using their experience to progress elsewhere. Whatever they do, by showing themselves keen to learn, these Water Monkeys will see new possibilities opening up. The Tiger year is no time for standing still.

As far as money matters are concerned, the Water Monkey will need to be disciplined and keep a tight control over his spending. With his many ideas and an often active social life, he should be wary of buying on impulse or taking risks. Also, should he take on any new financial agreement, he needs to check the terms and implications and take appropriate advice. In matters of finance, this is a year for care and thoroughness.

Another awkward aspect concerns the Water Monkey's relations with others. Sometimes a difference of opinion or misunderstanding will arise, petty jealousy will surface or there will be a clash of interests or personality. Although these could cause him some anguish, the Water Monkey should try to deal with them as they occur and keep them in perspective. Also, whenever he has concerns or worries, whether over a friendship, romance or other matter, he should remember he has some excellent friends willing to support and advise.

However, although the Water Monkey will need to remain aware of the year's cautionary aspects, for the most part he will value his social life. The changes of the year can lead to him getting to know new people and forming some close friendships. March, June and August to mid-October will see the most social activity.

Another important feature of the Tiger year will be the possibilities it can open up. These could involve the Water Monkey using recreational facilities where he is studying or working or in his local area. Some could get the opportunity to take up a new pursuit, and by making the most of such chances, they can derive much satisfaction from what they do. Some could also be attracted by travel opportunities. The Tiger year can bring some very attractive possibilities which, with the Water Monkey's enthusiastic nature, he will be keen to make the most of.

Overall, the Water Monkey can fare well over the year, with what he achieves helping both his present and future prospects. However, he will need to remain disciplined in his activities and use his time well. Provided he is wary of distractions and is careful, then this can be a productive, interesting and rewarding year.

TIP FOR THE YEAR
Seek advice and listen to it. With help and support your decisions will be easier and that much better for you.

The Wood Monkey

The Wood Monkey has a keen nature and enjoys a wide range of interests and pursuits. During the Tiger year he will have the chance to spend time on activities he enjoys as well as further certain skills and strengths. Also, with the Tiger year favouring new pursuits, creative and expressive Wood Monkeys could find something they do could receive an encouraging response.

For Wood Monkeys who have recently retired or who retire this year, the Tiger year is an excellent one for considering ways of using the extra time they now have. In particular if there is a course in their area that appeals to them or a local society or interest group they could join, they should find out more. By taking positive action and following up their ideas and opportunities, they can benefit greatly from what they do.

Another encouraging aspect of the year will be the level of support the Wood Monkey receives, whether from his partner, family members, close friends or those in a position to assist him. If at any time he is considering a particular idea or would welcome a second opinion on some matter, he should ask. Many Wood Monkeys will particularly welcome the social element that new or existing interests can bring and for the lonely Wood Monkey, a new interest could bring an important new friend.

The Wood Monkey would also do well to give some consideration to his well-being and if he feels that modifications to his diet or improving his exercise levels would help, he should seek medical guidance on how best to proceed. This is a year for action and follow-through.

There will also be some good travel opportunities over the year and whether he is invited to stay with others or go away for a holiday, the Wood Monkey should make the most of his opportunities. Some Wood Monkeys may also decide to combine an interest or event with their travels and so give their time away additional meaning.

However, while the Tiger year will contain some very pleasurable and satisfying times, it also has its more cautionary aspects. In money matters in particular the Wood Monkey should avoid risk or acting too hastily and when making major purchases should allow himself the time to consider the options, terms and implications. Haste can lead to regret. He should also attend to financial paperwork carefully and if he has doubts or concerns, seek further advice. The more thorough he is, the better.

For Wood Monkeys who decide to move this year, the process could be vexing. There could be delays, difficulties in coming to an agreement or settling terms as well as snags in packing, storage and the inevitable sorting out. This is a time when the Wood Monkey will need considerable patience as well as professional assistance.

Even those Wood Monkeys who do not move could experience the Tiger year's trickier aspects. There could be a disagreement with another person, problems over a transaction or contract, or plans having to be altered or postponed. At such times, the Wood Monkey will need to be wary and careful not to exacerbate the problem. This is a year for care and, where necessary, appropriate advice.

However, while the aspects may be mixed, a lot will go in the Wood Monkey's favour over the year and this can be a busy and satisfying time, particularly in his home life, with family successes and developments that will especially please him, including the progress made by younger relations. Sharing activities and encouraging each other can be of great help.

Overall, the Wood Monkey will need to be careful and thorough in the Tiger year. This is a time when problems can suddenly arise or mistakes be made through rush. However, there are many positive aspects. Both existing and new pursuits can bring especial pleasure and the Wood Monkey will value the support and encouragement he receives from those around him. With this backing, combined with his own earnest nature, he will find the Tiger year holds considerable possibility. It is a time to be vigilant but to make the most of his opportunities.

TIP FOR THE YEAR
Be thorough and draw on the willingness of others to advise or help. When under pressure or considering possible plans and activities, remember that those around you can do much to assist.

The Fire Monkey
This will be a significant year for the Fire Monkey and while it can bring many pressures, his decisions during it can lead to some particularly important developments. This often demanding year is also one of great possibility.

One area which will see considerable activity will be work. Changes will affect almost all Fire Monkeys, with new ways of working being introduced or a restructuring taking place where they work. Over the year it is important that the Fire Monkey keeps informed about developments and is prepared to adapt as required. Also some changes, particularly in staff, could open up promotion opportunities. By keeping alert and being prepared to adapt, many Fire Monkeys will, after some anxious moments, be able to make headway.

For Fire Monkeys who feel the time is now right for them to move on from where they are, as well as those seeking work, the Tiger year can be significant. These Fire Monkeys should be prepared to look at the options available as well as obtain advice from relevant agencies. For some, training and refresher courses could be worth considering. With this being a year for innovation, a new position may well ask a lot of the Fire Monkey but can often be something he can build on and can give him the incentive he may have been lacking in recent years. The Tiger year will, for some, be a time of new starts. July and September to November could see some interesting possibilities.

Although the Fire Monkey enjoys good relations with many people, he also needs to pay careful attention to his relations with colleagues this year. This includes remaining aware of their views, being alert to possible pettiness or jealousy and being guarded in tense and volatile situations. A loss of temper could bring problems that will prove an unwelcome distraction, and over the year the Fire Monkey will need to be careful *and* aware.

This also applies to his relations with his friends. An inadvertent comment or lapse of judgement could undermine rapport. Fire Monkeys, do take note and be alert and mindful. However, for the most part the Fire Monkey will enjoy his social life. Certain interests and, for some, sport or keep-fit exercises can lead to some fun times. The Fire Monkey does enjoy company and, despite the year's need for care, joint pursuits can often bring him pleasure.

With the Tiger year favouring personal development, it could also be to the Fire Monkey's advantage to consider trying out new activities or studying a new subject. With good use of his free time, he can make this a constructive year.

The Fire Monkey's home life will see a great deal of activity and as a result there will need to be excellent communication and co-operation between everyone in his household. At times of pressure, often caused by some demanding days at work, the Fire Monkey will need to be careful that tensions do not lead to irritability and lack of patience. Some days will require careful handling.

The generally busy situation could also be made worse if the Fire Monkey moves to new accommodation or has any practical work carried out in his home. Some of the Tiger year can be stressful, but once situations settle, moves have taken place or improvements have been completed, many Fire Monkeys will be pleased with what has been achieved.

While parts of the year may be fraught, there will still be a lot for the Fire Monkey to value and enjoy, including special times spent with his loved ones, any holidays and breaks and some well-deserved success. Amid all the activity, there will be times the Fire Monkey will particularly savour.

With some of the accommodation expenses that may arise and the commitments he has, he will, however, need to pay careful attention to his financial situation. When entering into agreements or embarking on costly under-takings, he does need to compare terms as well as check any obligations. This is no year for risk or carelessness.

Also, in order to go ahead with certain plans, including travel, he should aim to budget well in advance. This is a year for prudent management of his finances.

In general, the Year of the Tiger will be a demanding one, with the Fire Monkey having a lot to do and decide on. However, while the year will bring its pressures, it can also create some interesting possibilities, many of which can be to the Fire Monkey's present and future advantage. A busy but potentially significant year.

TIP FOR THE YEAR
Be adventurous. Look at new possibilities – fresh interests, projects you could start or skills you could learn. Although a busy year, this is a time of personal development and important choices. Use it well, for there is much you can ultimately gain from it.

The Earth Monkey

During the Tiger year the Earth Monkey will find it helpful to keep in mind the Chinese proverb, 'Caution is the vehicle for a long journey.' The next 12 months will be eventful, and while he may achieve a lot, this is no time for throwing caution to the wind or embarking on hasty and ill thought-out actions.

However, while the Earth Monkey will need to be vigilant, the Tiger year can bring some interesting opportunities. At work many Earth Monkeys will be encouraged to widen their experience and put their skills to other uses. By making the most of their opportunities, including taking advantage of any training that is available, many will prepare the way for taking on greater responsibilities later. Also, some of the pressures of the year will give the Earth Monkey the chance to use his skills and demonstrate his worth, which again can be to his future benefit. Work-wise, this may not always be an easy or straightforward year, but what the Earth Monkey accomplishes can have future significance, especially in the following Rabbit year.

One of the Earth Monkey's strengths is his ability to relate well to other people and over the year he should continue to work closely with colleagues and be an active team-member. Getting to know new people can also help his prospects.

Many Earth Monkeys will remain with their current employer over the year, building on their skills and making headway where they are, but for those who are unhappy, feel unsettled by recent developments or are seeking work, the Tiger year can be a significant juncture. For these Earth Monkeys this is a year to take stock, carefully consider what they now want to do and draw on the advice available to them. By considering their position and following up suggestions, many will find their efforts setting important wheels in motion. Obtaining a new position may not be easy, but many will be successful in securing something they can build on in the future. A cautious and carefully considered approach can pay dividends, with July and late August to November seeing the best chances.

The Earth Monkey will also need to remain disciplined in money matters. With possible increased family expenses, additional accommodation costs and the other commitments he will face, he will have many demands on his resources. As a result he should keep careful track of his outgoings and, where possible, make advance provision for forthcoming expenses. Many Earth Monkeys are vigilant when dealing with finance and the greater care they can take this year, the better.

The Tiger year can also bring some good travel opportunities and the Earth Monkey will often enjoy the chance to see new areas as well as have a rest from his usual routine. A short break in the last quarter of the year could be particularly delightful.

With all the activity, the Earth Monkey may decide to keep his social life relatively low key this year. However he should still keep in regular contact with his friends as well as go to events that appeal to him and allow himself time for his interests and recreational pursuits. These can do him a lot of good as well as help keep his lifestyle in balance.

The Earth Monkey's domestic life will also be particularly busy and he will not only be heavily involved in family activities but also do much to assist another person. Here his insights and ability to empathize will be of particular value. By keeping well-organized, prioritizing at busy times and encouraging everyone in his household to co-operate, he will not only see a lot happen but also enjoy some special occasions. As with so much this year, the more that can be planned in advance, the better.

The Tiger year can be a demanding one for the Earth Monkey, but by remaining aware of developments and liaising well with others, he can do a lot to counter some of its more negative aspects. Should problems arise, he does need to deal with these as quickly as he can or they could escalate. In addition, minor differences of opinion which the Earth Monkey may quite happily dismiss could become more serious. This is a year to tread carefully and the Earth Monkey's alert and canny nature will be a great advantage.

The Tiger year will ask a lot of the Earth Monkey but it will give him a good chance to draw on his skills and gain valuable experience. Demanding though it may be, he can take a great deal from it which he will be able to build on in the more favourable Rabbit year which follows.

TIP FOR THE YEAR
You have many aspirations and a keenness to succeed. Be cautious, proceed steadily and learn from the experiences of the year. These will stand you in excellent stead for the future. Do not underestimate the importance of the present time.

FAMOUS MONKEYS

Gillian Anderson, Jennifer Aniston, Christina Aguilera, Patricia Arquette, José Manuel Barroso, Joe Cocker, Colette, Patricia Cornwell, Daniel Craig, Joan Crawford, Leonardo da Vinci, Timothy Dalton, Bette Davis, Danny De Vito, Celine Dion, Michael Douglas, Mia Farrow, Carrie Fisher, F Scott Fitzgerald, Dick Francis, Jake Gyllenhaal, Jerry Hall, Tom Hanks, Harry Houdini, P. D. James, Katherine Jenkins, Julius Caesar, Buster Keaton, Alicia Keys, Don King, Gladys Knight, Bob Marley, Kylie Minogue, V. S. Naipaul, Peter O'Toole, Lisa Marie Presley, Debbie Reynolds, Little Richard, Mickey Rooney, Diana Ross, Tom Selleck, Wilbur Smith, Rod Stewart, Elizabeth Taylor, Dame Kiri Te Kanawa, Justin Timberlake, Harry Truman, Venus Williams.

8 FEBRUARY 1921 ～ 27 JANUARY 1922 *Metal Rooster*

26 JANUARY 1933 ～ 13 FEBRUARY 1934 *Water Rooster*

13 FEBRUARY 1945 ～ 1 FEBRUARY 1946 *Wood Rooster*

31 JANUARY 1957 ～ 17 FEBRUARY 1958 *Fire Rooster*

17 FEBRUARY 1969 ～ 5 FEBRUARY 1970 *Earth Rooster*

5 FEBRUARY 1981 ～ 24 JANUARY 1982 *Metal Rooster*

23 JANUARY 1993 ～ 9 FEBRUARY 1994 *Water Rooster*

9 FEBRUARY 2005 ～ 28 JANUARY 2006 *Wood Rooster*

THE
ROOSTER

THE PERSONALITY OF THE ROOSTER

With a clear destination
and firm will,
I raise my sails
to the winds of fortune.

The Rooster is born under the sign of candour. He has a flamboyant and colourful personality and is meticulous in all that he does. He is an excellent organizer and wherever possible likes to plan his various activities well in advance.

The Rooster is usually highly intelligent and very well read. He has a good sense of humour and is an effective and persuasive speaker. He loves discussion and enjoys taking part in any sort of debate. He has no hesitation in speaking his mind and is forthright in his views. He does, however, lack tact and can easily damage his reputation or cause offence by some thoughtless remark or action. He has a very volatile nature and should always try to avoid acting on the spur of the moment.

He is usually very dignified in his manner and conducts himself with an air of confidence and authority. He is adept at handling financial matters and organizes his financial affairs with considerable skill. He chooses his investments well and is capable of achieving great wealth. Most Roosters save or use their money wisely, but there are a few who are the reverse and are notorious spendthrifts. Fortunately, the Rooster has great earning capacity and is rarely without sufficient funds to tide himself over.

Another characteristic of the Rooster is that he invariably carries a notebook or scraps of paper around with him.

He is constantly writing himself reminders or noting down important facts lest he forgets – the Rooster cannot abide inefficiency and conducts all his activities in an orderly, precise and methodical manner.

The Rooster is usually very ambitious, but can be unrealistic in some of what he hopes to achieve. He occasionally lets his imagination run away with him and while he does not like any interference from others, it would be in his own interests to listen to their views a little more often. He also does not like criticism, and if he feels anybody is doubting his judgement or prying too closely into his affairs, he is certain to let his feelings be known. He can also be rather self-centred and stubborn over relatively trivial matters, but to compensate for this he is reliable, honest and trustworthy, and this is appreciated by all who come into contact with him.

Roosters born between the hours of five and seven, both at dawn and sundown, tend to be the most extrovert of their sign, but all Roosters like to lead an active social life and enjoy attending parties and big functions. The Rooster usually has a wide circle of friends and is able to build up influential contacts with remarkable ease. He often belongs to several clubs and societies and involves himself in a variety of different activities. He is particularly interested in the environment, humanitarian affairs and anything affecting the welfare of others. He has a very caring nature and will do much to help those less fortunate than himself.

He also gets much pleasure from gardening, and while he may not spend as much time in the garden as he would like, his garden is invariably well kept and productive.

The Rooster is generally very distinguished in his appearance and if his job permits he will wear an official uniform with great pride and dignity. He is not averse to publicity and takes great delight in being the centre of attention. He often does well at PR work or any job which brings him into contact with the media. He also makes a very good teacher.

The female Rooster leads a varied and interesting life. She involves herself in many different activities and there are some who wonder how she can achieve so much. She often holds very strong views and, like her male counterpart, has no hesitation in speaking her mind or telling others how she thinks things should be done. She is supremely efficient and well organized and her home is usually very neat and tidy. She has good taste in clothes and usually wears smart but very practical outfits.

The Rooster usually has a large family and takes a particularly active interest in the education of his children. He is very loyal to his partner and will find that he is especially well suited to those born under the signs of the Snake, Horse, Ox and Dragon. Provided they do not interfere too much in his various activities, the Rat, Tiger, Goat and Pig can also establish a good relationship with him, but two Roosters together are likely to squabble and irritate each other. The rather sensitive Rabbit will find the Rooster a bit too blunt for his liking, and the Rooster will quickly become exasperated by the ever-inquisitive and artful Monkey. He will also find it difficult to get on with the anxious Dog.

If the Rooster can overcome his volatile nature and exercise tact, he will go far in life. He is capable and talented and will make a lasting – and usually favourable – impression almost everywhere he goes.

THE FIVE DIFFERENT TYPES OF ROOSTER

In addition to the 12 signs of the Chinese zodiac there are five elements and these have a strengthening or moderating influence on the signs. The effects of the five elements on the Rooster are described below, together with the years in which the elements were exercising their influence. Therefore those Roosters born in 1921 and 1981 are Metal Roosters, those born in 1933 and 1993 are Water Roosters, and so on.

Metal Rooster: 1921, 1981

The Metal Rooster is a hard and conscientious worker. He knows exactly what he wants in life and sets about everything in a positive and determined manner. He can at times appear abrasive and he would almost certainly do better if he were more willing to reach a compromise with others rather than hold so rigidly to his beliefs. He is very articulate and most astute when dealing with financial matters. He is loyal to his friends and often devotes much energy to working for the common good.

Water Rooster: 1933, 1993

This Rooster has a very persuasive manner and can easily gain the co-operation of others. He is intelligent, well read and enjoys taking part in discussions and debates. He has a seemingly inexhaustible amount of energy and is prepared to work long hours in order to secure what he wants. He can, however, waste a lot of valuable time worrying over minor and inconsequential details. He is approachable, has a good sense of humour and is highly regarded by others.

Wood Rooster: 1945, 2005

The Wood Rooster is honest, reliable and often sets himself high standards. He is ambitious, but he is also more prepared to work in a team than some of the other types of Rooster. He usually succeeds in life but does have a tendency to get caught up in bureaucratic matters and attempt too many things at the same time. He has wide interests, likes to travel and is very caring and considerate towards his family and friends.

Fire Rooster: 1957

This Rooster is extremely strong-willed. He has many leadership qualities, is an excellent organizer and is most efficient in his work. Through sheer force of character he often secures his objectives, but he does have a tendency to be very forthright and not always consider the feelings of others. If he can learn to be more tactful he can often succeed beyond his wildest dreams.

Earth Rooster: 1909, 1969

This Rooster has a deep and penetrating mind. He is efficient, perceptive and particularly astute in business and financial matters. He is also persistent and once he has set himself an objective, he will rarely allow himself to be deflected from achieving his aim. He works hard and is held in great esteem by his friends and colleagues. He usually enjoys the arts and takes a keen interest in the activities of the various members of his family.

PROSPECTS FOR THE ROOSTER IN 2010

The Ox year (26 January 2009 to 13 February 2010) favours order and method and, being the keen planner that he is, the Rooster will generally fare well during it. The aspects are particularly encouraging for the closing months.

With his active and enquiring nature, the Rooster will find himself in demand at this time. At work many Roosters could have additional responsibilities and pressures to cope with and while these may be demanding, the Rooster could enjoy some personal success in a task or project he is involved with. For Roosters who are keen on making progress in their career or are looking for work, September could be a key month with some good possibilities to pursue.

The Rooster could also benefit from some additional funds towards the end of the year or be given a bonus or surprise gift. Also, if there is a particular purchase he is keen to make, by keeping alert he could secure just what is looking for, often at an advantageous price.

The Rooster's domestic and social life can also bring him considerable pleasure at this time. Again there will be a lot for him to do, but by keeping well-organized and planning ahead, he will not only be able to fit in a great deal but will particularly appreciate some special treats, parties or travel opportunities. August, December and January could be especially pleasurable months and for many Roosters the love they have for another person can make the closing months of the Ox year very special.

It is often said that life is a series of ups and downs and this will be very true for the Rooster in the Tiger year, which begins 14 February. Events can happen at a heady pace and for one who likes to plan and remain organized, this can be a tricky time. However, while the aspects may be mixed, amid all the activity (and, to the Rooster's mind, sometimes chaos) there will be some successes and occasions the Rooster will particularly appreciate.

One characteristic of the Rooster is that he keeps his wits very much about him. He is observant and perceptive and these traits will serve him well over the next 12 months. This is very much a year to remain aware and adapt as necessary. Also, in his relations with others, it is important that the Rooster consults *and listens*. The Rooster is a dominant personality and has very definite views, but to fare well this year he does need to liaise well with others, consider their advice and suggestions and build up support. This is no time to go it alone.

In his domestic life consultation and co-operation will be particularly important. With the busy nature of the year, everyone in the Rooster's household will need to pull together and be prepared to help one another. Joint projects can be particularly successful and should the Rooster have home improvements or other plans he would like to get underway, if these are tackled together, more will be accomplished. Also, if the Rooster is under strain at any time or concerned about a particular matter, a willingness to discuss this fully can do a lot of good. The Rooster's awareness and ability to empathize with others will once again be a valuable asset this year.

With all the activity of the year it is also important that he preserves quality time for sharing with others rather than remaining continually busy. Here mutual interests or an occasional treat could be especially appreciated. This can be a rewarding year domestically, but consultation and co-operation will be key.

The Tiger year can also be an active one as far as the Rooster's social life is concerned. Not only will there be chances to go out and enjoy a wide range of interesting and sometimes work-related events, but friends will often be keen to seek out the Rooster's views on certain situations or be grateful for a listening ear. The Rooster's talents will be in demand, although in some matters he does need to be considered in his response. To be too forthright could cause hurt or undermine rapport. The Rooster means well, but sometimes more tact would be wise. This necessity for mindfulness also applies to Roosters enjoying romance, whether well established or more recent. Relationships can flourish in the Tiger year, but the Rooster does need to be attentive and watch his sometimes too candid nature. February, particularly around the start of the Tiger year, March, August and December could be the busiest months socially, although such is the nature of the year that social opportunities can arise suddenly and, if they appeal, should be taken up.

This also applies to certain interests the Rooster may be considering. Chances to try out new activities could arise quickly and, if the Rooster is to benefit, he does need to act. The Tiger year is not one for delay, and opportunities and invitations need to be taken up when they arise. The Rooster may prefer more advance warning, but Tiger years favour spontaneity.

In work matters the Rooster will again need to keep his wits firmly about him. Developments can happen quickly and while the Rooster may like to follow set procedures, the Tiger year will require greater flexibility. Sometimes this will involve adapting to new work practices, dealing with alterations in his role or contending with some challenging situations. There will certainly be times in 2010 when the Rooster will have misgivings about what is happening or how certain tasks or plans are being rushed. The frenetic pace of the Tiger year does not always suit the Rooster personality. However amid all the activity, there will be excellent chances for the Rooster to learn about other aspects of his work, add to his skills and make reasonable headway, often with his present employer.

There will also be opportunities for Roosters who decide to further their career elsewhere or are seeking work. The Tiger year can have some surprises in store and by widening the scope of what they are prepared to consider, these Roosters could be given the chance to use their skills in different ways or acquire new ones. A key feature of the Tiger year is that it does favour personal growth and for quite a few Roosters it will bring a change in the nature of what they do. April, July, August and October could see some interesting chances, but in view of the fast-moving nature of the year, these do need to be acted upon when they arise.

The progress the Rooster makes at work will often bring an increase in income, although to reap the benefits, he will need to be disciplined in managing his money. Some Roosters do tend to spend quite freely and greater control over their purse-strings would not only be wise but often allow them to make better decisions and purchases. This is a year for good financial management and control.

The Rooster will certainly see a lot happen in the Tiger year and when he looks back he will often be surprised at all the changes he has been involved in and what has opened up for him. While some years favour planning, this is more a time to go with the flow and make the best of situations. This may not be to the Rooster's taste, but with willingness and good liaison with others, he will be able to take considerable satisfaction in his achievements and his domestic and social life and personal interests.

The Metal Rooster

The Metal Rooster has a very determined nature and is prepared to work hard for what he wants. In the past, his fortitude and strong convictions have not only allowed him to achieve a lot but also helped him to stay focused and motivated. And while this may not be the easiest of years for him, it can prepare the way for some significant personal success in the future. In this respect, it will be an important and instructive time.

A major feature of the Tiger year is that it is a time of change and while some of the year will be pressured and sometimes uncomfortable for the Metal Rooster, by making the best of what happens, he could find himself benefiting from new possibilities or a change in direction. As the saying goes, 'Everything happens for a reason,' and the events of 2010 will often have present *and* future value.

In his work the Metal Rooster tends to be very focused, concentrating on his own duties and responsibilities. However, over the year it is important that he keeps himself informed of the developments going on around him, including any impending changes or staff movements. By doing so he will not only be better prepared for the changes that take place but could find himself well placed to benefit. Should training be offered or senior personnel suggest it may be useful for him to gain experience in a different area of his work, he should follow this up. For many Metal Roosters the Tiger year can mark an important shift in what they do, and by making the most of this, they will not only be helping their prospects but also increasing their scope for later. This is not a year to be resistant to change.

Many Metal Roosters will benefit from opportunities provided by their present employer this year but for those who feel ready to move on or are seeking work, again this is a time for exploring new possibilities. By widening the scope of what they are prepared to consider, following up areas of interest, making enquiries and, for some, taking advantage of training or refresher courses, they may secure an important base to build on in the future. What opens up may not always be what the Metal Rooster envisaged, but everything happens for a reason and he can learn a lot from the opportunities of the Tiger year. April to mid-May, July, August and October will see some particularly interesting developments.

Throughout the year the Metal Rooster should work closely with colleagues and use any chances he has to build up connections and make contacts. By doing so he will not only benefit from the support and advice others give but also make some potentially valuable friendships.

In addition many Metal Roosters will find that both new and existing interests are good ways to meet and spend time with others. February, March, August and December will see the most social activity.

In addition to making time for his friendships and personal interests, it is also important that the Metal Rooster gives some consideration to his diet and level of exercise. With the pressures and activity of the year he does need to pay attention to his well-being and should he have any concerns or decide to make modifications, he should seek medical advice.

He also needs to be attentive when dealing with financial matters. Although many Metal Roosters will enjoy an increase in income, this will be an expensive year with increased accommodation costs, additional personal expenses and, for some, deposits to put down. Accordingly, the Metal Rooster will need to be disciplined in his spending. Also, if possible, he should try to save for his future requirements. With care and good management, he will find he is able to go ahead with many of his plans, including a possible holiday, but it would be wise to exercise prudence and resist impulse purchases. Metal Roosters, do take note.

Domestically, this will be an eventful year marked by some important personal developments. For some Metal Roosters these could involve a move while others may become parents or see an addition to their family. For the unattached, the year could bring new love and, for some, their future partner. While busy and sometimes pressured, these can still be special and rewarding times.

Also, although the Metal Rooster has a very determined nature and clear views, it is important that he consults his loved ones, whether his partner or more senior relations, and listens to their views. Their words can help him considerably, but to benefit he does need to be receptive. Similarly, should he have any pressures or concerns, it would be better for him to speak of them and give others the opportunity to help rather than dwell on them alone. This frequently eventful year is not a time for being too independent in approach.

Overall, the Tiger year is one of great possibility for the Metal Rooster and during it he will need to keep alert to all that is going on around him and make the most of current developments. With flexibility, backed by support and self-belief, he can accomplish a great deal that will be of present *and* future value. In addition, busy though he may be, he can look forward to some significant developments in his personal life which can add some excitement to the year.

TIP FOR THE YEAR

Be flexible and open to opportunity. This can be an important year and of great future value. Use your strengths and
this Tiger year well.

The Water Rooster

This will be an important year for the Water Rooster and
to make the most of it he will need to remain focused and
disciplined. In the Tiger year distractions can all too easily
arise and to succumb to too many could affect his progress.
This is very much a year for concentrating on priorities
and making the best use of his time.

Water Roosters in education will often have important
exams to take and course work to complete, and in order to
get the best results will need to put in the effort and work
consistently. With discipline and good use of their study
time, they will find that some of their results could exceed
expectations as well as indicate certain strengths and
subjects it would be worth taking further. As the Chinese
proverb reminds us, 'Diligence leads to riches,' and good
work throughout the year can bear considerable fruit.
However, for those who slack or lack the necessary application, the Tiger year can provide some salutary reminders.
This is not a year to waste.

An encouraging feature of the year will be the opportunities it will bring. The Tiger year does have a buzz to it
and if the Water Rooster has the chance to try new interests, join an activity group or use specialist facilities and
equipment, he should make full use of this. If he is willing
to try things out, he will not only enjoy himself but often

make new friends in the process. Also, if there is a particular skill he would like to learn or improve on, he should look at ways of doing this. If he is active and enterprising, a lot can open up for him.

However, while the Tiger year can be positive and encouraging, the Water Rooster will need to remain disciplined and manage his time well. Sometimes personal interests, casual employment or certain friends can eat into his time and, without care, prevent him from doing all he has to do. Over the year he does need to keep his lifestyle in balance and make sure he gives sufficient time to his priorities. With the active nature of the Tiger year this may sometimes be difficult, but if he is to realize his potential, good time management will be so very important.

In his home life it is important that the Water Rooster is open and forthcoming, and should he have any concerns or pressures, he should be prepared to speak of them. This way others will not only be better able to understand but can also make some helpful suggestions or assist. Similarly, when considering future options, if the Water Rooster mulls over his choices with others, some interesting possibilities can arise and helpful decisions be made. Even though sometimes a gap in ages or different outlooks may cause some awkward moments, with openness, care and involvement, the Water Rooster's home life and relations with others will be generally positive and there will be some good family times to enjoy.

The Water Rooster can also look forward to an interesting social life over the year and will particularly value the support and camaraderie of one or two special friends. Again, by sharing concerns or confidences, he will be especially grateful for the empathy and understanding of others. February to early April, August and December will see the most social activity.

The Tiger year also contains a strong element of adventure and for many Water Roosters there will be the chance to travel and visit new areas. These trips can often be interesting and fun and the Water Rooster would do well to take up any opportunities that come his way.

With so much that he wants to do and so many temptations in the shops, however, he will need to be disciplined when he goes out and keep a close watch on his spending. If he has any concerns or is perhaps attracted by some 'too good to be true' opportunities, he would do well to seek advice. Money-wise, this is a year for care.

For Water Roosters in work or seeking work, the Tiger year can be important, particularly as it will give them the chance to gain experience and develop new skills. Sometimes the work they are currently doing may be routine, but by showing commitment and reliability, they will find other opportunities starting to open up for them. Focus, discipline and a willing approach will pay off. Mid-March to April, July, August and October could see some interesting openings, but in the Tiger year opportunities can arise at any time and need to be taken quickly. Also, even if certain applications do not go the Water Rooster's way, he should not lose heart. Sometimes in the wake of disappointment, more suitable openings can arise. The Tiger year will bring some interesting possibilities and can reward the keen and diligent Water Rooster well.

In general, the Year of the Tiger holds much potential for the Water Rooster, but throughout he will need to make the most of his time and be disciplined in what he has to do. With effort, backed by the support and goodwill of those around him, this can be an eventful and personally rewarding year.

TIP FOR THE YEAR
Rise to the challenges before you. Make full use of the chances you have to learn and develop your skills. With good use of your time and opportunities, you will find the rewards of the Tiger year can be substantial and far-reaching.

The Wood Rooster

The Year of the Tiger has a considerable energy to it and a lot is set to happen in the Wood Rooster's life during it. This is a time of change and exciting possibility.

Quite a few Wood Roosters will decide to retire or reduce their working commitments over the year, and they will welcome the chance to do something new, often including activities and projects they have long considered. Some may still have the chance to use their skills in other ways and perhaps work on a more casual basis, without the pressures seen in more recent years. As many Wood Roosters will find, the Tiger year can bring some interesting opportunities and by following up those that appeal, they can make this a personally rewarding time.

A feature of the year is that it favours new directions and if there is a skill the Wood Rooster has considered learning or a subject he would like to find out more about, this would be an excellent year in which to do so. As the saying reminds us, 'There's no time like the present,' and for the eager Wood Rooster, this can be a constructive time. If he is able to join others, whether on a course or at a local group, he can also benefit from some social opportunities. Wood Roosters who have let their interests lapse or who feel bored or unfulfilled will find that a new activity taken up now can make a considerable difference to their outlook as well as give them greater purpose.

Travel can also figure prominently in the Tiger year and many Wood Roosters are likely to receive invitations to visit others as well as take advantage of opportunities to go on holiday or take a short break. Some could be particularly tempted by last minute offers or decide to go away for a few days on a whim. The Tiger year does favour spontaneity.

The Wood Rooster's social life can also enjoy a fillip this year. In addition to enjoying times with his friends, he will find that new activities can introduce him to others. For those who may be lonely or dispirited, the Tiger year can mark an upturn in their situation and positive action will often reward them well. February, March, August, December and early January will see some particularly fine social occasions.

This can also be an eventful year as far as the Wood Rooster's domestic life is concerned. With the Tiger year favouring change, some Wood Roosters could be tempted to move and so mark a new chapter in their lives. For those who do move, this could take up considerable time as well as be stressful, but once installed in their new home, they will soon come to appreciate what they have achieved.

Those who remain where they are will not escape the activity of the year. Many will embark on ambitious home projects and, once under way, these can often lead on to other undertakings and ideas. Busy though the Tiger year may be, the Wood Rooster will often be pleased with the improvements he has made.

In view of all the plans he has in mind over the year, it is important that there is good co-operation with others in his household. Here discussion and careful consideration of options will be helpful. Also, while the Wood Rooster may be eager for his plans to go ahead, he does need to be flexible in making arrangements and to fit in with those around him as well as avoid having too much happening at once. Sometimes he will need to keep his zealous nature in check. Should any problems or disagreements arise (often as a result of pressure), if he addresses these and talks them through, he will often find that solutions can be reached and in some instances a compromise will ultimately work out better for everyone. Discussion, awareness and flexibility will be key this year. Amid all the activity, there will, however, be some fine family occasions which will mean a lot to the Wood Rooster and here his talent for making arrangements and coming up with ideas will be especially valued. The last few months of the Tiger year could be particularly special.

With all the activity of the year this will be an expensive time, though, and just as one practical project can lead on to another, so one expense can lead on to another. As a result, the Wood Rooster will need to keep a close watch on his outgoings and, if authorizing any work, obtain several quotations and check what is covered. This is a year for control and vigilance, and if the Wood Rooster has concerns or uncertainties over any financial matter, he should seek advice.

This need for care also applies to his well-being and over the year the Wood Rooster should aim to give some consideration to his diet and level of exercise. If he feels either could be improved or has any concerns, he should seek medical advice. He should also be careful if involved in any strenuous undertaking and obtain additional help if necessary.

The Tiger year is one of considerable possibility for the Wood Rooster and by making the most of his opportunities and being flexible in his planning he can gain a lot from it. This is a time for launching plans, following up ideas and taking up new interests and challenges. For the willing and eager, this can be a satisfying and constructive year.

TIP FOR THE YEAR
Seize the initiative and the spirit of this vibrant, active year. Act upon your ideas, launch projects and enjoy and develop your interests. This is a time for action and you can make it a personally rewarding one.

The Fire Rooster

This will be a year of encouraging developments for the Fire Rooster and by being prepared to adapt and make the most of emerging situations, he can fare well. In addition, he will often be encouraged by the support of those around him.

In his work the Tiger year can bring some important changes. In some cases colleagues will leave and open up promotion opportunities or new schemes and initiatives – and the Tiger year can see plenty – could allow him to adapt his role and take on other responsibilities. To benefit, he will need to act quickly and be flexible.

Throughout the year the Fire Rooster will also be helped by the experience he has built up and the support of colleagues. In some cases, a more senior colleague could be particularly instrumental in helping him progress, whether through giving advice, putting in a recommendation or alerting him to a possibility. If he is ever in a quandary over a work matter or decision, if the Fire Rooster seeks the views of those with experience, he can be well advised and supported.

The aspects are also promising for Fire Roosters who are keen to make a change or seeking a position. They, too, should obtain advice, either from employment agencies, professional organizations or contacts they have. That way, they may not only be advised of possibilities and the best approach to take but also be given the introduction or reference they may need. In work matters this is no year for the Fire Rooster to go it alone, but with good backing and his own earnest nature, he may find important doors opening up for him. April, July, August and October could see important developments, but the key to success in the Tiger year is to act quickly, to have faith *and to persist*.

Throughout the year events can happen at a fast pace and while he is usually thorough, the Fire Rooster should be careful and vigilant in his work, financial matters or when dealing with important correspondence. Moments of inattention could create problems. Also, with some of the plans and domestic expenses he has, he will need to keep careful control of his budget and, where possible, make advance provision for forthcoming expenses. With some of his more expensive purchases, he could save himself considerable outlay by waiting for sales and favourable buying opportunities rather than proceeding too hurriedly. Many Fire Roosters will have some additional family expenses during the year and whether they are contributing to an important family event or assisting another person, their generosity will be appreciated.

Over the year the Fire Rooster's organizational talents will also be particularly valued, especially as his home life may be busy. Amid all the activity, it is important that he makes sure that quality time is set aside for everyone to enjoy together. Again his thoughtfulness, ideas and time will make a difference.

The Fire Rooster should also make sure his social life does not suffer due to the pressures of the year and that he keeps in regular contact with his friends as well as takes up any invitations that appeal to him. Not only can his social life help keep his lifestyle in balance, but the support of friends can be helpful and sometimes reassuring. The opening weeks of the Tiger year to early April and then August and December could be the most active times socially.

Similarly, with personal interests, the Fire Rooster should not only aim to set a regular time aside for these but also, if a new one appeals, follow it up. The Tiger year favours activity and experimentation and by using his time well, the Fire Rooster stands to benefit from it.

Overall, this will be a busy and often eventful year for the Fire Rooster. In his work there will be new opportunities to pursue and his domestic life will also see much activity. Many Fire Roosters will be involved in an important family occasion as well as do a lot to assist their loved ones. In the Tiger year the Fire Rooster's careful and thoughtful nature, together with his organizational talents, will be in demand and appreciated by many.

TIP FOR THE YEAR

In this busy year, do keep your lifestyle in balance and preserve time for your interests and loved ones. Also, when considering options or making decisions, listen to the views of those who are close to you. Their input can make a considerable difference to how you fare this year.

The Earth Rooster

The Earth Rooster is alert and aware and these traits will serve him well this year. By making the most of opportunities he can enjoy some notable successes. Many Earth Roosters could also benefit from some strokes of good fortune, either by being in the right place at the right time or having a hunch pay off. The Tiger year can often be both eventful and rewarding.

Although the Earth Rooster, like all Roosters, likes to plan and look ahead, he should not feel tied to existing ideas should situations change or new possibilities open up. To benefit from the current year he will need to be flexible.

This particularly applies to his work. In recent years he will have added to his skills and experience and this year he may well have the chance to take these further. Some Earth Roosters, because of recent successes, will find themselves earmarked for a particular role or objective, while others will be well placed for promotion. In order to progress, the Earth Rooster should not be too narrow in what he is prepared to consider. By making the most of what becomes available, he can take his career to a new stage. Similarly, if he has the chance to go on courses or learn about other aspects of his work, he should make the most of it. Positive action on his part can be to his present and future advantage.

For those Earth Roosters who feel they have achieved all they can with their present employer and are ready for change or seeking work, the Tiger year can again provide some good openings. As it is a year favouring change, these Earth Roosters should give careful thought to what it is they really want to do as well as other ways in which they could use their skills. Registering with employment agencies and talking to contacts could also alert them to possibilities. By giving their situation careful thought and remaining alert, many will find a type of work which will allow them to develop in new ways and have scope for the future. Work-wise, this is a promising year and with willingness, initiative and the desire to move forward, many Earth Roosters can make headway. Late March to early May, July, August and October could see some positive developments.

The Earth Rooster's progress at work can often lead to an increase in his income, although to benefit he will need to remain disciplined in money matters. In addition to his existing plans he could face costs for repairing or replacing equipment and have certain family commitments to contend with. To meet these and do all he wants, he should try to make advance provision for known expenses as well as save for contingencies. This is a year for financial prudence.

With work pressures and all his other activities, the Earth Rooster should also try to take a break over the year.

By going away, even if not too far, he will benefit from the change of scene and will often enjoy visiting areas new to him.

An important feature of Tiger years is that it encourages personal development and not only will many Earth Roosters have the opportunity to develop their work skills but also to take their personal interests further. This could be by taking up a new recreational pursuit, starting a new fitness discipline or advancing a current interest in some way. Although Earth Rooster's free time may be limited, giving some attention to his interests, level of exercise and general lifestyle can be very beneficial. He should also keep in regular contact with his friends. These can be very supportive and sometimes share his activities. Mid-February to early April, August and December could see the most social activity and chances to meet new people.

This will also be a busy year as far as the Earth Rooster's home life is concerned and here his alert and caring nature can be especially helpful. If he feels another person is under strain or preoccupied, he will often be able to help by talking and offering support. Many will have reason to be grateful for his advice and attention over the year. However, while domestic life will often be conducted at a heady pace, if the Earth Rooster makes sure there is time to spend sharing news and interests with his loved ones, he will enjoy some special moments.

Overall, the Tiger year has considerable potential for the Earth Rooster and if he adopts a positive approach and seizes his opportunities, some interesting possibilities can open up for him.

Be active and vigilant, for this is a year of potentially rewarding developments, whether in your work or personal interests. Also, liaise with others. Your colleagues can be helpful and your loved ones often very special to you.

FAMOUS ROOSTERS

Mohamed al Fayed, Fernando Alonso, Beyoncé, Cate Blanchett, Barbara Taylor Bradford, Sir Michael Caine, Enrico Caruso, Christopher Cazenove, Eric Clapton, Joan Collins, Rita Coolidge, Craig David, Daniel Day Lewis, Minnie Driver, the Duke of Edinburgh, Gloria Estefan, Roger Federer, Errol Flynn, Benjamin Franklin, Dawn French, Stephen Fry, Melanie Griffith, Josh Groban, Deborah Harry, Goldie Hawn, Katherine Hepburn, Paris Hilton, Catherine Zeta Jones, Quincy Jones, Diane Keaton, Søren Kierkegaard, D. H. Lawrence, David Livingstone, Jayne Mansfield, Steve Martin, James Mason, W. Somerset Maugham, Paul Merton, Kate Middleton, Bette Midler, Van Morrison, Willie Nelson, Kim Novak, Yoko Ono, Dolly Parton, Matthew Perry, Michelle Pfeiffer, Priscilla Presley, Mary Quant, Joan Rivers, Kelly Rowland, Jenny Seagrove, George Segal, Carly Simon, Britney Spears, Johann Strauss, Verdi, Richard Wagner, Serena Williams, Neil Young, Renée Zellweger.

28 JANUARY 1922 ⌢ 15 FEBRUARY 1923   *Water Dog*

14 FEBRUARY 1934 ⌢ 3 FEBRUARY 1935   *Wood Dog*

2 FEBRUARY 1946 ⌢ 21 JANUARY 1947   *Fire Dog*

18 FEBRUARY 1958 ⌢ 7 FEBRUARY 1959   *Earth Dog*

6 FEBRUARY 1970 ⌢ 26 JANUARY 1971   *Metal Dog*

25 JANUARY 1982 ⌢ 12 FEBRUARY 1983   *Water Dog*

10 FEBRUARY 1994 ⌢ 30 JANUARY 1995   *Wood Dog*

29 JANUARY 2006 ⌢ 17 FEBRUARY 2007   *Fire Dog*

THE
DOG

THE PERSONALITY OF THE DOG

I have my values
and beliefs.
These are my beacon
in an ever-changing world.

The Dog is born under the signs of loyalty and anxiety. He usually holds very firm views and beliefs and is the champion of good causes. He hates any sort of injustice or unfair treatment and will do all in his power to help those less fortunate than himself. He has a strong sense of fair play and will be honourable and open in all his dealings.

The Dog is very direct and straightforward. He is never one to skirt round issues and speaks frankly and to the point. He can be stubborn, but he is prepared to listen to the views of others and will try to be as fair as possible in coming to his decisions. He will readily give advice where it is needed and will be the first to offer assistance when things go wrong.

The Dog instils confidence wherever he goes and there are many who admire him for his integrity and resolute manner. He is a very good judge of character and can often form an accurate impression of someone very shortly after meeting them. He is also very intuitive and can frequently sense how things are going to work out long in advance.

Despite his friendly and amiable manner, the Dog is not a big socializer. He dislikes having to attend large functions or parties and much prefers a quiet meal with friends or a chat by the fire. He is an excellent conversationalist and is often a marvellous raconteur of amusing stories and anecdotes.

The Dog is also quick-witted and his mind is always alert. He can keep calm in a crisis and although he does have a temper, his outbursts tend to be short-lived. He is loyal and trustworthy, but if he ever feels badly let down or rejected by someone, he will rarely forgive or forget.

The Dog usually has very set interests. He prefers to specialize and become an expert in a chosen area rather than dabble in a variety of different activities. He usually does well in jobs where he feels that he is being of service to others and is often suited to careers in the social services, the medical and legal professions and teaching. He does, however, need to feel motivated in his work. He has to have a sense of purpose and if ever this is lacking he can quite often drift through life without ever achieving very much. Once he has the motivation, however, very little can prevent him from securing his objective.

Another characteristic of the Dog is his tendency to worry and to view things rather pessimistically. Quite often his worries are totally unnecessary and are of his own making. Although it may be difficult, worrying is a habit that all Dogs should try to overcome.

The Dog is not materialistic or particularly bothered about accumulating great wealth. As long as he has the money necessary to support his family and to spend on the occasional luxury, he is more than happy. However, when he does have any spare money he tends to be rather a spendthrift and does not always put it to its best use. He is also not a very good speculator and would be advised to get professional advice before entering into any major long-term investment.

The Dog will rarely be short of admirers, but he is not an easy person to live with. His moods are changeable and his standards high, but he will be loyal and protective to his partner and will do all in his power to provide a comfortable home. He can get on extremely well with those born under the signs of the Horse, Pig, Tiger and Monkey, and can also establish a sound and stable relationship with the Rat, Ox, Rabbit, Snake and another Dog, but will find the Dragon a bit too flamboyant for his liking. He will also find it difficult to understand the imaginative Goat and is likely to be highly irritated by the candid Rooster.

The female Dog is renowned for her beauty. She has a warm and caring nature, although until she knows someone well she can be both secretive and very guarded. She is highly intelligent and despite her calm and tranquil appearance she can be extremely ambitious. She enjoys sport and other outdoor activities and has a happy knack of finding bargains in the most unlikely of places. She can also get rather impatient when things do not work out as she would like.

The Dog usually has a very good way with children and can be a doting parent. He will rarely be happier than when he is helping someone or doing something that will benefit others. Providing he can cure himself of his tendency to worry, he will lead a very full and active life, and in that life he will make many friends and do a tremendous amount of good.

THE FIVE DIFFERENT TYPES OF DOG

In addition to the 12 signs of the Chinese zodiac there are five elements and these have a strengthening or moderating influence on the signs. The effects of the five elements on the Dog are described below, together with the years in which the elements were exercising their influence. Therefore those Dogs born in 1970 are Metal Dogs, those born in 1922 and 1982 are Water Dogs, and so on.

Metal Dog: 1970

The Metal Dog is bold, confident and forthright and sets about everything he does in a resolute and determined manner. He has a great belief in his abilities and has no hesitation about speaking his mind or devoting himself to some just cause. He can be rather serious at times and can become anxious and irritable when things are not going according to plan. He tends to have very specific interests and it would certainly help him if he were to broaden his outlook and become more involved in group activities. He is extremely loyal and faithful to his friends.

Water Dog: 1922, 1982

The Water Dog has a very direct and outgoing personality. He is an excellent communicator and has little trouble in persuading others to fall in with his plans. He does, however, have a somewhat carefree nature and is not as disciplined or as thorough as he should be in certain matters. Neither does he keep as much control over his finances as he should, but he can be most generous to his family and friends and will make sure that they want for nothing. He is usually very good with children and has a wide circle of friends.

Wood Dog: 1934, 1994

This Dog is a hard and conscientious worker and will usually make a favourable impression wherever he goes. He is less independent than some of the other types of Dog and prefers to work in a group rather than on his own. He is popular, has a good sense of humour and takes a keen interest in the activities of the various members of his family. He is often attracted to the finer things in life and can obtain much pleasure from collecting items of interest, beauty or antiquity. He prefers to live in the country rather than the town.

Fire Dog: 1946, 2006

This Dog has a lively, outgoing personality and is able to establish friendships with remarkable ease. He is an honest and conscientious worker and likes to take an active part in all that is going on around him. He also likes to explore new ideas and providing he can get the necessary support and advice, he can often succeed where others have failed. He does, however, have a tendency to be stubborn. Providing he can overcome this, he can often achieve considerable fame and fortune.

Earth Dog: 1958

The Earth Dog is very talented and astute. He is methodical and efficient and is capable of going far in his chosen profession. He tends to be rather quiet and reserved, but has a very persuasive manner and usually secures his objectives without too much opposition. He is generous and kind and always ready to lend a helping hand when it is needed. He is also held in very high esteem by his friends and colleagues and is usually most dignified in his appearance.

PROSPECTS FOR THE DOG IN 2010

The Year of the Ox (26 January 2009 to 13 February 2010) is one of the more difficult Chinese years for the Dog. Progress can be slow, problems likely and his good intentions sometimes ignored. Ox years can be challenging, but there is now excellent reason for the Dog to take heart, as his prospects are far more encouraging in the Tiger year.

In the remaining Ox months the Dog will, though, need to remain careful and alert. This is no time for risk or jeopardizing his prospects by some hasty or ill thought-out action. Although it may not always suit his nature, sometimes keeping a low profile and remaining discreet would be the best policy.

However, while the aspects are cautionary, the Dog can still use the remaining Ox months profitably. At work, if he uses his skills well and helps more at busier times, he can do a lot to help his standing and prospects. Good work carried out in the closing Ox months can bring later reward, with October to December seeing some interesting possibilities emerging.

The Dog always sets much store by his relations with others and in the frequently demanding Ox year he will especially value his home life. By being open, sharing his thoughts and talking over his ideas, he will be particularly grateful for the love, support and understanding shown him, as well as some of the occasions that take place. In this mixed year his home life can be very special to him. And although he may be selective in his socializing, September, December and January could see a flurry of invitations and chances to meet up with friends.

The remaining Ox months do require the Dog to tread carefully, but better times are on the way.

The Tiger year starts on 14 February and will see an upturn in the Dog's fortunes. This is a much brighter and more progressive year for him and will give many Dogs the chance to make up for lost ground as well as enjoy success in both their personal and working lives. For those who start the year disillusioned or nursing disappointments, this is a time to draw a line under what has gone before and focus on the present. With a positive and willing approach, the Dog can achieve a lot over the next 12 months.

The Dog's personal life is particularly favourably aspected and the positive relations he enjoys with many people will not only mean a lot to him but also encourage him in what he sets out to do. While some Dogs may be reticent about asking for advice or sharing what is on their mind, in the Tiger year they really do need to be more forthcoming. This way others will be better able to advise as well as reciprocate the Dog's own kindness and support. Similarly, in social situations and when meeting others for the first time, the Dog can sometimes appear reserved and not always show his personality to best advantage. Again in the Tiger year it would be worth him making an effort so that others can better appreciate his true nature. This way he will not only impress – and first impressions *do* count – but also make some valuable contacts and friendships over the year. For unattached Dogs, the prospects for romance are especially encouraging, with some meeting their future partner, often in the most unusual of ways. March to May and August could be active and interesting months and those Dogs who have let their social life lapse will find that by going out more and meeting others with similar interests, perhaps at a local group, they can see a considerable improvement in their situation.

The Dog's home life can also be special this year. As always he will take considerable interest in the activities of his loved ones and give much in the way of support and advice. Those who are parents can find that the encouragement they give to their children can make a real difference. Also, tackling projects jointly will not only help rapport but also allow everyone to appreciate what takes place and enjoy the time spent together.

The Tiger year can also be marked by some notable family achievements. Not only will his loved ones be keen to celebrate the Dog's own successes, but they, too, could make good progress or enjoy some strokes of good fortune. In many a Dog household this can be an active and pleasing year.

However, while the aspects are positive, no year is ever free from problems and when these do arise, the Dog would do well to talk them over rather than allow them to linger in the background. Similarly, if he has any concerns or feels he is shouldering too many domestic responsibilities, he should speak out and ask for help. This is a year favouring joint effort.

The Dog should also make sure he allows time over the year for his personal interests. These can not only bring him pleasure but also be a good way for him to relax and unwind. Any Dogs who are feeling bored or discontented should actively seek out new interests and pursuits to take up. A new activity could both improve their outlook and sometimes help them in other ways. Dogs, do take note and aim to make good use of your free time.

The Tiger year also holds considerable potential as far as the Dog's work prospects are concerned and for those who have languished in recent years and are ready for change, there can be some important developments. However, to benefit the Dog will need to take positive action and not feel fettered by any recent disappointments or under-performance. With determination and initiative, this is a year when many Dogs can find themselves in the right place at the right time and make a real impression. Not only should the Dog keep alert for positions that will allow him to make progress but he should also seek out the views of senior colleagues and useful contacts. In the Tiger year he will have much on his side, with his reputation, support and experience all serving him well. March, May, September and November could see some interesting opportunities, but the Tiger year is fast-moving and whenever the Dog sees something that interests him, he should act. In 2010 many Dogs will be able to make the headway that has eluded them in recent years.

This also applies to those Dogs seeking work. Some may be feeling disillusioned, especially if they had been looking for some time or recently lost a position, but the Tiger year can be one of new opportunities. It is also a time when some Dogs will decide to take their career in a new direction. A lot is possible this year and again, by getting good advice, having faith in their own abilities and acting determinedly, many Dogs will find their efforts well rewarded. After several difficult years, the Tiger year will see their prospects brightening.

Progress at work can also have a positive effect on the Dog's finances, with many seeing an increase in income and some also receiving a bonus or gift. However, to reap the full benefits of any improvement, the Dog does need to control his spending, otherwise anything extra could easily be frittered away. Also, if he takes on any new financial commitment, he does need to check the terms. The aspects may be on his side, but this is no year to be lax in money management or matters which could have long-term implications.

Overall, the Dog can do well in the Tiger year. With self-belief and positive action, he will find chances opening up for him. And on a personal level, the love, support and encouragement he receives can be a useful spur.

The Metal Dog

This year will not only mark the start of a new decade in the Metal Dog's life but often a new chapter as well. This will be a significant year, bringing change *and* the chance to move forward. For those Metal Dogs who have found progress difficult in recent years or lacked enthusiasm or incentive, the Tiger year can see a transformation. In this, his fortieth year, the Metal Dog will feel more motivated than he has for a long time.

As the Tiger year starts he would do well to think about what he would like to see happen over the next 12 months. With some clear ideas and aims he will not only be able to direct his energies in a more purposeful way but also be more impelled to act. As the Chinese proverb reminds us, 'Well begun is half done,' and thinking about the changes he wants to make will help the Metal Dog get the year off to a positive start.

The aspects are particularly encouraging in work matters, and for Metal Dogs who have struggled recently, this is a year offering hope. These Metal Dogs should focus on the present and act determinedly to bring about the improvements they want. With self-belief, willingness and persistence (all qualities the Metal Dog has), they will find that doors will open. For those keen to advance their career, make a change or obtain work, this is a year to put themselves forward, persevere and show their true worth. Admittedly, there will be some setbacks, but the Tiger year can open up exciting possibilities and give these Metal Dogs the chance to establish themselves in a different and often more fulfilling position. March, May, September and November could see some positive developments, although such is the nature of the year that once the Metal Dog starts to make enquiries the wheels of change will quickly begin to turn.

For those Metal Dogs who are established in a career this can again be a significant year, with an excellent chance of promotion. Some Metal Dogs could have waited years for the opportunities that are now opening up and many will be rewarded for their loyalty and experience.

All Metal Dogs, whether settled in a career or considering change, should make the most of any training they may be offered or ways in which they could further certain skills. Sometimes this could be something they could do themselves, perhaps through self-tuition, online courses or an evening class. By seeking to learn, they will be reinforcing the progressive nature of the year.

Another area the Metal Dog might consider improving is his well-being. If he does not get much regular exercise or is reliant on convenience foods, he should look at ways of improving his diet and level of exercise. Swimming, cycling or walking further could be worth considering. Here again the Metal Dog has it within him to make a real difference this year, but it does call on him to act.

With many Metal Dogs taking on greater responsibilities at work, it is also important that they allow themselves time for relaxation and recreational pursuits. These can not only help to keep their lifestyle in balance but also be an enjoyable outlet for their talents. And with this being a year of possibility, if something new appeals to the Metal Dog, he should follow it up.

For Metal Dogs who have neglected their social life of late, are nursing some personal disappointment or would welcome new friends, the Tiger year can be a time of change, and by taking up invitations and following up ideas, they can see a considerable improvement in their situation and restore an element of their life which may have suffered in recent years. March to early June and August could see the most social opportunities and, for the unattached, the Tiger year could also bring some excellent romantic possibilities.

The Metal Dog will also see considerable activity in his home life. This may involve embarking on practical projects or even moving to somewhere more convenient. This can be an eventful year and once the Metal Dog decides on certain courses of action, all sorts of possibilities can start to arise. In view of this, it is especially important that he liaises closely with his loved ones. With discussion and co-operation, a great deal can be accomplished.

The Metal Dog will also value the quality time he spends with his loved ones, whether sharing interests, following others' progress or enjoying special occasions, breaks and holidays. In addition his loved ones could be keen to mark his fortieth birthday in style.

Although a lot can go in the Metal Dog's favour in 2010, one thing he does need to be wary of is rush. This particularly applies to financial matters. If conducting large transactions, he does need to take the time to check the details and any obligations he may be taking on. Haste can lead to oversights and additional expense. Also, by managing his financial situation carefully and, if he is able, setting sums aside for particular plans or taking advantage of tax incentives to save or add to his pension, he can not only do more now but also improve his prospects in the future.

The Year of the Tiger holds much promise for the Metal Dog and with clear aims and the determination to make things happen, he can get this new decade in his life off to an encouraging start.

This can be a special year for you. In 2010 you are very much in the driving seat and it rests with you to make the most of yourself and your considerable talents.

The Water Dog

This is a year of considerable opportunity for the Water Dog and will allow him to make progress as well as take some important decisions about his future. Much can be achieved this year and the Water Dog can reap some fine rewards.

Although many Water Dogs will have made headway in recent years, there will still be quite a few who do not yet feel fulfilled. For these Water Dogs, as well as those who may have experienced recent reversals, the Tiger year can bring some significant opportunities. For some, it could mark a change in direction, and for the determined, it can have far-reaching value.

This particularly applies to work prospects. With the experience they have behind them and the pressures and sometimes uncertainty they have recently had to deal with, many Water Dogs will not only feel well qualified to move on but also consider that the time is now right. Often they will be in an excellent position to put in for promotion, with their reputation and in-house knowledge making them strong candidates. Many will also find senior colleagues supportive and they should take note of any advice given. Over the year many will have the chance to make important headway.

For Water Dogs who consider they have accomplished all they can in their present area of work or feel staid or bored, this is again a year for decisive action. These Water Dogs, as well as those seeking work, should give serious thought to what they now want to do. By contacting professional organizations and agencies for advice, many could be alerted to types of work that they have not considered before but are ideal for them. In some cases this could involve additional training and a steep learning curve, but by being open to possibilities, these Water Dogs could set their career off on a potentially more rewarding path. The Tiger year is one of change and progress, with opportunities arising quickly and sometimes taking the Water Dog by surprise. March, May, late August to the end of September and November could see important developments.

Another key feature of the year is that it favours personal development and not only will the Water Dog have the opportunity to further his work skills but he could also find his personal interests rewarding. A new recreational activity could be especially enjoyable and sometimes very different. Again, by being active and using his time to advantage, the Water Dog can reinforce the constructive nature of the year.

Another positive aspect will be the travel opportunities that arise. Although some could be work related, if the Water Dog receives invitations to stay with relatives or friends or sees a special offer that appeals to him, he should follow it up. As well as enjoying visiting areas new to him, he could benefit from the chance to spend time away from everyday pressures.

The Water Dog will also appreciate his social life during the year and although other commitments may mean he is selective in his socializing, by keeping in regular contact with his friends and going to events that appeal to him, he will often enjoy himself. His interests and changes at work can also lead to him making some new friendships, and for the unattached, Cupid's arrow could suddenly strike. The Tiger year can be a very special one for the Water Dog, with February to May and August seeing the most social activity.

For those Water Dogs with a partner, there could be celebrations in store. These could include an addition to the family, a move to better accommodation or some personal success. Domestically, this can be an eventful year. During it, if the Water Dog ever feels under strain or has important decisions to take, he should talk to others as well as take up offers of help from senior relations or close friends. The support he receives can be an important factor in his success, as well as give him the backing and confidence he needs, especially if taking on new responsibilities or embarking on change.

Progress at work will allow many Water Dogs to increase their earnings this year and an enterprising idea or spare-time interest could also bring in something extra. However, while the Water Dog's earning abilities will be on good form, with the commitments and expensive plans he has, he will need to keep careful control of his budget. If he has any financial uncertainties, he should seek professional advice. This is a year for good financial management. Water Dogs, take note.

The Water Dog will have much in his favour this year and by remaining active and looking at ways in which he can progress, he can achieve a lot. He will also be encouraged by the support of those around him and many Water

Dogs will enjoy exciting developments in their personal life. A year of considerable promise.

TIP FOR THE YEAR
Take action and be the instigator of improvement. Positive action can open up exciting possibilities. Believe in yourself and aim to move forward.

The Wood Dog

There is a Chinese proverb that will be especially apt for the Wood Dog this year. It is, 'High aspirations are as essential for a man as persistence is essential for learning.' By giving himself worthy aspirations and persisting in his learning, the Wood Dog can make this a significant and rewarding year. The aspects are on his side, and with a 'can do' attitude, great headway can be made.

In his education the Wood Dog will need to be disciplined and thorough. By putting in the effort and working consistently he can not only make good progress but also take greater satisfaction in what he is doing. During the year certain strengths could emerge and these could indicate future paths and possibilities. This can be a significant year in the Wood Dog's personal development.

Also, as the proverb notes, 'persistence is essential for learning', and while the Wood Dog will have his favourite subject areas, he should not give up on those he finds more difficult or lose heart if certain pieces of work do not get the marks he had hoped for. Instead, it is worth rising to the challenge and showing what he is capable of. As a Dog he has a tenacious side to his nature and during the year he will have excellent opportunity to prove himself as well as to correct certain weaknesses. In the Tiger year effort and persistence really will deliver.

The Chinese proverb also suggests that 'high aspirations are essential' and it is important that the young Wood Dog believes in himself and has aspirations. If he sets himself certain objectives, whether passing exams or developing particular interests, he will find that such goals help him to keep focused.

His personal interests can bring him much pleasure this year and not only should he make the most of chances to add to his knowledge but also explore other ideas and opportunities. With a willingness to learn, he can find a lot opening up for him.

The Wood Dog will also appreciate some of the good friendships he has. Not only can much fun be had by sharing interests, but sometimes just the chance to talk, exchange secrets, seek opinions or receive support will mean a lot. There will also be opportunities for the Wood Dog to get to know new people and while he does take his time in selecting and making friends, he may form a very good bond with some of those he meets this year. On a personal and social level he will find himself in increasing demand.

In view of all the Wood Dog is involved with, he should also be forthcoming with those at home. This includes talking about his studies, any difficulties he may have and any interests he may be keen to develop. If he is open and communicative, those around him will be better able to guide and assist. A willingness to participate in home life and help with certain tasks will also help rapport. The greater the Wood Dog's involvement, the more value he can get from the year.

For Wood Dogs born in 1934, the Tiger year will also have its highlights. For many these will be family related, with the Wood Dog taking a keen interest in the progress of loved ones as well as offering what can be some quite pertinent advice. In spite of a considerable gap in years, some younger relations could be especially grateful for assistance he is able to give.

He will also derive much satisfaction from certain personal interests, especially those that allow him to explore ideas and use his creative talents. Many Wood Dogs will enjoy a holiday or short break they are able to take and by choosing their destination carefully will not only delight in what they get to see but also in the camaraderie of other travellers and people they meet while away.

The Tiger year can be a satisfying one for the more senior Wood Dog, although should he have any concerns, particularly with detailed correspondence or financial matters, he should seek advice. Additional care and scrutiny can help prevent mistakes.

Whether born in 1934 or 1994, this can be an interesting year for the Wood Dog and exploring their ideas and talents will bring particular pleasure. For the younger Wood Dog, the commitment they give to their education can help open up important possibilities for the future. For these Wood Dogs, it is a year to keep those aspirations in mind and to show what they are capable of. For all Wood Dogs, the Tiger year can be a rewarding and personally very satisfying one.

Do draw on the support of others. You may be keen to do a lot on your own, but by being forthcoming, you will find so much more becoming possible. With openness and involvement, you can make this an exciting and pleasing year.

The Fire Dog

Quite a few Fire Dogs will have felt buffeted by events in recent years, with pressures to cope with and certain plans not going as well as they may have hoped. However, now is a time when they can take heart, as this is a much more favourable year.

As the Tiger year starts, if not slightly before, many Fire Dogs will sense a change in their situation. Rather than feeling frustrated, they will set about their activities with greater purpose and energy. And their attitude will make a difference.

The Fire Dog will also be helped considerably by the support and advice of family, friends and colleagues. Over the year he will certainly have a lot in his favour, and with this comes a time for action and initiative.

For those Fire Dogs in work, the Tiger year can bring some significant choices. For some there will be the opportunity to retire and to devote more time to plans they have long wanted to carry out. For others, changes in their workplace can give them a greater chance to concentrate on their area of expertise and make this a more fulfilling time. Some may also have the opportunity to rearrange their working schedule and perhaps reduce their hours. What opens up for the Fire Dog can suit him well, and while adjustments will need to be made, he will no longer feel so frustrated or lacking in incentive.

The Tiger year can also produce some surprises and new possibilities could emerge, particularly for Fire Dogs who retire. Quite a few Fire Dogs will find fresh ways to use their experience and skills over the year. Events can move in curious ways, with some decisions the Fire Dog takes setting some interesting wheels in motion. As far as work developments are concerned, March, May, September and November could be key months.

The Fire Dog could also enjoy some positive financial news over the year, possibly involving a bonus, gift or the fruition of a policy. In addition some may be able to supplement their income through an idea or interest they have. However, to make the most of his situation the Fire Dog will need to stay disciplined and set money aside for particular plans and, if possible, the longer term.

With the promising aspects, however, if he sees a competition which appeals to him, he would do well to enter it. For quite a few Fire Dogs the Tiger year will contain an element of good fortune.

The Fire Dog's personal interests can also bring him a lot of pleasure. Not only will he enjoy exploring his ideas and skills, but they can often bring him into contact with others. For those Fire Dogs who are keen to extend their knowledge and social life, joining a local interest group would be well worth considering. By making the most of his opportunities, the Fire Dog can add another positive strand to his year.

The Tiger year will also bring some good travel opportunities and not only should the Fire Dog try to take a holiday over the year but if he receives an invitation to visit others or go away at short notice, he should take it up. The Tiger year favours spontaneity.

In so much of what the Fire Dog does this year, he will be grateful for the encouragement he receives from those around him. This is a year for joint effort, particularly in his domestic life. By sharing ideas and discussing possibilities, he will find that so much more will happen. In addition, when he is considering possible changes, especially connected with his work or interests, his loved ones could bring to his notice implications he may not have fully considered. This year again, Fire Dog's relations with others can be both special and meaningful.

This also applies to the good friendships the Fire Dog is likely to have. Those who know him well will often be keen to support and advise, and this will be another helpful factor during the year. His interests and any travels can also bring opportunities for him to meet others and for those Fire Dogs who would welcome new friends or have had some recent personal difficulty to contend with, the Tiger year can see a considerable brightening in their situation. Late February to May and August could see the most social activity.

The Year of the Tiger is one of hope and opportunity, but to benefit the Fire Dog does need to act. With a willing and positive approach, however, much can be achieved. In addition the Fire Dog can be considerably helped by the love, support and goodwill of others. This is a year for positive action.

TIP FOR THE YEAR
Do not let your hopes come to nothing. By seizing your opportunities you could enjoy some particularly pleasing results. Also, do draw on the willingness of others to help and support you. Their input can assist you in many ways, including making certain decisions and plans easier.

The Earth Dog

One feature of Tiger years is that events happen quickly and throughout 2010 the Earth Dog will need to keep alert and be prepared to move smartly. When opportunities arise, they do need to be taken quickly, before the moment is lost or another person takes advantage. This is no year for delay or wavering, and for many Earth Dogs it holds considerable possibility.

In the Earth Dog's work the aspects are promising and with the experience and depth of knowledge he has, he may well find himself taking on greater responsibilities during the year. For some this could be through promotion or transfer to other duties. By showing willing, many Earth Dogs can make important and deserving headway. Also, should the Earth Dog hear of an opening that appeals to him, he should be quick to signal an interest. As the saying goes, 'The early bird catches the worm,' and in work matters, by being swift the Earth Dog can substantially improve his chances.

Many Earth Dogs will benefit from opportunities in their current place of work, but for those who feel they have achieved all they can where they are, the Tiger year can present some excellent possibilities. Again these Earth

Dogs will need to be quick in following up anything of potential interest. Time will be of the essence and events can move swiftly. Applications may be processed faster than the Earth Dog may have anticipated and offers may be put to him unexpectedly. Tiger years can bring some surprising and often fortuitous developments.

Another factor in the Earth Dog's favour will be the contacts and colleagues who think so highly of him. Some could even put in recommendations for him without his knowledge or provide references which can help his progress.

Earth Dogs seeking work should also act quickly and, with this being a year favouring innovation, seek advice on other ways in which they could use their skills. Many will be successful in securing a new position. For all Earth Dogs, late February, March, September and November could see some important work developments, but such is the nature of the year that opportunities can occur at almost any time.

Another important feature of the year will be the opportunity many Earth Dogs will have to develop certain skills. Whether established in a particular career or moving to something new, by taking advantage of any training that may be offered they can enhance their prospects for the future.

With this being a year favouring personal development, the Earth Dog can also gain a lot by giving time to his interests, including looking at ways in which he could further his knowledge, develop skills or take up new activities. Over the year his interests can provide him with considerable satisfaction as well as help to keep his lifestyle in balance.

Socially, the Tiger year can be far livelier than more recent ones and for Earth Dogs who are alone, their interests can lead to new friendships and, for some, romance. These are encouraging times, with late February to May and August seeing the most social activity.

While a lot can go well for the Earth Dog over the year, if he has any uncertainties over what is happening around him, it is important that he checks the details. With so much activity this year, arrangements can get muddled and facts confused, so the Earth Dog should make sure everything is clear and agreed beforehand.

This need for clarity also applies to finance. Although many Earth Dogs will enjoy a rise in income, the Earth Dog should be his vigilant and thorough self when dealing with financially related correspondence. In this busy year it can be tempting to skip details or delay a response, but this could leave the Earth Dog at a disadvantage.

The Tiger year will also see a lot of activity in the Earth Dog's domestic life, with those close to him often involved in change and important decisions. Here the Earth Dog will be able to give much useful support and others will set great store by his judgement. With certain plans of his own, whether involving family activities or more practical projects, he will need to be flexible. Although he may be a keen planner, the Tiger year favours spontaneity. Home life this year may be conducted at a fast pace, but there will be much that the Earth Dog will appreciate, with shared interests and activities, including travel, bringing him particular pleasure.

Overall, the Year of the Tiger can be a successful and rewarding one for the Earth Dog. If he seizes his opportunities, important progress can be made, and his interests and relations with others will continue to mean a great deal.

This is a fast-moving year requiring fast responses. Act quickly and look to move forward. With your experience and talents you have much in your favour and your initiative can lead to some well-deserved success.

FAMOUS DOGS

King Albert II of Belgium, Brigitte Bardot, Gary Barlow, Candice Bergen, Andrea Bocelli, David Bowie, George W. Bush, Kate Bush, Laura Bush, Naomi Campbell, Fabio Capello, Mariah Carey, King Carl Gustaf XVI of Sweden, José Carreras, Paul Cézanne, Cher, Sir Winston Churchill, Bill Clinton, Leonard Cohen, Jamie Lee Curtis, Matt Damon, Charles Dance, Claude Debussy, Dame Judi Dench, Joseph Fiennes, Robert Frost, Ava Gardner, Judy Garland, George Gershwin, Anne Hathaway, Lenny Henry, O. Henry, Victor Hugo, Barry Humphries, Holly Hunter, Michael Jackson, Al Jolson, Felicity Kendal, Jennifer Lopez, Sophia Loren, Joanna Lumley, Shirley MacLaine, Andie McDowell, Madonna, Norman Mailer, Barry Manilow, Freddie Mercury, Liza Minelli, Simon Pegg, Billie Piper, Sydney Pollack, Elvis Presley, Tim Robbins, Paul Robeson, Andy Roddick, Susan Sarandon, Jennifer Saunders, Claudia Schiffer, Dr Albert Schweitzer, Sylvester Stallone, Robert Louis Stevenson, Sharon Stone, David Suchet, Donald Sutherland, Chris Tarrant, Mother Teresa, Uma Thurman, Donald Trump, Voltaire, Prince William, Shelley Winters.

30 JANUARY 1911 ⌣ 17 FEBRUARY 1912   *Metal Pig*

16 FEBRUARY 1923 ⌣ 4 FEBRUARY 1924   *Water Pig*

4 FEBRUARY 1935 ⌣ 23 JANUARY 1936   *Wood Pig*

22 JANUARY 1947 ⌣ 9 FEBRUARY 1948   *Fire Pig*

8 FEBRUARY 1959 ⌣ 27 JANUARY 1960   *Earth Pig*

27 JANUARY 1971 ⌣ 14 FEBRUARY 1972   *Metal Pig*

13 FEBRUARY 1983 ⌣ 1 FEBRUARY 1984   *Water Pig*

31 JANUARY 1995 ⌣ 18 FEBRUARY 1996   *Wood Pig*

18 FEBRUARY 2007 ⌣ 6 FEBRUARY 2008   *Fire Pig*

THE
PIG

THE PERSONALITY OF THE PIG

It's the doing,
the giving,
the playing the part,
that makes life what it is.
And what it can be.

The Pig is born under the sign of honesty. He has a kind and understanding nature and is well known for his abilities as a peacemaker. He hates any sort of discord or unpleasantness and will do everything in his power to sort out differences of opinion or bring opposing factions together.

He is also an excellent conversationalist and speaks truthfully and to the point. He dislikes any form of falsehood or hypocrisy and is a firm believer in justice and the maintenance of law and order. In spite of these beliefs, however, he is reasonably tolerant and often prepared to forgive others for their wrongdoings. He rarely harbours grudges and is never vindictive.

The Pig is usually very popular. He enjoys other people's company and likes to be involved in joint or group activities. He will be a loyal member of any club or society and can be relied upon to lend a helping hand at functions. He is also an excellent fundraiser for charities and is often a great supporter of humanitarian causes.

The Pig is a hard and conscientious worker and is particularly respected for his reliability and integrity. In his early years he will try his hand at several different jobs, but he is usually happiest where he feels that he is being of service to others. He will unselfishly give up his time for the common good and is highly valued by his colleagues and employers.

The Pig has a good sense of humour and invariably has a smile, joke or some whimsical remark at the ready. He loves to entertain and to please others, and there are many Pigs who have been attracted to careers in show business or who enjoy following the careers of famous stars and personalities.

There are, unfortunately, some who take advantage of the Pig's good nature and impose upon his generosity. The Pig has great difficulty in saying 'no', and although he may dislike being firm, it would be in his own interests to say occasionally, 'Enough is enough.' He can also be rather naïve and gullible; however, if at any stage in his life he feels that he has been badly let down, he will try to become self-reliant. There are many Pigs who have become entre- preneurs or forged a successful career on their own after some early disappointment in life. Although the Pig tends to spend his money quite freely, he is usually very astute in financial matters and there are many Pigs who have become wealthy.

Another characteristic of the Pig is his ability to recover from setbacks reasonably quickly. His faith and his strength of character keep him going. If he thinks that there is a job he can do or there is something that he wants to achieve, he will pursue it with dogged determination. He can also be stubborn and no matter how many may plead with him, once he has made his mind up he will rarely change his views.

Although the Pig may work hard, he also knows how to enjoy himself. He is a great pleasure-seeker and will quite happily spend his hard-earned money on a lavish holiday or an expensive meal – for the Pig is a connoisseur of good food and wine – or a variety of recreational activities. He also enjoys small social gatherings and if he is in company he likes he can very easily become the life and soul of the party. He does, however, tend to become rather withdrawn at larger functions or when among strangers.

The Pig is a creature of comfort and his home will usually be fitted with all the latest in luxury appliances. Where possible, he will prefer to live in the country rather than the town and will opt to have a big garden, for the Pig is usually a keen and successful gardener.

The Pig is very popular with others and will often have numerous romances before he settles down. Once settled, however, he will be loyal to his partner and he will find that he is especially well suited to those born under the signs of the Goat, Rabbit, Dog and Tiger and also to another Pig. Due to his affable and easy-going nature he can also establish a satisfactory relationship with all the remaining signs of the Chinese zodiac, with the exception of the Snake. The Snake tends to be wily, secretive and very guarded, and this can be intensely irritating to the honest and open-hearted Pig.

The female Pig will devote all her energies to the needs of her children and her partner. She will try to ensure that they want for nothing and their pleasure is very much her pleasure. She can be a caring and conscientious parent and has very good taste in clothes. Her home will either be very clean and orderly or hopelessly untidy. Strangely, there seems to be no in between with Pigs – they either love housework or detest it! The female Pig does, however, have considerable talents as an organizer and this, combined with her friendly and open manner, enables her to secure many of her objectives.

The Pig is usually lucky in life and will rarely want for anything. Provided he does not let others take advantage of his good nature and is not afraid of asserting himself, he will go through life making friends, helping others and winning the admiration of many.

THE FIVE DIFFERENT TYPES OF PIG

In addition to the 12 signs of the Chinese zodiac there are five elements and these have a strengthening or moderating influence on the signs. The effects of the five elements on the Pig are described below, together with the years in which the elements were exercising their influence. Therefore those Pigs born in 1911 and 1971 are Metal Pigs, those born in 1923 and 1983 are Water Pigs, and so on.

Metal Pig: 1911, 1971
The Metal Pig is more ambitious and determined than some of the other types of Pig. He is strong, energetic and likes to be involved in a wide variety of different activities. He is very open and forthright in his views, although he can be a little too trusting at times and has a tendency to accept things at face value. He has a good sense of humour and loves to attend parties and other social gatherings. He has a warm, outgoing nature and usually has a large circle of friends.

Water Pig: 1923, 1983

The Water Pig has a heart of gold. He is generous and loyal and tries to remain on good terms with everyone. He will do his utmost to help others, but sadly there are some who will take advantage of his kind nature and he should, in his own interests, be a little more discriminating and be prepared to stand firm against anything that he does not like. Although he prefers the quieter things in life, he has a wide range of interests. He particularly enjoys outdoor pursuits and attending parties and social occasions. He is a hard and conscientious worker and invariably does well in his chosen profession. He is also gifted in the art of communication.

Wood Pig: 1935, 1995

This Pig has a friendly, persuasive manner and is easily able to gain the confidence of others. He likes to be involved in all that is going on around him but can some-times take on more responsibility than he can properly handle. He is loyal to his family and friends and derives much pleasure from helping those less fortunate than himself. He is usually an optimist and leads a very full, enjoyable and satisfying life. He also has a good sense of humour.

Fire Pig: 1947, 2007

The Fire Pig is both energetic and adventurous and sets about everything he does in a confident and resolute manner. He is very forthright in his views and does not mind taking risks in order to achieve his objectives. He can, however, get carried away by the excitement of the moment and ought to exercise more caution in some of the enterprises in which he gets involved. He is usually lucky in money matters and is well known for his generosity. He is also very caring towards the members of his family.

Earth Pig: 1959

This Pig has a kindly nature. He is sensible and realistic and will go to great lengths in order to please his employers and to secure his aims and ambitions. He is an excellent organizer and is particularly astute in business and financial matters. He has a good sense of humour and a wide circle of friends. He also likes to lead an active social life, although he does sometimes have a tendency to eat and drink more than is good for him.

PROSPECTS FOR THE PIG IN 2010

The Ox year (26 January 2009 to 13 February 2010) requires effort and the hardworking Pig will have achieved a lot during it. In the remaining months he can look forward to making some useful gains as well as enjoying pleasing developments in his personal life.

At work many Pigs will see an increase in activity as the Ox year draws to a close, with some additional pressures and sometimes complex matters to deal with. However, while this can often be a demanding time, by focusing on what needs to be done and using their judgement (Pigs do have good business sense), many can look forward to some satisfying results and receiving recognition and sometimes a financial bonus for what they do. For those wanting to advance their career or seeking work, October and November could contain some interesting possibilities.

The closing months of the year could also see increased spending and in addition to seasonal purchases, many Pigs will be involved in a sizable transaction. Where possible, the Pig should try to budget ahead for this as well as keep alert for favourable buying (or travel) opportunities. His judgement and canny sense can serve him well.

He will also find himself in demand, and in addition to the social events he attends, his home life will see much activity. Here some advance planning would be helpful, particularly as this can prevent a lot of activity being concentrated in just a short space of time. Many Pigs can also look forward to seeing relations or friends they have not seen for some time and the closing Ox weeks can bring some often special times.

Pigs like activity and the Tiger year, which begins in 14 February, will certainly contain a lot of it. However, the fast pace of the year and its many demands can make this a challenging time. Progress will not be easy and at times the Pig may feel that he is putting in a lot of effort for little return. The Tiger year may be frustrating, but on the positive side, it can be instructive and usher in some important changes.

One area in which the Pig will need to be especially careful is finance. Tiger years can bring additional expenses and whether these are connected with accommodation, personal plans or assisting loved ones, there will be many demands on the Pig's resources. As a result he does need to keep a close watch on his spending and think carefully if tempted by impulse purchases. This is a year for tight control of the purse-strings.

The Pig also needs to be vigilant when dealing with correspondence which could have financial implications. To delay a response or give it scant attention could cause problems later and sometimes incur additional cost. Similarly, he should make sure insurance policies are maintained and that important documents are kept safely. Should he have concerns over any financial or bureaucratic matter, he would do well to seek clarification. Without care, problems can all too easily arise. Pigs, do take note.

Although the Pig has a superb personal manner and enjoys good relations with many people, in the Tiger year he needs to keep his wits about him. In particular he should be wary about speaking too freely or passing on information in confidence. As the saying goes, 'Walls have ears,' and an indiscretion could cause embarrassment. Also, there is the risk of another person letting him down. While the Pig has a trusting nature, over the year he should be more guarded and circumspect. Should he find himself in a situation about which he has reservations, he should follow his judgement and, if necessary, stand firm. Lapses can lead to difficulties later.

In the Pig's domestic life he should also make sure that despite his many commitments he gives time to his loved ones. Fortunately Pigs are usually careful in this respect, but if they become preoccupied with other matters, tetchy due to pressure or not as aware of the opinions of others as they should be, tensions can arise. In the Tiger year the Pig will need to be aware and attentive. In addition home life may not be helped by equipment breaking, faults occurring or disruption being caused by some projects. The Tiger year can bring some trying moments, but if everyone in the Pig's household supports each other and does their best, difficulties can be overcome. In some cases problems can even turn out to be blessings in disguise as equipment is replaced with something better or tasks that have been put off are finally tackled.

However, while the Tiger year can bring its irritations, it will also contain many times that the Pig will enjoy, including possible spontaneous trips or breaks. Despite the year's pressures the Pig's capacity for fun will not be diminished and will be something everyone will appreciate. In addition, successes achieved either by the Pig himself or those around him will often feel more special this year and be marked in fine style.

With the various pressures of the year it is also important that the Pig preserves time for recreational pursuits which allow him to rest and unwind. Fortunately most Pigs do keep their lifestyle in balance, but in this particularly busy year this is important.

In his work the Pig is conscientious, sets high standards and has high expectations. However, progress will not be easy this year. Some Pigs could have to cope with increased bureaucracy, complications caused by new working methods or the unhelpful attitude of some colleagues. Parts of the Tiger year can be frustrating, but by doing what he can and being flexible in approach, the Pig can benefit from the chance to gain experience. Amid the pressures and exasperations, headway can be made and many Pigs will succeed in moving their career forward in some way. April, July, mid-October to early December and January could see some interesting developments.

Pigs who are intent on change or seeking work will also need to be flexible and widen the scope of what they are prepared to consider. This is no year for being too narrow in their approach. By keeping alert to possibility, many will gain the chance to use their skills in other ways. The Tiger year may be challenging, but the experience the Pig gains can be instrumental in some of the success he will enjoy in following years. For all its difficulties, the Tiger year can be instructive *and* important in the longer term.

During the year the Pig will need to be attentive and aware in both his relations with those around him and the situations in which he finds himself. With care and his usually good judgment, he can do a lot to negate the more difficult aspects of the year and emerge from it wiser, more experienced and with personal gains he can take further, especially in the more promising Year of the Rabbit that follows.

The Metal Pig

The Metal Pig will have experienced a lot in recent years, including some fine personal successes but also a few disappointments. The Tiger year is one to take stock, consolidate his position and look ahead. It may not be an easy time, but it can prepare the Metal Pig for the more substantial advances he is to enjoy towards the end of the Tiger year and more notably in 2011.

One characteristic of Tiger years is the speed with which things happen. Changes can suddenly be thrust on the Metal Pig and over the year he will need to be flexible in his approach. Parts of the year can be exasperating, but will help demonstrate some of the Metal Pig's finer strengths, including his resourcefulness.

This particularly applies to his work. Although the Metal Pig may like to immerse himself in his own duties, he should keep alert to what is happening around him. The more aware and informed he is, the better he will be able to adjust to changing situations as well as take advantage of proposals put forward. Also, at busy times or as colleagues move on, he could be asked to alter his role or take on increased duties, and by showing willing he can not only benefit from the additional experience but also improve his prospects. Some of the year can be hectic, but it can prepare the way for future progress.

Most Metal Pigs will remain with their present employer over the year, but for those who are keen to move elsewhere or are seeking work, the Tiger year calls for patience and flexibility. With often limited openings in the type of work these Metal Pigs are trying to obtain, they should take careful note of the advice agencies or contacts give, as well as consider other ways in which they could use their skills. While their quest will not be easy, an opportunity could arise unexpectedly and have potential for the future. April, July, mid-October to early December and January could see some interesting developments.

With financial matters, the Metal Pig will need to be careful. With his existing commitments and plans, his outgoings this year could be considerable, and if he does not do so already, he could find it helpful to keep a set of accounts. This way he will not only have better control over his budget but also be able to make allowance for forthcoming plans. Also, paperwork needs to be dealt with thoroughly and promptly. Delay or inattention could result in additional expense. Metal Pigs, do take note.

This need for care also applies to the Metal Pig's domestic life. Although he is usually very mindful, sometimes, due to pressure or the long hours he keeps, he could find certain matters trying his patience or disagreements arising over some plans. At such times he does need to show greater understanding and talk things through. This will not only lead to better domestic arrangements but also to better decisions.

Also, if the Metal Pig should feel overwhelmed by all he has to do, again he should speak to his loved ones. That way they may be able to do more and so ease certain pressures. Busy though the year may be, the Metal Pig should also aim to make sure he and his loved ones appreciate the fruits of what they work so hard for. An occasional family treat can do everyone a lot of good.

The Metal Pig should also make sure his own interests do not get sidelined due to the activity of the year. Not only can these sometimes give him the chance to get out of doors but the satisfaction of being able to use his skills in other ways or just enjoy some relaxing activities can be important.

He will also appreciate the social events he attends over the year and if he sees something that appeals to him, he should do his best to go. It is important that he keeps his lifestyle in balance. However, when in company he does need to remain tactful and wary of rumour. Without a certain guardedness, there is a risk that he could be misled or have his words misconstrued. Metal Pigs, do take note. March, June, August and December will see the greatest social activity.

This may not be the easiest of years for the Metal Pig and throughout he will need to be alert and cautious. However, by doing his best and making the most of situations, he can gain valuable experience and help prepare the way for later successes, especially those that await next year. The long-term benefits of the Tiger year can be considerable.

TIP FOR THE YEAR
Spend time with your loved ones and speak of any concerns. With good communication, those close to you will be better able to understand and assist. Also, make sure time is set aside for recreation. It is important in this busy year to keep your lifestyle in balance.

The Water Pig

The Water Pig has a great many strengths and virtues. He is keen, willing and thoughtful. He is also well regarded by many and his ability to relate well to others is a real asset which will help him throughout his life. He is also a realist and recognizes that while some times are favourable for making progress, at others it would be wiser to hold back and watch developments unfold. And in the Tiger year this is what many Water Pigs will opt to do.

In their work, this is a year for focusing on their duties and dealing with the sometimes complex situations and pressures that will arise. Work-wise, this can be a demanding year, but it will give the Water Pig an excellent chance to build on his experience and acquire some valuable skills. Also, by working closely with colleagues and showing himself a good team-member, he will strengthen his reputation and make some important new contacts.

Many Water Pigs will decide to remain where they are this year and in the process become more established in their line of work. For Water Pigs who do decide to make a change, as well as those seeking work, the Tiger year will not be an easy or straightforward one. Opportunities could be limited, and in the face of fierce competition it could be difficult for these Water Pigs to make the breakthrough they want. They could find it helpful to research the companies they are applying to and so make their application more relevant and informed. Also, by seeking advice and widening the type of work they are prepared to consider, they could get the chance to move to a completely different field. What is accomplished now can have important future implications. April, late June, July, mid-October to early December and January could see interesting possibilities, but such is the nature of the year that developments could take the Water Pig by surprise.

With financial matters, he will need to be disciplined in his spending and set money aside for specific requirements. This is a year for good management. Also, if he takes on any new commitment, he does need to check the terms and implications and seek advice if anything is unclear. This is no year for risk or making assumptions.

The Water Pig is blessed with a trusting and good-hearted nature, and while this is an aspect of his character that endears him to many, unfortunately there are some who will be prepared to take advantage of it. In the Tiger year the Water Pig would do well to be more circumspect than usual in his relations with others. There is a risk that another person could let him down or confidences could be betrayed. Water Pigs, do take note and be guarded and discreet.

However, while the aspects may be cautionary, there will still be a lot for the Water Pig to enjoy. Certain interests in particular can be a source of much pleasure as well as bring him into contact with others. Any Water Pigs who are hoping for new friendships or a more fulfilling social life will find their interests can often be a good way to meet those who are like-minded. March, June, August and December could see a lot of social activity, although when in the company of those he does not know well the Water Pig would be wise to be discreet.

The Tiger year will also bring a lot of activity in the Water Pig's home life. As well as work pressures, for those who are parents or become parents this year, there could be the prospect of disturbed nights. As a result there will be occasions when tiredness gives way to irritability or little niggles escalate. Although usually so thoughtful, the Water Pig does need to watch this and make a point of talking through any concerns. Some Water Pigs could be especially grateful for practical assistance offered by more senior relations. However, while the Tiger year can be demanding – and occasionally exhausting – there will also be many pleasing moments, including some joint achievements and the fruition of important plans.

The key message for the Water Pig this year is to be thorough and careful. Lapses, indiscretions or risks are liable to cause problems and he will need to be on his guard. However, this can still be a constructive time. Work experience can bring later reward and personal interests can not only be beneficial but often lead to social opportunities. In his domestic life, there will again be a lot that the Water Pig will value. Overall, a busy and sometimes trying year, but often also a satisfying and instructive one.

TIP FOR THE YEAR

Draw on the support that is available and do not shoulder too much alone. Also, take advantage of ways in which you can further your knowledge and skills. Positive action now can be a real investment in your future and experience gained this year can stand you in excellent stead for some of the exciting opportunities that await in 2011.

The Wood Pig

This will be a full and interesting year for the Wood Pig, although it will require effort. Results will need to be worked for and the Wood Pig could also face some difficulties. However, provided he is prepared to rise to the challenge and be adaptable in his approach, he can learn a great deal.

For Wood Pigs born in 1995 this will be a significant year in their education. With important exams to be prepared for and much material to be covered, a lot will be asked of the Wood Pig. Also, while he will have his strengths, he could find some subjects difficult, especially if they are having to be covered quickly or he does not feel confident in that area. However, by making a concerted effort and not closing his mind to certain topics, he may not only make encouraging progress but also find this having a positive effect on other parts of his education. As he will find now and throughout his life, when his mind is focused he is capable of some truly great things.

Another positive feature of the year will be the opportunities that open up for the young Wood Pig. These may include the chance to use the facilities where he is studying, and by taking advantage of these and the support and instruction available, he can have a good deal of fun. Some Wood Pigs could be tempted by new pursuits over the year and will particularly enjoy the challenge these give. There is a strong element of personal discovery in the Tiger year which, for the keen and willing, can make this an interesting time.

The Wood Pig will also value the support his friends can give and especially the good times that shared interests can bring. However, while his social life will be mostly positive, he needs to be wary of rumour, the mischief-making of others or being misled. If he has doubts over anything he hears, he should check it out for himself. Also, should he find himself in any situation about which he has misgivings, he should listen to his better judgement. Lapses or risks could lead to difficulties. Wood Pigs, do take note and do draw on the support that is available to you.

In his home life the Wood Pig should also be open with others. This includes talking about what he is doing at school and letting others share in his successes as well as help him if he has any concerns. If there are activities he would like to try, again he should let others know. If he is forthcoming, those around him will be better able to advise and assist.

For Wood Pigs born in 1935, this can be a reasonable year, but requires care. Again, if there is any matter causing concern or doubt, the more senior Wood Pig should check it out and, if appropriate, seek advice, otherwise problems could linger and prey on his mind. It is important that the Wood Pig avails himself of advice and support if necessary.

The Tiger year can also be an expensive one, particularly as items may need repairing or replacing and the Wood Pig may have certain plans he may want to proceed with, including travel. Whenever he is considering a large transaction or having work carried out, he should take the time to consider options, compare costs and check that his requirements are being met. Similarly, if he receives forms relating to pensions or benefits, he should deal with these carefully and obtain guidance if need be. The Tiger year does require care and thoroughness.

More positively, the Wood Pig will follow the activities of family members with especial delight and could be involved in a memorable celebration during the year. Some younger relations could be particularly grateful for his advice, and his ability to empathize, despite a sometimes considerable gap of years, will be especially valued.

The Wood Pig will also derive much pleasure from certain interests he pursues, and whether spending time enjoying his garden, using his creative talents in some way or setting himself a particular goal, he will find his various activities can often be a source of much pleasure. The Wood Pig has a knack for using his time and strengths wisely.

For all Wood Pigs, whether born in 1935 or 1995, the Tiger year can bring some rewarding times, especially in developing their interests and skills. However, it is also a year for caution and the Wood Pig will need to remain alert, seek advice on any matter causing concern and be thorough in his various undertakings. With care, he can do much to negate some of the trickier aspects of the year and will be generally pleased with how he fares.

TIP FOR THE YEAR
At all times remember that help is there should you need it. If you are forthcoming, problems and pressures can often be eased. Wood Pigs born in 1995, nurturing your skills will enable you to reap rewards both now and in the future. In the Tiger year it is worth putting in the effort.

The Fire Pig
The element of Fire can give a sign a more pioneering, adventurous quality and when combined with the genial and hardworking nature of the Pig, this produces a Pig with a great many fine qualities. And while the Tiger year signifies caution, it will also encourage the Fire Pig to grow, develop *and* venture forth.

For Fire Pigs in work this can be an important and decisive year. Tiger years bring change and few Fire Pigs will remain untouched by developments, whether the introduction of new working methods, company restructuring or staff moving on. As a result many Fire Pigs will be considering their options. For some, new initiatives or changes in staffing can give them the chance to use their expertise in another way. Others, though, may decide that current developments are not for them and choose to move elsewhere or perhaps take early retirement. The Tiger year will contain some important decisions. While these may be difficult, by following their instincts and seeking appropriate advice, these Fire Pigs will often be able to make the most of the possibilities that will open up for them. Those who choose to move on will have an opportunity to reassess what they want to do and perhaps choose something very different from what they have been doing. The Tiger year can bring significant change and while readjusting can be demanding, the Fire Pig will often feel ready for the new challenge. April, July and last quarter of the Tiger year could see some important developments.

For those Fire Pigs who retire, there will be some major adjustments to make. To help, these Fire Pigs should consider which activities they would now like to pursue. Many will already have some thoughts in mind and with the Tiger year favouring experimentation and personal development, this is a year for following up ideas and making enquiries. Some Fire Pigs could be tempted by self-development or interest-related courses that are available online or in their local area. Positive action can make this a personally satisfying time.

In addition, all Fire Pigs should give some consideration to their well-being over the year, including reviewing their diet and level of exercise. If they feel changes could be helpful or they have any concerns, they should seek medical guidance. If they are to do all they want, they would benefit from paying some attention to their lifestyle.

With financial matters, the Fire Pig will need to be careful and avoid risk or haste. For those who change their work or retire, there could be financial adjustments to be made, and when dealing with paperwork concerning employment or pensions, they need to be thorough and if in doubt seek advice. Also, if involved in any costly purchase, the Fire Pig should check the details and any obligations he may be taking on. Where finance is concerned, Tiger years can be problematic.

Some of the Fire Pig's spending will be on his accommodation, with possible repair and replacement costs or changes to certain rooms. Some Fire Pigs may opt to move altogether. In all his practical undertakings, the Fire Pig will need to carefully consider the costs and implications as well as consult both his loved ones and, where relevant, the professionals. With careful planning, he can enjoy some pleasing results.

The Fire Pig has a great knack for coming up with ideas and if, as a respite from some of the pressure and disruption of the year, he suggests possible treats for his loved ones, perhaps a trip or a social event, his input can lead to some good times that will be appreciated by everyone.

The Fire Pig will also enjoy the social opportunities of the year and for those who retire or are feeling lonely this is very much a time for going out more and making the most of activities and amenities in their area. March, June, August and December could see much social activity. However, while the Fire Pig's relations with others can bring him pleasure, as with all Pigs, he does need to be wary of rumour and indiscretion. Without care, his trust could be misplaced. Fire Pigs, enjoy your socializing, but do be guarded and circumspect.

In general, the Tiger year will certainly be a full and interesting one. It will also be a time of change and if the Fire Pig draws on the advice of others and proceeds carefully, his decisions can be both important and beneficial. The Tiger year is one that can, despite its pressures, open up some excellent possibilities and the earnest Fire Pig will be keen to make the most of them.

TIP FOR THE YEAR

With important decisions to be made and plans to consider, do consult others and, if necessary, seek professional advice. With careful thought and good guidance, what is decided this year can lead to some positive developments. Also, consider developing your interests. These can be satisfying as well as often personally beneficial.

The Earth Pig

This will be a busy and sometimes demanding year for the Earth Pig, but it will not be without some appreciable benefits. It is a year to keep alert, be flexible and make the most of unfolding situations. With care, progress made now can have later significance.

At work this is a year for proceeding carefully. With changes in the air, it is important that the Earth Pig keeps himself informed of developments and is prepared to adapt as necessary. This is no year for him to immerse himself so fully in his own activities that he remains unaware of what is happening around him. Also, while he may be experienced in his present role, he should make the most of any training available or any chances to vary his work. This way he will not only keep his skills up to date but could also gain valuable experience in another area. In addition, some of the duties and problems he has to tackle over the year will give him the chance to develop his skills and so further his reputation. Work-wise, this may not be an easy year, but his achievements can pave the way for future progress.

Many Earth Pigs will remain with their present employer over the year, but for those who choose to move or are seeking work, this can be a significant time. These Earth Pigs would do well to assess what they have achieved and consider the direction they would now like their life to take. They could find it helpful to talk to those qualified to advise and, if thinking of making a career change, undertake any relevant courses or training. By giving careful thought to their future, they will come up with some new ideas that will be worth following up. Although making a change will not be easy, these Earth Pigs could find it helpful to remember the Chinese proverb, 'No task is too difficult if you are patient.' With patience, persistence and self-belief, they will eventually prevail. April, July, mid-October to early December and January could see some key developments, but work-wise all Earth Pigs will need to show flexibility and make the most of chances to extend their skills. Again, headway made this year can prove instrumental in some of the success enjoyed in 2011.

The Tiger year can be an expensive one and many Earth Pigs will face increased accommodation costs as well as expenses to do with family activities. As a result they will need to keep a close watch on their outgoings and budget accordingly. This is a year for good control and advance planning. Also, when entering into agreements or dealing with important correspondence, the Earth Pig should take the time to check that all is in order. With the aspects as they are, this is no time for risk or carelessness.

One of the more satisfying areas of the year will concern the Earth Pig's personal interests and he should aim to set time aside for these. Whether enjoying the more social aspects of his hobbies, setting himself a new personal goal or using his knowledge and ideas to good effect, what he does can not only bring him pleasure but also be a good way for him to relax and enjoy some of the rewards he works so hard for. Earth Pigs who have neglected their interests in recent years would do well to rectify this.

If possible, the Earth Pig should also try to go away for a break or holiday over the year. It is again important that he has an occasional respite from his active lifestyle, and his travels can do him a lot of good. Some Earth Pigs could particularly enjoy short breaks or visits to local attractions which are arranged almost at the last moment and have a delightful air of spontaneity about them.

There will also be some excellent chances for the Earth Pig to meet new people over the year, perhaps through his interests, work or travel. With his sincere and genial manner, he is set to impress and add to his social circle. March, June, August, December and early January could see the most social activity, although the Earth Pig does need to remain alert and be wary of placing himself in potentially awkward situations.

This need for mindfulness also applies to his domestic life. Over the year he should regularly consult others over his plans and ideas and take on board their viewpoints. In particular with any family plans that need arranging or home projects the Earth Pig may be considering, there needs to be good discussion, agreement and a certain flexibility. In addition, while the Earth Pig will often be occupied with work and other commitments, he should try to make sure quality time is preserved for sharing with his loved ones. By giving time and being involved, he can enjoy many pleasurable occasions. In addition many Earth Pigs will have some pleasing family news during the year which could be marked in fine style.

Overall, the Tiger year will bring its pressures, but these will give the Earth Pig the chance to further his knowledge and prepare himself for future progress. The Tiger year may test him in many ways, but by using his strengths and opportunities to advantage he will acquit himself well and take much of lasting value from the year.

TIP FOR THE YEAR
This will be a busy year and you should follow unfolding situations closely and adapt as necessary. What opens up for you now can have later significance. Also, keep your lifestyle in balance and make sure you give time to those who are important to you as well as enjoy and develop your personal interests.

FAMOUS PIGS

Bryan Adams, Woody Allen, Julie Andrews, Marie Antoinette, Fred Astaire, Humphrey Bogart, James Cagney, Maria Callas, Hillary Rodham Clinton, Glenn Close, Sacha Baron Cohen, Alice Cooper, the Duchess of Cornwall, Noël Coward, Simon Cowell, Oliver Cromwell, Billy Crystal, the Dalai Lama, Ted Danson, Dido, Richard Dreyfuss, Ben Elton, Ralph Waldo Emerson, Henry Ford, Stephen Harper, Emmylou Harris, William Randolph Hearst, Ernest Hemingway, Henry VIII, Conrad Hilton, Alfred Hitchcock, Sir Elton John, Tommy Lee Jones, Carl Gustav Jung, Stephen King, Kevin Kline, Hugh Laurie, Nigella Lawson, David Letterman, Jerry Lee Lewis, Meat Loaf, Ewan McGregor, Ricky Martin, Johnny Mathis, Dannii Minogue, Wolfgang Amadeus Mozart, Michael Parkinson, James Patterson, Luciano Pavarotti, Iggy Pop, Maurice Ravel, Ronald Reagan, Ginger Rogers, Winona Ryder, Françoise Sagan, Carlos Santana, Arnold Schwarzenegger, Kevin Spacey, Steven Spielberg, Sir Alan Sugar, David Tennant, Emma Thompson, Jules Verne, David Walliams, Amy Winehouse, Michael Winner, the Duchess of York.

APPENDIX

———◆◆◆———

The relationships between the 12 animal signs, both on a personal level and business level, are an important aspect of Chinese horoscopes and in this appendix the compatibility between the signs is shown in the two tables that follow.

Also included are the names of the signs ruling the hours of the day and from this it is possible to find your ascendant and discover yet another aspect of your personality.

Finally, to supplement the earlier chapters on the personality and horoscope of the signs, I have included a guide on how you can get the best out of your sign and the year.

RELATIONSHIPS BETWEEN THE SIGNS

Personal Relationships

KEY

1 Excellent. Great rapport.

2 A successful relationship. Many interests in common.

3 Mutual respect and understanding. A good relationship.

4 Fair. Needs care and some willingness to compromise in order for the relationship to work.

5 Awkward. Possible difficulties in communication with few interests in common.

6 A clash of personalities. Very difficult.

	Rat	Ox	Tiger	Rabbit	Dragon	Snake	Horse	Goat	Monkey	Rooster	Dog	Pig
Rat	1											
Ox	1	3										
Tiger	4	6	5									
Rabbit	5	2	3	2								
Dragon	1	5	4	3	2							
Snake	3	1	6	2	1	5						
Horse	6	5	1	5	3	4	2					
Goat	5	5	3	1	4	3	2	2				
Monkey	1	3	6	3	1	3	5	3	1			
Rooster	5	1	5	6	2	1	2	5	5	5		
Dog	3	4	1	2	6	3	1	5	3	5	2	
Pig	2	3	2	2	2	6	3	2	2	3	1	2

Business Relationships

KEY

1 Excellent. Marvellous understanding and rapport.
2 Very good. Complement each other well.
3 A good working relationship and understanding can be developed.
4 Fair, but compromise and a common objective are often needed to make this relationship work.
5 Awkward. Unlikely to work, either through lack of trust, understanding or the competitiveness of the signs.
6 Mistrust. Difficult. To be avoided.

	Rat	Ox	Tiger	Rabbit	Dragon	Snake	Horse	Goat	Monkey	Rooster	Dog	Pig
Rat	2											
Ox	1	3										
Tiger	3	6	5									
Rabbit	4	3	3	3								
Dragon	1	4	3	3	3							
Snake	3	2	6	4	1	5						
Horse	6	5	1	5	3	4	4					
Goat	5	5	3	1	4	3	3	2				
Monkey	2	3	4	5	1	5	4	4	3			
Rooster	5	1	5	5	2	1	2	5	5	6		
Dog	4	5	2	3	6	4	2	5	3	5	4	
Pig	3	3	3	2	3	5	4	2	3	4	3	1

YOUR ASCENDANT

The ascendant has a very strong influence on your personality and will help you gain an even greater insight into your true personality according to Chinese horoscopes.

The hours of the day are named after the 12 animal signs and the sign governing the time you were born is your ascendant. To find your ascendant, look up the time of your birth in the table below, bearing in mind any local time differences in the place you were born.

11 p.m.	to	1 a.m.	The hours of the Rat
1 a.m.	to	3 a.m.	The hours of the Ox
3 a.m.	to	5 a.m.	The hours of the Tiger
5 a.m.	to	7 a.m.	The hours of the Rabbit
7 a.m.	to	9 a.m.	The hours of the Dragon
9 a.m.	to	11 a.m.	The hours of the Snake
11 a.m.	to	1 p.m.	The hours of the Horse
1 p.m.	to	3 p.m.	The hours of the Goat
3 p.m.	to	5 p.m.	The hours of the Monkey
5 p.m.	to	7 p.m.	The hours of the Rooster
7 p.m.	to	9 p.m.	The hours of the Dog
9 p.m.	to	11 p.m.	The hours of the Pig

RAT

The Rat ascendant is likely to make the sign more outgoing, sociable and careful with money. A particularly beneficial influence for those born under the signs of the Rabbit, Horse, Monkey and Pig.

OX

The Ox ascendant has a restraining, cautionary and steadying influence that many signs will benefit from. This ascendant also promotes self-confidence and willpower and is especially good for those born under the signs of the Tiger, Rabbit and Goat.

TIGER

The Tiger ascendant is a dynamic and stirring influence that makes the sign more outgoing, action-orientated and impulsive. A generally favourable ascendant for the Ox, Tiger, Snake and Horse.

RABBIT

The Rabbit ascendant has a moderating influence, making the sign more reflective, serene and discreet. A particularly beneficial influence for the Rat, Dragon, Monkey and Rooster.

DRAGON

The Dragon ascendant gives strength, determination and ambition to the sign. A favourable influence for those born under the signs of the Rabbit, Goat, Monkey and Dog.

SNAKE

The Snake ascendant can make the sign more reflective, intuitive and self-reliant. A good influence for the Tiger, Goat and Pig.

HORSE

The Horse ascendant will make the sign more adventurous, daring and on some occasions fickle. Generally a beneficial influence for the Rabbit, Snake, Dog and Pig.

GOAT

The Goat ascendant will make the sign more tolerant, easy-going and receptive. It could also impart some creative and artistic qualities. An especially good influence for the Ox, Dragon, Snake and Rooster.

MONKEY

The Monkey ascendant is likely to impart a delicious sense of humour and fun to the sign. It will make the sign more enterprising and outgoing – a particularly good influence for the Rat, Ox, Snake and Goat.

ROOSTER

The Rooster ascendant helps to give the sign a lively, outgoing and very methodical manner. Its influence will increase efficiency and is good for the Ox, Tiger, Rabbit and Horse.

DOG

The Dog ascendant makes the sign more reasonable and fair-minded as well as giving an added sense of loyalty. A very good ascendant for the Tiger, Dragon and Goat.

PIG

The Pig ascendant can make the sign more sociable and self-indulgent. It is also a caring influence and one that can make the sign want to help others. A good ascendant for the Dragon and Monkey.

HOW TO GET THE BEST FROM YOUR CHINESE SIGN AND THE YEAR

Each of the 12 Chinese signs possesses its own unique strengths and by identifying them you can use them to your advantage. Similarly, by becoming aware of possible weaknesses you can do much to rectify them and in this respect I hope the following sections will be useful. Also included are some tips on how you can get the best from the Year of the Tiger.

The Rat

The Rat is blessed with many fine talents, but his undoubted strength lies in his ability to get on with others. He is sociable, charming and a good judge of character. He also possesses a shrewd mind and is good at spotting opportunities.

However, to make the most of his abilities, he does need to impose some discipline upon himself. He should resist the (sometimes very great) temptation of getting involved in too many activities all at the same time and should decide upon his priorities and objectives. By concentrating his energies on specific matters he will fare much better as a result. Also, given his personable manner, he should seek out positions where he can use his personal relations skills to good effect. For a career, sales and marketing could prove ideal.

The Rat is astute in dealing with finance, but while often thrifty, he can sometimes give way to moments of indulgence. Although he deserves to enjoy the money he has so carefully earned, it would sometimes be in his interests to exercise restraint when tempted to satisfy too many expensive whims!

The Rat's family and friends are important to him and while he is loyal and protective towards them, he does tend to keep his worries and concerns to himself and would be helped if he were more willing to discuss his anxieties. Others think highly of him and are prepared to do a lot to help him, but for them to do so the Rat does need to be less guarded.

With his sharp mind, keen imagination and sociable manner, he does, however, have much in his favour. When he has commitment, he can be irrepressible and, given his considerable charm, often irresistible as well! Provided he channels his energies wisely, he can make much of his life.

Advice for the Rat's Year Ahead

GENERAL PROSPECTS

Rats are well known for their resourcefulness and during the year they should keep alert and make the most of what opens up for them. This may be a demanding year, but it is one for moving forward.

CAREER PROSPECTS
Change is all around, often happening at a fast pace, and there will be chances for the Rat to extend his skills. This is a year to build on his position and make headway.

FINANCE
The Rat should be disciplined in his everyday spending and make advance provision for more expensive plans and purchases. He should also avoid unnecessary risk. With travel well aspected, though, he should, where possible, save up for a holiday.

RELATIONS WITH OTHERS
The Rat has great personal skills, but this year he will need to be particularly attentive towards others. This is not a year for single-mindedness or becoming so involved in his own activities that his relations with others begin to suffer. Rats, take note. Care and attentiveness will be so very important this year.

The Ox
Strong-willed, determined and resolute, the Ox certainly has a mind of his own! He is persistent and sets about achieving his objectives with dogged determination. In addition he is reliable and tenacious and is often a source of inspiration to others. He is an achiever, and he often achieves a great deal. However, to really excel, he would do well to try and correct some of his weaknesses.

Being so resolute and having such a strong sense of purpose, the Ox can be inflexible and narrow-minded. He can be resistant to change and prefers to set about his activities in his own way rather than be dependent on others. His dislike of change can sometimes be to his detriment and if he were prepared to be more adaptable and adventurous he would find his progress easier.

The Ox would also be helped if he were to broaden his range of interests and become more relaxed in his approach. At times he can be so preoccupied with his own activities that he is not always as mindful of others as he should be, and his demeanour can sometimes be studious and serious. There are times when he would benefit from a lighter touch.

However, the Ox is true to his word and loyal to his family and friends. He is admired and respected by others and his tremendous willpower usually enables him to achieve a great deal in life.

Advice for the Ox's Year Ahead

GENERAL PROSPECTS

The Ox is a redoubtable character and he may sometimes find himself at odds with the fast pace of the year. This is a year of change and throughout the Ox will need to keep alert and be flexible. To be intransigent could prevent him from getting the most from the year.

CAREER PROSPECTS

The Ox needs to keep informed of developments and be willing to act when opportunities arise. There is good scope for progress and personal development, but it is a case of adapting to the times.

FINANCE

The Ox needs to remain his disciplined and thorough self and be wary of rush or haste. This is a year to watch spending and to save towards more major purchases.

RELATIONS WITH OTHERS

The Tiger year will bring its pressures and irritations, and during it the Ox will need to show patience and some forbearance and remain aware of the views of others. Good communication and shared activities will be helpful in many ways. A year to tread carefully and listen closely to loved ones.

The Tiger

Lively, innovative and enterprising, the Tiger enjoys an active lifestyle. He has a wide range of interests, an alert mind and a genuine liking of others. He loves to live life to the full. However, despite his enthusiastic and well-meaning ways, he does not always make the most of his considerable potential.

By being so versatile, the Tiger does have a tendency to jump from one activity to another or dissipate his energies by trying to do too much at the same time. To make the most of himself he should try to exercise a certain amount of self-discipline. Ideally, he should decide how best he can use his abilities, give himself some objectives and then stick to them. If he can overcome his restless tendencies, he will find he will accomplish far more as a result.

Also, in spite of his sociable manner, the Tiger likes to retain a certain independence in his actions, and while few begrudge him this, he would sometimes find life easier if he were more prepared to work in conjunction with others. His reliance upon his own judgement does sometimes mean that he excludes the views and advice of those around him, and this can be to his detriment. The Tiger may possess an independent spirit, but he must not let it go too far!

The Tiger does, however, have much in his favour. He is bold, original and quick-witted. If he can keep his restless nature in check, he can enjoy considerable success. In addition, with his engaging personality, he is well liked and much admired.

Advice for the Tiger's Year Ahead

GENERAL PROSPECTS

The Tiger will be keen to make his own year special and will set about his activities with verve, resolve and purpose. And he will be well rewarded. This is very much a year for acting on his ideas. Throughout, he will also be encouraged by the support and goodwill of others.

CAREER PROSPECTS

A favourable year, with the Tiger often having more chance to build on his strengths than of late. This is a year to stay alert for ways to move forward. It is a time for the Tiger to show his true and wonderful capabilities. Luck will favour the bold.

FINANCE

Money may flow in the Tiger's direction this year, but with accommodation plans and an often active lifestyle, he needs to control his spending and would find it helpful to set funds aside for specific purposes, including travel, and if able, the longer term.

RELATIONS WITH OTHERS

The Tiger's relations with others can make this a special year. Many will have a personal event or celebration to look forward to and romance can play an especially big part. For the unattached, this can be an eventful year, with many meeting someone who is destined to become significant. With the generally busy nature of the year the Tiger should be open and communicative as well as use his chances to get to know others. In his own year his personal skills will serve him well.

The Rabbit

The Rabbit is certainly one who appreciates the finer things in life. With his good taste, companionable nature and wide range of interests, he knows how to live well – and usually does!

However, for all his finesse and style, the Rabbit does possess traits he would do well to watch. His desire for a settled lifestyle makes him err on the side of caution. He dislikes change and as a consequence can miss out on opportunities. Also, there are many Rabbits who will go to great lengths to avoid difficult and fraught situations, and again, while few may relish these, sometimes in life it is necessary to take risks or stand your ground. At times it would certainly be in the Rabbit's interests to be bolder and more assertive in going after what he desires.

The Rabbit also attaches great importance to his relations with others and while he has a happy knack of getting on with most people, he can be sensitive to criticism. Difficult though it may be, he should really try to develop a thicker skin and recognize that criticism can provide valuable learning opportunities, as can some of the problems he strives so hard to avoid.

However, with his agreeable manner, keen intellect and shrewd judgement, the Rabbit does have a lot in his favour and invariably makes much of his life – and enjoys it too!

Advice for the Rabbit's Year Ahead

GENERAL PROSPECTS

The Rabbit may not always feel at ease with the fast pace of the Tiger year, but it can be a significant one for him. By making the most of his opportunities, he can gain experience and the long-term benefits of what he does now should not be underestimated, particularly with some of the successes that await in 2011.

CAREER PROSPECTS

Change is on the agenda. The Rabbit will have the chance to make progress and in the process take on new responsibilities and learn new skills. This can be a demanding year, but it will be instructive and help the Rabbit's reputation and prospects.

FINANCE

With increased accommodation costs and possible home purchases, the Rabbit will need to keep track of his everyday spending as well as check the terms of any agreements he may enter into. If in doubt, he should take advice.

RELATIONS WITH OTHERS
The Rabbit will particularly value the support of those around him and when under pressure or making decisions, he should involve others. His family and social life will be busy but often very rewarding. Many Rabbits will also have the chance to help another person and demonstrate the true value of love and friendship.

The Dragon

Enthusiastic, enterprising and honourable, the Dragon possesses many admirable qualities and his life is often full and varied. He always gives his best and even though not all his endeavours meet with success, he is nonetheless resilient and hardy, and is much admired and respected.

However, for all his qualities, the Dragon can be blunt and forthright and, through sheer strength of character, sometimes domineering. It would certainly be in his interests to listen more closely to others rather than be so self-reliant. Also, his enthusiasm can sometimes get the better of him and he can be impulsive. To make the most of his abilities, he should give himself priorities and set about his activities in a disciplined and systematic way. More tact and diplomacy might not come amiss either!

However, with his lively and outgoing manner, the Dragon is popular and well liked. With good fortune on his side (and the Dragon is often lucky), his life is almost certain to be eventful and fulfilling. He has many talents, and if he uses them wisely he will enjoy much success.

Advice for the Dragon's Year Ahead

GENERAL PROSPECTS

The Dragon will welcome the progressive nature of the Tiger year and be keen to make the most of his opportunities. However, he will need to be flexible and put in the effort. The Tiger year has considerable potential, but it can be demanding. It is important that the Dragon keeps his lifestyle in balance.

CAREER PROSPECTS

Important progress can be made, with the Dragon often having the chance to take on greater duties, secure promotion and considerably widen his experience. The year calls for effort, but the rewards can be considerable.

FINANCE

In view of the opportunities of the year, including travel, the Dragon will need to keep a close watch on his spending and manage his outgoings carefully. This is a time for financial discipline.

RELATIONS WITH OTHERS

The Dragon can look forward to some special times in both his family and social life and the chance to make new friends and, for the unattached, find romance. However, he does need to give time to those who are important to him. To be distracted, preoccupied or continually busy could affect rapport. In this positive year it is essential that the Dragon keeps his lifestyle in balance.

The Snake

The Snake is blessed with a keen intellect. He has wide interests, an enquiring mind and good judgement. He tends to be quiet and thoughtful and plans his activities with considerable care. With his fine abilities he often does well in life, but he does possess traits which can undermine his progress.

The Snake is often guarded in his actions and sometimes loses out to those who are more action-oriented and assertive. He also likes to retain a certain independence in his actions and this too can hamper his progress. It would be in his interests to be more forthcoming and involve others more readily in his plans. The Snake has many talents and possesses a warm and rich personality, but there is a danger that this can remain concealed behind his often quiet and reserved manner. He would fare better if he were more outgoing and showed others his true worth.

However, the Snake is very much his own master. He invariably knows what he wants in life and is often prepared to journey long and hard to achieve his objectives. He does, though, have it in his power to make that journey easier. Lose some of that reticence, Snake, be more open and assertive, and do not be afraid of the occasional risk!

Advice for the Snake's Year Ahead

GENERAL PROSPECTS

The cautious ways of the Snake could be thrown into confusion by the heady pace of the Tiger year. However, despite his misgivings, some important possibilities can open up for him and by being prepared to act on these, the Snake stands to benefit.

CAREER PROSPECTS

The Snake may feel buffeted by events, but with change comes possibility, and there will be some excellent chances to make progress and gain new experience. Some Snakes could change the nature of their career completely. For the willing, much is possible. For the creative, certain ideas could be worth taking further.

FINANCE

An expensive year with possible repair costs, purchases, commitments and family expenses. This is a time for discipline, planning and budgeting ahead.

RELATIONS WITH OTHERS

With so much happening, the Snake will be grateful for the support of others this year. And despite the many pressures, it is important that he gives quality time to his loved ones. Socially, much can be gained by meeting up with others and some good friendships can be formed. The attention the Snake gives to others this year will reward him well.

The Horse

Versatile, hardworking and sociable, the Horse makes his mark wherever he goes. He has an eloquent and engaging manner and makes friends with ease. He is quick-witted, has an alert mind and is certainly not averse to taking risks or experimenting with new ideas.

He possesses a strong and likeable personality, but he does also have his weaknesses. With his wide interests he does not always finish everything he starts and he would do well to be more persevering. He has it within him to achieve considerable success, but to make the most of his talents he does need to overcome his restless tendencies. When he has made plans, he should stick with them.

The Horse loves company and values both his family and friends. However, there will have been many a time when he will have lost his temper or spoken in haste and regretted his words later. Throughout his life he needs to keep his temper in check and be diplomatic in tense situations. If not, he could risk jeopardizing the respect and good relations he so values.

However, the Horse has a multitude of talents and a lively and outgoing personality. If he can overcome his restless and volatile nature, he can lead a rich and highly fulfilling life.

Advice for the Horse's Year Ahead

GENERAL PROSPECTS

This will be a busy year and with some good opportunities. To benefit, the Horse should be prepared to put himself forward and act on his aims and objectives. As Virgil wrote,

'Fortune favours the bold,' and this will hold true for the bold and determined Horse this year.

CAREER PROSPECTS

This is a year of change and by being flexible and willing to make the most of what happens, the Horse can not only make progress but also gain some valuable experience, often in a new area. A year offering considerable possibility.

FINANCE

An expensive year and, with an often busy social life plus many other activities, the Horse will need to manage his money well. A year for discipline and care.

RELATIONS WITH OTHERS

With a busy home life, changes in his work situation and his often considerable social life, the Horse will find himself in demand. There will also be many opportunities to make new friends and, for some, good prospects for romance. Amid all the activity, there will be times when the Horse will be tired and under pressure, and he must be careful not to take this out on others. If he does, relationships could be undermined. Horses, take careful note. Do not let a loss of temper mar an otherwise great personal year.

The Goat

The Goat has a warm, friendly and understanding manner and gets on well with most people. He is generally easy-going, has a fond appreciation of the finer things in life and possesses a rich imagination. He is often artistic and enjoys the creative arts and outdoor activities.

However, despite his engaging manner, there lurks beneath his skin a sometimes tense and pessimistic nature. The Goat can be a worrier, and without the support and encouragement of others can feel insecure and be hesitant in his actions.

To make the most of himself he should aim to become more assertive and decisive as well as more at ease with himself. He has much in his favour, but he really does need to promote himself more and be bolder. He would also be helped if he were to sort out his priorities and set about his activities in an organized and disciplined manner. There are some Goats who tend to be haphazard in the way they go about things and this can hamper their progress.

Although the Goat will always value the support of others, it would also be in his interests to become more independent and not be so reticent about striking out on his own. He does, after all, possess many talents, as well as a sincere and likeable personality, and by always giving his best he can make his life rich, rewarding and enjoyable.

Advice for the Goat's Year Ahead

GENERAL PROSPECTS

Hold tight! Goats may not like the turbulence and pace of the Tiger year, but it can lead to new experiences and possibilities. This is not a time to be resistant to change. By rising to the challenges, the Goat stands to gain a great deal.

CAREER PROSPECTS

The Goat may feel uneasy about the developments or pressures of the Tiger year, but with a 'can do' attitude and willingness to make the most of his situation, he can gain experience that will stand him in excellent stead for the future. A year to learn and develop.

FINANCE

Paperwork and financial transactions need great care this year. Delay or inattention could leave the Goat at a disadvantage. He also needs to remain disciplined in his spending and take the time to plan important purchases. This is no year for rush or risk.

RELATIONS WITH OTHERS

The Goat has great personal skills and the time and attention he gives to family life will be especially appreciated, with him playing an often pivotal role in the home. Also, by networking and socializing he will get to impress many and benefit from the support he receives.

The Monkey

Lively, enterprising and innovative, the Monkey certainly knows how to impress. He has wide interests, a good sense of fun and relates well to others. He also possesses a shrewd mind and often has a happy knack of turning events to his advantage.

However, despite his versatility and considerable gifts, he does have his weaknesses. He often lacks persistence, can get distracted easily and also places tremendous reliance upon his own judgement. While his belief in himself is a commendable asset, it would certainly be in his interests to be more mindful of the views of others. Also, while he likes to keep tabs on all that is going on around him, he can be evasive and secretive with regard to his own feelings and activities, and again a more forthcoming attitude would be to his advantage.

In his desire to succeed the Monkey can also be tempted to cut corners or be crafty and he should recognize that such actions can rebound on him!

However, he is resourceful and his sheer strength of character will ensure that he has an interesting and varied life. If he can channel his considerable energies wisely and overcome his sometimes restless tendencies, his life can be crowned with success and achievement. And with his amiable personality, he will have many friends.

Advice for the Monkey's Year Ahead

GENERAL PROSPECTS

The Monkey is keen and likes to keep active, but despite his best intentions, plans and problems can occur in Tiger years. This one may not be an easy time for him, but by adapting and being flexible, he can still profit from its opportunities. A potentially rewarding year, but one to be aware and cautious.

CAREER PROSPECTS

A year of movement and change. While the pressure may be great, the Monkey will have the opportunity to develop his skills and make headway. With willingness and flexibility, he can find the Tiger year opening up some important possibilities, some of which can have important long-term value.

FINANCE

With finance, the Monkey needs to avoid risk or haste. When involved in any major transaction he should take the time to check the details and implications. This is a year to be thorough.

RELATIONS WITH OTHERS

Although the Monkey can look forward to some meaningful times in his domestic and social life, he does need to be alert. Misunderstandings can all too easily arise and when under pressure the Monkey should be careful not to take his irritations out on others. It would benefit him to be open and allow others to assist more.

The Rooster

With his considerable bearing and incisive and resolute manner, the Rooster cuts an impressive figure. He has a sharp mind, is well informed on many matters and expresses himself clearly and convincingly. He is meticulous and efficient in his undertakings and commands a great deal of respect. He also has a genuine and caring interest in others.

The Rooster has much in his favour, but there are some aspects of his character that can tell against him. He can be candid in his views and over-zealous in his actions, and sometimes he can say or do things he later regrets. His high standards also make him fussy, even pedantic, and he can get diverted into relatively minor matters when in truth he could be occupying his time more profitably. This is something all Roosters would do well to watch. Also, while the Rooster is a great planner, he can sometimes be unrealistic in his expectations. In making plans – indeed, in most of his activities – he would do well to consult others. He would benefit greatly from their input.

The Rooster has many talents as well as commendable drive and commitment, but to make the most of himself he does need to channel his energies wisely and watch his candid and sometimes volatile nature. With care, however, he can make a success of his life, and with his wide interests and outgoing personality, he will enjoy the friendship and respect of many.

Advice for the Rooster's Year Ahead

GENERAL PROSPECTS

The hectic activity of the Tiger year may not always make this a comfortable time for the Rooster, but despite his misgivings, this can be a constructive and rewarding year. It is very much one to act on ideas and seize opportunities. With willingness, backed by the support of others, the Rooster can benefit from some important and sometimes far-reaching possibilities.

CAREER PROSPECTS

A year of change. By looking to move forward, the Rooster can make important progress. The Tiger year favours activity and for Roosters who are willing to put themselves forward, the benefits can be substantial.

FINANCE

With some often large family expenses and existing commitments, the Rooster will need to be disciplined in his spending. This is a year for good control and vigilance.

RELATIONS WITH OTHERS

The Rooster can gain a lot from the support of others and should draw on the help available. Developments in his work or new interests can be good ways for him to make new friendships. For the unattached, there is the possibility of romance. With care, including watching his sometimes candid tongue, the Rooster can make this a busy and rewarding year.

The Dog

Loyal, dependable and with a good understanding of human nature, the Dog is well placed to win respect and admiration. He is a no-nonsense sort of person and hates any sort of hypocrisy and falsehood. With the Dog you know where you stand and, given his direct manner, where he stands on any issue. He also has a strong humanitarian nature and often champions good causes.

The Dog has many fine attributes, although there are certain traits that can prevent him from either enjoying or making the most of his life. He is a great worrier and can get anxious over all manner of things. Although it may not always be easy, he should try to rid himself of the 'worry habit'. Whenever he is tense or concerned, he should be prepared to speak to others rather than shoulder his worries all by himself. In some cases, they could even be of his own making! Also, he has a tendency to look on the pessimistic side and he would certainly be helped if he were to view his undertakings more optimistically. He does, after all, possess many skills and should have faith in his abilities. Another weakness is his tendency to be stubborn over certain issues. If he is not careful, at times this could undermine his position.

If the Dog can reduce the pessimistic side of his nature, he will not only enjoy life more but also find he is achieving more. He possesses a truly admirable character and his loyalty, reliability and sincerity are appreciated by all he meets. In his life he will do much good and befriend many people – and he owes it to himself to enjoy life too. Sometimes it might help him to recall the words of another Dog, Sir Winston Churchill: 'When I look back on all these worries I remember the story of the old man who said on his deathbed that he had had a lot of trouble in his life, most of which never happened.'

Advice for the Dog's Year Ahead

GENERAL PROSPECTS

A promising year. With determination and belief, the Dog can make real progress, but he does need to act. With a resolute approach and the support of others, he will find a lot going in his favour.

CAREER PROSPECTS

Events can happen quickly in the Tiger year and by keeping alert the Dog can make important headway. A progressive year, with the Dog's achievements often helping his longer-term prospects.

FINANCE

The Dog's successes this year can bring an increase in income and some Dogs could also enjoy some financial good fortune. However, the Dog does need to keep a close watch on his spending and check the details and implications of any new agreement he may enter into. In money matters, this is a year to be thorough.

RELATIONS WITH OTHERS

Loyal and caring, the Dog does a lot for others and this year there will be excellent chances for others to do a lot for him. He will be encouraged in his activities and really should draw on the support available. Domestically and socially, this can be a pleasing year, with new friends and contacts being helpful. For the unattached, romance can make this already positive year even more special.

The Pig

Genial, sincere and trusting, the Pig gets on well with most people. He has a kind and caring nature, a dislike of discord and often a good sense of humour. In addition, he has a fondness for socializing and enjoying the good life!

The Pig possesses a shrewd mind, is particularly adept at dealing with business and financial matters and has a robust and resilient nature. Although not all his plans may work out as he would like, he is tenacious and will often rise up and succeed after experiencing setbacks and difficulties. In his often active and varied life he can accomplish a great deal, although there are certain aspects of his character that can tell against him. If he can modify these or keep them in check then his life will certainly be easier and possibly even more successful.

In his activities the Pig can sometimes over-commit himself and while he does not want to disappoint, he would certainly be helped if he were to set about his activities in an organized and systematic manner and give himself priorities at busy times. He should also not allow others to take advantage of his good nature and it would be in his interests to be more discerning. There will have been times when he has been gullible and naïve; fortunately, though, he quickly learns from his mistakes. However, he possesses a stubborn streak and if new situations do not fit in with his line of thinking, he can be inflexible. Such an attitude may not always be to his advantage.

The Pig is a great pleasure-seeker and while he should enjoy the fruits of his labours, he can sometimes be self-indulgent and extravagant. This is also something he would do well to watch.

However, though the Pig may possess some faults, those who come into contact with him are invariably impressed by his integrity, amiable manner and intelligence. If he uses his talents wisely, his life can be crowned with considerable achievement and he will also be loved and respected by many.

Advice for the Pig's Year Ahead

GENERAL PROSPECTS

A tricky year. The Pig will need to pay particular attention to the events happening around him and adapt as necessary. Demanding though the year can be, it can also be instructive and the experience the Pig gains will be instrumental in his future success, especially next year.

CAREER PROSPECTS

With increased pressure and problems, the Pig will have excellent chances to demonstrate his skills and gain important new experience. This is a year to keep alert and make the most of his situation. What is achieved now can have great bearing on his future prospects.

FINANCE

With accommodation, family expenses and other outgoings, the Pig will need to keep careful control over his finances. Care also needs to be taken with correspondence with financial implications.

RELATIONS WITH OTHERS

The Pig enjoys good relations with many, but this year he does need to be on his guard. Indiscretion, rumour and people proving unreliable could all cause him anguish and pain. Pigs, do remember this and be discreet and circumspect. The Pig should also keep his lifestyle in balance and preserve time for his loved ones, social life and interests. These can often be special in this busy and sometimes demanding year.